I CALL THE SHOTS

I CALL THE SHOTS

Straight Talk About the Game of Golf Today

JOHNNY MILLER

with Guy Yocom

G O T H A M   B O O K S

GOTHAM BOOKS
Published by Penguin Group (USA) Inc.
375 Hudson Street, New York, New York 10014, U.S.A.
Penguin Group (Canada), 10 Alcorn Avenue, Toronto, Ontario, Canada M4V 3B2 (a division of Pearson Penguin Canada Inc.); Penguin Books Ltd, 80 Strand, London WC2R 0RL, England; Penguin Ireland, 25 St Stephen's Green, Dublin 2, Ireland (a division of Penguin Books Ltd); Penguin Group (Australia), 250 Camberwell Road, Camberwell, Victoria 3124, Australia (a division of Pearson Australia Group Pty Ltd); Penguin Books India Pvt Ltd, 11 Community Centre, Panchsheel Park, New Delhi—110 017, India; Penguin Group (NZ), Cnr Airborne and Rosedale Roads, Albany, Auckland, New Zealand (a division of Pearson New Zealand Ltd); Penguin Books (South Africa) (Pty) Ltd, 24 Sturdee Avenue, Rosebank, Johannesburg 2196, South Africa

Penguin Books Ltd, Registered Offices: 80 Strand, London WC2R 0RL, England

Published by Gotham Books, a division of Penguin Group (USA) Inc.
Previously published as a Gotham Books hardcover edition.

First Gotham trade paperback printing, 2005

10 9 8 7 6 5 4 3 2 1

The Library of Congress has cataloged the hardcover edition of this title as follows:

Miller, Johnny, 1947–
I call the shots : straight talk about the game of golf today / Johnny Miller with Guy Yocom.
p. cm.
ISBN 1-592-40065-5 (hardcover : alk. paper) 1-592-40072-8 (pbk.)
1. Golf. I. Title: Straight talk about the game of golf today. II. Yocom, Guy. III. Title.
GV965.M4685 2004
796.352—dc22

Printed in the United States of America
Set in Berkeley Medium with Bodoni Old Face
Designed by Sabrina Bowers

This book is printed on acid-free paper. ♾

In memory of my father, Laurence Otto Miller.
Dad was a great teacher of golf and life.
He was simply the greatest man I ever knew.

Contents

Foreword

JOHNNY MILLER HAS always had a knack for making difficult things look easy. That was especially true with golf. During his prime in the 1970s, he played the game brilliantly, yet almost effortlessly. Of all the guys I went up against, John was, arguably, blessed with the most talent.

I first met Johnny at the 1966 U.S. Open at the Olympic Club when he was just a nineteen-year-old amateur and finished in the top 10. A short five years later, he and I tied for second at the 1971 Masters, and after that performance, I knew Johnny had all the physical gifts. Then, to see his marvelous performance at Oakmont in the 1973 U.S. Open, I knew he also had the heart and the head to go with those gifts. When Johnny was on his game, he made the rest of us question what we were doing out there. You've no doubt heard what a wonderful iron player he was and it's true; he'd go on streaks where he just knocked down the flagsticks with almost every shot. You've also heard that he wasn't a very good putter—John will tell you that himself—but don't always believe what you hear. There were weeks when he made everything with that Bulls Eye putter of his. You don't win more than twenty tournaments, including two majors, if you aren't a good putter, and a good pressure putter Johnny is—one of the greatest competitors I have ever met and certainly played against. All I know is, my playing record would look a lot better if I hadn't had to go up against John all those years. As it is, several of my victories were made even more memorable simply because of Johnny's presence down the stretch. I have always said that my victory in the 1975 Masters came with one of the most thrilling final-round duels I have ever faced, and Johnny played a starring role.

John's greatest strengths have always been his decisiveness and aggressiveness, which stemmed from enormous self-confidence. He knew how good he was and it was reflected in his bearing, speech, and bold playing style. Some people thought he was cocky, but I never viewed him that way at all. He was merely honest, and he never talked about other players in a deprecating way. He was a great sportsman who always treated the game and its players with respect. There is also a humility about John that I've found appealing. He's a very unselfish person who has always placed the priority of family over golf. That's what impressed me most about John when I first met him. Our friendship, which has lasted thirty-five years, is founded on this and other common values.

I wasn't at all surprised when John became the game's best TV analyst. The personality traits that made him a great player translated into a terrific announcing style. He's quick, honest, insightful, and very self-assured, yet rarely offends. He supplements those qualities with a deep understanding of the game and the way top players think and behave under pressure. Having dabbled briefly in the broadcast booth, I can assure you his job is tougher than it looks, but like I said earlier, John has a way of making difficult things look easy.

As a golfer, I'm thankful to have had Johnny around all these years, and look forward to more of his great commentary in the future.

Good golfing,
JACK NICKLAUS

North Palm Beach, Florida
February 2004

Introduction

I WAS WATCHING the classic golf movie *Follow the Sun* the other day, and was captivated by the fact that there actually was a time when golf tournaments were covered by radio. Watching Ben Hogan (played by actor Glenn Ford) play shots with a radio announcer whispering the action in the background made me understand why golf is no longer covered by radio. The announcing was dreadful.

On the other hand, I felt a bit envious of the radio guy being able to talk so much. As lead golf analyst for NBC's golf coverage, I've lost count of how many times I've described a shot a player had made and wished I could say more about it. But TV is a visual medium in which the picture is always the star. The image you see tells most of the story, and my role is merely to amplify the image with words. Often, though, there's much more to what you see than meets the eye—or in the case of my brief commentary on a player's on-course predicament—the ear.

The things I've wanted to say—the deep background I wanted to relate but couldn't—are covered in this book. My career has brought me to a time and place where I can sit back and assess the whole of golf as it is today. My experience as a player has given me a sound perspective on many of the issues that are of concern and interest to the everyday golfer. My thoughts on individual players, the media, etiquette, the PGA Tour, and trends in equipment, instruction, and architecture often come across as strong opinion—not that anyone will be surprised by that. But they've been formed by what I think is fair and what is good for the game of golf.

Golf has been omnipresent in my life as early as I remember. Some aspect of the game has always been there as a full-time job. My twenty-five years as a touring professional followed a ten-year quasi-career as a junior and college golfer. During that time I traveled the world and either saw or competed against many of the greatest players in history. Along the way I've designed more than thirty courses. I taught the game in books, magazines, and videos. I served on boards and committees, endorsed products, and made commercials. I have a long resume, and it's getting longer every year. I sometimes feel I've packed three lifetimes of experiences into the one short life I've had, and it blows me away that it all was made possible by a wonderful game.

Over the last fifteen years, the game has grown enormously. We're living in a time of tremendous economic prosperity, and with it has come greater opportunities for kids and adults to take up the game—to travel; to use it as a means to get an education and employment; to generally bring all it has to offer within reach. The influx of new players, the growth of the PGA and LPGA Tours, and the increased exposure on TV and in the print media means the game has reached a critical stage. I want people to understand where the game has been so that they can understand the challenges that confront golf today and shape a good course for the future.

In this book I have done my best to be truthful, and I try not to identify a problem without also offering a solution. I love the game more than anything except my church and family, and I want it to remain the wonderful vehicle for camaraderie, fun, competition, good health, and sportsmanship that it is. The game truly is a microcosm of life, and the principles that govern both are remarkably similar.

I'm very much at peace with my accomplishments as a player and announcer. As for being an author, I've tried to deliver some great material. But you can call the shots on that.

JOHNNY MILLER

Salt Lake City, Utah
January 2004

CHAPTER 1

Welcome to Smackdown Golf

The Decline of Etiquette in Today's Game

THE BEST U.S. OPEN performance of all time was by Tiger Woods at Pebble Beach in 2000. The worst performance at a U.S. Open was also provided by Woods that same year. Teeing off on the 18th hole at the conclusion of the second round, Tiger pulled his drive to the left of the famous par 5 and onto the beach. That's when he let himself have it with as vile a stream of profanity as I've ever heard on a golf course. Everyone in the broadcast booth was so stunned we didn't know what to say. So we said nothing.

Tiger is not the first golfer to swear after a bad shot, and a case can be made that maybe the microphone shouldn't have been positioned so close to him. What surprised me though was the way some people flew to his defense when the episode came widely to light. I heard things like, "He's only human" and "It just shows how competitive he is." When someone pointed out that some kids were probably tuning in to see their hero and role model, the reply was, "Every kid has heard those words before." The implications of the outburst came and went pretty quickly—clearly, a lot of people thought it was OK.

Here's the deal: Tiger's swearing was *not* OK. I don't buy that it's merely the language of the GenX crowd. The people who defended Tiger are the same people who swear at their kids or at least swear in front of them. The rationale to my objection is simple: Did the incident elevate golf or bring it down? What if all golfers swore at the top of their lungs when they hit a bad shot?

That episode was symptomatic of a recent decline in etiquette and behavior in the world of golf that has to be watched. It isn't a crisis yet, but as golf more and more becomes a "sport" as opposed to a "game," it's taking on some of the more unsavory features common to the NBA and NFL. This isn't true so much with PGA Tour players as it is the newest wave of fans and amateurs just taking up the game. One thing is for sure: I don't think the people who play golf already are doing a very good job of educating the newcomers.

This isn't a wholesale indictment of Tiger Woods. For the most part, he is one of the class acts in golf. His work with the Tiger Woods Foundation proves he cares about people and loves the game deeply. On the course, he is the one who revived the classy act of removing his hat when he holes out on 18, shaking hands with his fellow competitor, and acknowledging the crowd. He even removed his hat when he lost to Darren Clarke at the 2000 World Golf Championship Match Play. He also has toned down the defiant, fist-pumping, in-your-face displays he regularly made early in his career. Like Walter Payton in football, he began to behave like he'd been in the end zone before.

Deep down, I believe Tiger was embarrassed by the swearing incident, and at the time I predicted we wouldn't hear any more cussing out of him. And indeed, we didn't hear many epithets from Tiger for a time. But at Olympia Fields at the 2003 U.S. Open, as Tiger struggled with his game, he let the four-letter words fly again—albeit not on national TV but certainly within earshot of some eleven-year-old kids. Had that not happened, I probably wouldn't hold his behavior up as an example of a problem that's becoming all too common on golf courses everywhere.

Golf probably is the most frustrating game of all, and it's rare to find a golfer who hasn't sworn out loud on occasion. But it is also the ultimate game of self-control, of keeping your composure. I've always believed that swearing can be controlled. For example, a person can learn to implement milder words into his vocabulary. The odd "crap" or "you stinking hacker" aren't very offensive and can give full vent to your frustration and anger, if you make a habit of it. In all my years of playing with Jack Nicklaus, I never once heard him swear on the golf course. His style was to moan, "Oh, Jack," and that was it. Craig Stadler, who gets so mad he can't see straight, has never been one to swear much, and in fact, very few players of my era did. They knew it would make them look ridiculous and immature.

Golf has always held itself to a very high standard. For example, it's probably the easiest game in the world to cheat at if you are inclined to do so, and consequently it is played on an honor system. Along with the honor system comes a code the players and fans must abide by if the game is to be any good at all. But there are signs it is deteriorating.

The low point probably occurred at the 1999 Ryder Cup at The Country Club. Not among the players, though everyone running onto the green when Justin Leonard holed that monster putt against Jose Maria Olazabal was definitely out of line. The real problem on that occasion was the fans. To say players were heckled would be putting it mildly; the spectators yelled some pretty awful things at the European players and for good measure insulted their wives, too. The wife of European captain Mark James was even spat upon. It was a little scary, because no one could say for sure if the European fans would take revenge three years later at The Belfry. Fortunately, nothing of note happened. But fan behavior remains an issue; you only have to see galleries throwing empty beer cups at the 16th hole at the Phoenix Open to wonder where it might end. That kind of stuff never happened fifteen years ago, and there's no question that it hurts golf.

Even caddies get out of line. When Matt Kuchar had his father caddie for him in his first Masters a few years ago, the dad's demonstrative cheerleading did not please Matt's fellow competitors. You can understand his dad's excitement and I'm inclined to give him a pass, but on the other hand, caddies are supposed to be like a referee in boxing—invisible..

In some ways golf has been victimized by its own success. Everyone wants the game to grow in popularity, but one of the consequences of that is people diving headlong into the game without proper direction. Golf is a game you learn by experiencing more than memorizing conduct rules from a book of etiquette. It takes a while for even a conscientious person to take part without disrupting anything or anyone. So in some ways disruptions are inevitable. Take, for example, the local newspaper photographers who are assigned to cover tournaments. Many of them are new to golf and cover it only once a year when the PGA Tour comes to town. How are they to know that clicking their shutter at the top of a player's backswing is an absolute no-no? It takes time for them to become educated, and hopefully that education takes a softer form than that administered by Tiger's caddie, Steve Williams, to a fan in 2002. The spectator snapped a picture, causing Tiger to flinch on a shot near the green. Williams, identifying the culprit, walked over, grabbed the guy's camera, and threw it into a water hazard. Come to think of it, I don't know who behaved worse, the fan or Williams.

Boorish behavior can come across in many subtle ways. It's more common at the grassroots level than on the pro tours. None of the trends I see are serious in and of themselves, but collectively they've changed the game enough for the observant person to notice. The whole of golf is greater than the sum of its parts, but if you chip away at it long enough, you'll make the game less than it was—and definitely less than it could be.

A typical example is cell phones. I don't know why, but cell phones have almost become an appendage to people's bodies. When golfers make no allowance for the fact they're on a golf course and reach for their cell phone reflexively, it's a problem. Jackie Burke, the great Texas pro, complained ten years ago that that the golf course had become a "grassed-in office." I wonder what Jackie is thinking now. For some reason, when people have their cell phones with them, they are determined to use them whether they really have to or not. It's as if they *have* to call *somebody*. My friend Steve Young, the former quarterback for the San Francisco 49ers, was on his cell phone constantly when I played with him not long ago. I commented on his love of the cell phone, and Steve just laughed. There's a reason they are banned from a lot of public and private courses, and it's pretty obvious why they are banned at pro tour events. If one rang at the top of somebody's backswing, it could decide the outcome of a tournament.

You see the decorum deterioration in golf attire, too. It's not the clothes necessarily. Heck, the psychedelic stuff a lot of us wore in the 1970s was at least as wild as the pants Jesper Parnevik and Charles Howell wear today. It's more the way they wear them. Putting a cap on backward like a comic book character doesn't strike me as particularly stylish, though my son, Andy, did wear his cap backward during the 2002 U.S. Open at Bethpage Black. The difference with Andy was, it was raining. And he wore a bucket hat on top of the cap. I suppose someone is entitled to wear their cap any way they want, but when people do, it seems like a conscious effort to look like anything but a golfer, as opposed to wanting to look as golflike as possible. The same goes with shirttails hanging out. There have always been pro's who could be seen with their shirttails out. But in days past they at least started the round with them tucked in.

Another trend I don't care for is wraparound shades. I wear them on the course myself on occasion, but hey, I'm no longer a tour pro. Tour players who wear them seem aloof. The eyes are the windows to the soul, and I think it bothers fans when they look at a guy and see an expressionless RoboCop. How is this bad etiquette? Because the players don't care if the fans see into their soul or not. Tour pros are in the entertainment business, but imagine watching a movie where all the characters wore dark glasses. Maybe it's a way of hiding, an expression of their shyness. It does seem like the players who wear dark shades—David Duval, Karrie Webb, and Annika Sorenstam—are shy by nature.

Maybe I'm being too stuffy, but the PGA Tour agrees with me, at least in principle. After all, they still don't allow their players to wear shorts, and it's only been a couple of years since they started letting caddies wear shorts. That happened when Steve Williams, Tiger Woods's caddie, showed up in shorts on a sweltering day. The tour threatened to take action, but when Tiger intervened, the tour relented. That's another measure of Tiger's influence; I can't imagine another player having the juice to change a rule, just like that.

These days, people are slow to criticize clothing and behavior. This wasn't the case in the PGA Tour in 1969. Ben Hogan was famous for staring down guys like Grier Jones, a player of my era whose laid-back dress and long hair was not in keeping with Hogan's conservative standard. Beards didn't go down too well, either. I've never been too big on dress codes myself and frankly feel that some of them are too strict, especially at the club level. The practice of sending a woman to the pro shop for wearing shorts that are slightly more than one inch above her knee, or requiring men to wear collared shirts when some of the new, collarless styles really look pretty flattering, is ready for the junk pile. Why can't common sense prevail?

When it comes to playing the game, players are taught early on to replace divots, repair ball marks, and rake bunkers. Golfers do a pretty good job of this, especially at private clubs. But some of the most basic things, such as where to stand when other players are playing their shot, have fallen through the cracks. One of the great furors of the 2003 season occurred when Michelle Wie, a thirteen-year-old prodigy playing in the U.S. Women's Open, was paired with veteran Danielle Ammaccapane. Wie is a very long hitter, and she frequently walked past Ammaccapane's ball and stationed herself at her ball, well in Ammaccapane's field of vision. Once she reportedly walked across the fairway in front of Ammaccapane while Ammaccapane was preparing to play a shot. Wie also walked in Ammaccapane's "through line" on the putting green, a no-no which rankles some players. Ammaccapane does not suffer fools gladly, and she gave Wie a tough talking to after the round. Wie really deserved a pass on that. Very few thirteen-year-olds possess the all-encompassing awareness and experience that tells you where to stand and where to walk. Ammaccapane was wrong to expect as much out of Wie as she does an experienced adult. Wie is a good kid and will learn, but I will say this: By age thirteen, with a lot of tournament experience already behind her, she should know by now where to stand.

Then again, Wie is just a kid. Kids these days aren't bothered by anything. At my first U.S. Open in 1966, I was paired with Al Mengert, a veteran and fine player. On one green, I was standing well away from Mengert while he putted. Not thinking I was in his way, I was making practice strokes with my Bulls Eye putter. Mengert came over to me and told me to hold still, that my practice stroking was bothering him. I had no idea I was distracting him. At age nineteen nothing bothers you, and I was only behaving the way all us kids did.

On the other hand, one area that has improved is temper. If anything, players at all levels used to be worse than they are now. Pros don't throw clubs anymore, though I'm sure the threat of a fine has something to do with it. When I was a kid, tour players were much worse. Tommy Bolt's image revolved around his bad temper, and a good many pros threw clubs all the time. At one of the first pro tournaments my dad ever took me to, the Lucky International, I saw Arnold Palmer bury a club in the ground after he hit a bad shot. I thought that was what pros did, but you better believe my dad corrected me the first time I tried it.

Golf is naturally going to change a bit to reflect society, and that's OK to a point. The game today isn't diminished by its players no longer wearing neckties. The idea, though, is for golf to emulate the best parts of society, not the worst. Fans should respect the players. Players should respect each other. And everyday players should be taught to treat the game with reverence.

CHAPTER 2

The Dreaded "C" Word

A Primer on Choking

THERE WAS PETER JACOBSEN, standing in the 18th fairway with a long, tough shot over water he needed to pull off to win the 1990 Bob Hope Chrysler Classic. And there I was, sitting in the NBC TV tower at the first golf tournament I'd ever broadcast. I sized up the situation closely. I examined Jacobsen's downhill lie on the monitor in front of me. I got the distance to the pin: 225 yards. I checked out Jake's body language. That's when a goblin entered my body.

"This is absolutely the easiest shot to choke I've ever seen in my life," I said.

Jacobsen hit a beautiful shot and won the tournament, proving my prediction—or *possibility* as I saw it—wrong. But from the fallout that ensued over the next few months, you'd think I'd exposed warts on Miss America. Jacobsen didn't talk to me for eight months. The venerable Ken Venturi, the lead analyst over at CBS, said he'd never say such a thing. Writers jumped all over me. Judging by the mail that landed, a lot of golf fans didn't like it either.

Frankly, I didn't get it. From my first day in the booth, I've never intended to be sensationalist or to embarrass anybody. I've never been unduly harsh, except for the time at the Ryder Cup when I suggested that Justin Leonard should have stayed home—a comment I later apologized for. My goal is to be constructive, while pointing out honestly what might be going on in the player's mind and what emotions he may be experiencing. I don't take potshots, because I always have some evidence when a player is choking. If I see a telling idiosyncrasy in his behavior, such as taking an extra waggle, clearing his throat, or displaying trembling hands when he's teeing his ball, something is going on.

As a TV commentator, ignoring the fact that athletes choke is disingenuous. Gagging under pressure often determines the difference between first and second place. The most well-known cliché in golf is that the game is 90 percent mental, and it doesn't refer to figuring out the yardage to the green or pulling the right club. What it really means is that the game is largely emotional. It's about trust, believing in yourself, and playing good golf under the gun. Sometimes pressure gets the better of all of us. It's an issue with every single person who plays the game, and it's especially critical for professionals who have a lot at stake. When you're playing the game for a living and trying to fulfill a lifelong dream of winning a high-profile PGA Tour event, a little self-doubt is always stomping around the periphery of your brain. Sometimes a *lot* of self-doubt. The entire history of golf has been shaped by players who choked when it counted or else got a handle on it and survived.

I myself choked so many times over the years that it's a joke. It started with my putting at age nineteen. I had a fairly short, poplike stroke to begin with, and one day that stroke started to get a little yippy. I dealt with it successfully for many years and was a very good putter until I turned thirty, when my nerves began getting worse. Over time I choked in many different areas of my game, on so many occasions, in all sorts of scenarios. To me, it wasn't the result of a character flaw. It wasn't that I lacked courage. Choking isn't like that at all. It's merely stress manifesting itself mentally and physically. The truth is, the yips are the biggest reason I don't play on the Champions Tour.

Why be in denial about it? The way some tour players react to the suggestion they choked, you'd think they'd run out of a burning building and left their family behind. My feeling is, there is a lot to be learned by studying choking. I've been fascinated with the subject for thirty-five years and have studied it more than just about anyone. If they gave out Ph.D.s for knowledge about choking, the wall of my study would be full of degrees.

At the 1972 Crosby at Pebble Beach, I was tied with Jack Nicklaus with three holes left to play. On the par-4 16th hole, in front of a national television audience, I cold-shanked my approach into the trees. I made a great bogey to go behind my only one, and Jack three-putted the 17th to put us even again. He won the playoff on the first extra hole. From that day forward, I would never be in contention on the back nine on Sunday without thinking, "Am I going to shank this again?" I've always said that the hardest shot in golf is the one immediately following a shank. The clubface looks the size of a pea, while the hosel looks as big as an elephant. That's what choking is—having thoughts go through your mind that wouldn't be there during a casual round with your buddies. The shank at Pebble Beach wasn't a choke, but it led to some unnerving, choking thoughts. I contended in tournaments probably fifty times and every time after that, I worried about shanking. I never did shank again, but you can bet it was dancing around in my head.

My most extreme case of choking, in case you missed it, was against Nicklaus in a Shell's Wonderful World of Golf match in 1997. I'd looked forward to playing the match for a long time, because it was at the Olympic Club in San Francisco and I was playing against my hero. But I happened to have the worst putting day of my life. I three-putted so many times—seven in all—that when the show was edited for TV, they mercifully eliminated five of them. It was worse than embarrassing. From tee to green I played OK, but on the greens it was like I was holding a snake in my hands. I couldn't make a three-footer. There is no worse feeling than standing over a short putt and knowing you've got no chance to make it.

Playing with Nicklaus almost always brought out the best in me, but it also prompted all varieties of choking, usually with the putter. In a playoff against Jack and Frank Beard at the 1974 World Open at Pinehurst No. 2, I came to the 16th hole, which in those days was a par 5, looking for a birdie to win. I ripped a 3-wood about ten feet from the hole, which seemingly locked up the tournament for me. All I needed was two putts to win. But when I took my stance over the ball, I suddenly thought, "How do you two-putt?" When you're ten feet from the hole and the putt isn't particularly fast, you always make a nice run at the hole. Suddenly I wanted to lag the putt up close for an easy two-putt, a strategy my brain couldn't process. How hard do I hit it? Should I play any break? Mentally, sparks started flying. Not wanting to come up short, I blew the putt two feet by the hole. Now I was really nervous. I don't even remember the second putt. Somehow it went in, but I had no idea how. It was terrifying.

The same thing happened to Retief Goosen at the 2001 U.S. Open, but with a more disastrous result. Needing two putts from twelve feet to win, Goosen whacked his first putt two feet past the hole. Then the choking really set in. The groan of the crowd made a nasty little subliminal imprint on his mind. He had just seen his fellow competitor, Stewart Cink, miss from the same distance. Goosen was tired from the heat, humidity, and seventy-one holes of nerve-wracking, major championship golf. He pushed the two-footer badly, which, under pressure, is usually how good players miss putts. Now he had a three-footer left for a bogey and a chance to get in a playoff. At that point, Goosen got angry. One thing that helps defeat choking is to get mad. Goosen steadied himself, knocked in the three-footer, then beat Mark Brooks in a playoff the next day. I don't know how well I made the call from the booth. I was so immersed in Goosen's choking—I could see it coming a mile away—and wrapped up in my own feelings of déjà vu, that I had trouble finding words to describe what was transpiring.

Players will do anything to avoid giving the impression they're choking. I'll never forget the 1982 Andy Williams San Diego Open at Torrey Pines. I had a one-stroke lead over Tom Kite playing the last hole, a par 5 that is a real risk–reward hole because to get home in two you have to clear a pond fronting the green. I outdrove Kite by thirty yards and waited to see what he was going to do with his second shot. He had about 240 yards over water, which in the days of persimmon woods was a very long carry. It was, in fact, outside of his range. Amazingly, Kite pulled a 3-wood from his bag and had a go. He had absolutely no chance of getting over the water, and sure enough, he plopped his ball right in the middle of the drink. Why did he make that play if he had no chance? Simple: He didn't want to look like a chicken by laying up. I would have been much more fearful of Kite had he laid up, because he was (and still is) one of the best wedge players in the world and could have holed his third shot for an eagle.

It takes courage to lay up. David Toms showed a lot of guts when he laid up short of the water on the par-4 finishing hole of the 2001 PGA Championship at Atlanta Athletic Club. If Toms had laid up and lost, he would have been accused of not playing the hole like a man, just as Chip Beck was criticized for laying up on the 15th hole at Augusta in 1993. Kite's failure to lay up in San Diego was a form of choking, because he tried something that was impossible. It showed he wasn't thinking clearly.

It's important to point out that not all chokes are created equal. There are three distinct stages of choking, each having their own characteristics. I'll describe each level of gagging, providing some real-life examples along the way.

Stage One Choking

The player can't handle the visual intimidation of a hole. For example, say there is water running along the left side of a narrow par-4 hole. It scares you, so you aim a bit to the right. As you swing, the fear of the trouble intensifies so that you bail out even farther right. A player can survive Stage One Choking. His body is obeying the mental command to avoid the trouble and he makes a swing that takes him far away from it—sometimes too far away. He might make a bogey and lose the tournament, but very often he is able to make par.

Three examples of Stage One Choking come to mind, one involving a drive, a second involving an iron shot, and the third a putt.

The 18th hole at the Tournament Players Club at Sawgrass, home of The Players Championship, is a sensational choke hole. It sets up in classic fashion, a slight dogleg with a narrow fairway, water on the left and trees on the right. It's amazing how often the leaders find the fairway Thursday, Friday, and Saturday, but then find the right trees on Sunday afternoon. In 2002, Craig Perks came to the tournament having never won on the PGA Tour. A win for Perks meant a five-year exemption, not to mention $1,080,000 in prize money. He came to the 18th hole with a two-stroke lead over Stephen Ames. A pull or hook into the water probably meant a tie at best and maybe a loss. So Perks promptly drove his ball so far to the right that his only shot was a punch back to the fairway. Perks then hit his third shot over the green into a difficult lie from where, unbelievably, he chipped in for par and a two-shot win.

Perks survived. So did Larry Mize, whose choke on the second playoff hole in the 1987 Masters has been completely forgotten. Greg Norman had already hit his approach safely on the 11th green when Mize, needing to match that fine shot but wanting to avoid the pond to the left of the green, hit his middle-iron approach a mile to the right of the green. Mize was one angry dude, muttering in disgust a second after the ball left the clubface. Lo and behold, Mize chipped in for one of the luckiest birdies of all time. Of all the lucky shots inflicted on Norman, this one was the most devastating. Norman didn't choke, the other guy did, and he still lost. Mize survived Stage One Choking.

Davis Love III wasn't as fortunate. On the last hole of the 1996 U.S. Open at Oakland Hills, playing two groups ahead of the leaders, Love's approach to the 72nd hole stopped well above the hole, leaving him a quick downhill putt. Davis didn't know for sure he needed two putts to tie, but he did know it was crucial. Criticized for not yet winning a major, Davis looked at that slick downhill putt and surely thought, "Don't blow it six feet past the hole." So he didn't. He left the putt three feet short instead, something I don't think he would have done a day earlier. He missed the three-footer, and finished second to Steve Jones by a single stroke.

Stage Two Choking

The most common case. The player is so fearful of trouble on a hole that he can't erase it from his mind. Aware that there is trouble on the left, he aims well to the right. But the image of the trouble on the left is so powerful and omnipresent, he inadvertently makes a swing that makes the ball fly to the left anyway. The negative image pushes the positive image out of his mind. A golfer cannot survive this stage.

All of Greg Norman's disasters were of the Stage Two variety. At the 1996 Masters, he had lost all of his six-stroke lead by the time he arrived at the 12th hole, one of the hardest par 3s in all of golf, especially on Sunday. The flag on Sundays is always positioned on the right-hand side of the green, which is particularly shallow. It isn't a long shot, just 155 yards or so, but swirling winds between the tee and green make it very hard to get the distance right. There are many places to pick up birdies on the back nine at Augusta, but the 12th is not among them. The smart play is to the left side of the green, which is much broader. You take your two putts and get out of there.

Watching the telecast on CBS, I could hear Norman's caddie, Tony Navarro, tell Greg to favor the left side of the green. He was very emphatic. Somehow, Norman played his shot to the right anyway, and went in the water. He made a great up and down for a bogey, but it cost him dearly. The miss to the right was always Greg's bugaboo. At Winged Foot in the 1984 U.S. Open, he hit his approach shot to the final hole so far right it went into the gallery. On the last hole of the 1986 Masters, needing only a par to tie Jack Nicklaus and a birdie to win outright, his iron shot flew far right of the green again. The miss to the right under pressure, caused by Greg's failing to turn his lower body, was something he never learned to overcome.

Ray Floyd, who usually was ice under pressure, fell to the Stage Two Choking syndrome at the 1990 Masters. On his approach to the 11th green—the same one Larry Mize missed way to the right during his Stage One episode—Floyd missed his approach in the one place he knew he couldn't miss it: short and to the left, in the water. I don't doubt that water was lurking so vividly in his mind he subconsciously hit it there, even though he tried like crazy to play to the right.

Stage Three Choking

A total meltdown. This is where you're so nervous, your body basically ceases to obey any command from your brain—if your brain is thinking at all. You've heard of people who, in a life-threatening situation, lose control of their bowels? A very similar thing happens here. The player not only can't survive Stage Three Choking, it very often impacts their careers permanently.

Most TV guys don't dare acknowledge the Stage Three disasters. They treat it like sex education in the 1950s, where teachers explained everything except what actually causes a woman to get pregnant. The two most dramatic cases I've seen happened to occur while I was in the broadcast booth for NBC. Both occurred in the Ryder Cup and they involved Jay Haas and Mark Calcavecchia.

Haas's malfunction occurred at the 1995 Ryder Cup at Oak Hill in Rochester, New York. The outcome of the matches hinged almost totally on his singles showdown against Philip Walton. Haas was 1 down on the 18th tee. There, he hit one of the strangest shots I've ever seen, a popped-up drive that went deep into the left rough. One thing about pop-ups is they almost always go straight. As I said on television at the time, you know you're choking when your pop-ups start going crooked. I doubt Haas had hit a shot that poorly since he was ten years old. He lost the match, and Europe won the Ryder Cup by one point. I felt sorry for Jay, because he's one of the nicest guys in golf. And I admire the way he bounced back from that horrible episode. Haas, in fact, had five top-ten finishes on the PGA Tour in 2003, at the advanced age of forty-nine.

Calcavecchia's collapse is the worst I ever saw. It came at the 1991 Ryder Cup at Kiawah Island. It was the most heated Ryder Cup ever and the pressure was more intense than at any event in history, including the majors. Calcavecchia was 4 up in his singles match against Colin Montgomerie with only four holes left to play. At that point, all he needed to do was make a simple par on any hole coming in, and the United States would get a much needed point. Calcavecchia lost the 15th and 16th holes. At the par-3 17th hole, one of the toughest in Ryder Cup history at more than 200 yards and a strong ocean breeze always blowing, Montgomerie hit first and found the water. All Calcavecchia had to do was hit his shot on dry land, and the point was his. But Calcavecchia hit a sort of top-shank-push that barely got off the ground. He went in the water, too, and his next shot wasn't much better even though it stayed dry. Monty made a nice putt for double bogey, Calcavecchia three-putted, then lost the last hole as well to halve the match. It was one of the most terrible collapses in the history of pro golf, and I'll never forget the sight of Calcavecchia crying afterward. The United States won the Ryder Cup and Calcavecchia's day was saved, but it remains probably the most extreme case of choking most people have ever seen. Like Haas, Calcavecchia recovered. He won five tour events after that and is still going strong, but to many people, the Ryder Cup meltdown was the defining moment of his career.

Stage Three Choking isn't rare, really. How about Jean Van de Velde and his triple-bogey seven on the last hole of the 1999 British Open? This was a different variety of the Stage Three disaster; one where the brain shuts down and the player makes a terrible mental error. Van de Velde hit a 2-iron to the last green and he hit a poor shot, but the mistake was his hitting a 2-iron to begin with. He just wasn't thinking clearly. Pulling the wrong club is a very common mistake under pressure. When Jack Nicklaus made that 40-foot putt on the 16th green at the Masters in 1975, Tom Weiskopf's mind became terribly addled. The two of us were standing on the 16th tee waiting to hit when Jack's putt dropped, and the sight of it rattled Tom so badly he hit one club less than he should have. He three-putted the hole for a bogey and lost the tournament.

Although Van de Velde's decision to hit the 2-iron was a choke—if I were his caddie I would have snatched the 2-iron from his hands and broken it over my knee so he couldn't use it—he also suffered the worst break in the history of championship golf. Had Van de Velde's ball simply flown into the gallery, he would have gotten a free drop. He could have pitched onto the green, two-putted, and won by two shots. But his ball hit a metal railing about the width of a golf ball and bounced into junglelike rough short of a burn. Imagine the odds of hitting that skinny metal railing! Van de Velde choked, but it was magnified by extraordinary bad luck.

The roll call of Stage Three disasters is long indeed. How about Costantino Rocca laying the sod over a simple pitch on the final hole at St. Andrews in the 1995 British Open? Doug Sanders missing a three-foot putt that would have won the British Open twenty-five years earlier? Or Fred Couples at the 1989 Ryder Cup, who seeing Christy O'Connor Jr.'s ball close to the pin on the last hole and desperately needing a par to tie, blowing a simple 9-iron shot way right? I'm telling you, it happens all the time. And for a TV analyst to merely say, "He left the clubface open" is lousy reporting, because the viewers aren't getting the real story.

Even caddies choke. When Ian Woosnam discovered an extra driver in his bag on the second tee at the 2001 British Open, the two-stroke penalty that ensued took him out of contention. The caddie forgot to take the fifteenth club out of the bag when they left the practice range. The interesting thing about that incident to me was, if Woosnam was near the lead in the British Open—obviously he was playing great—why was he trying out a new driver?

The Agents of Doom

The golfer is more prone to choking than athletes in other sports. Because it's an individual game, you don't have teammates to fall back on. You absorb the full force of the pressure. There is no place to hide; when it's your turn to hit everyone is silent, still, and waiting to see whether you'll succeed or fall on your face. There also are more trigger points for choking than in other games. In baseball a few years ago, the former All-Star second-baseman for the Yankees, Chuck Knoblauch, developed a terrible problem throwing the ball to first base accurately. It was the only situation that caused him to tighten up, and the Yankees moved him to the outfield. In golf, there may be twenty different situations that make your nervous system go haywire. Then there's the fact you're dealing with a game that requires exacting control of the smallest muscles. That's the first place where physical symptoms of choking show up.

What situations bring about a choke? I can think of seven:

1. Fear of certain kinds of trouble. Just as monster movies scare some people and movies about the occult scare others, golfers vary as to what frightens them into choking. Personally, water always terrified me. I grew up playing at Lincoln Park and the Olympic Club in San Francisco, courses which had no water at all. When I began competition outside California and started confronting water hazards, I probably gave them more respect than they deserved. I couldn't stop thinking, "I can play my next shot from anywhere, but six feet of water is out of the question."

Out-of-bounds is a killer. When I won the U.S. Open at Oakmont with that final round 63, the guy I beat by one stroke, John Schlee, hit his opening tee shot that day out-of-bounds. I'm sure Schlee was overly aware of its presence. Bunkers also scare a few pros. Cary Middlecoff, who won two U.S. Opens, was about a 15-handicapper from sand. Hard as he practiced, he never found a technique that gave him confidence. Sometimes a certain kind of bad lie can summon a choke. The short chip from tall greenside rough gives a lot of players the heebie-jeebies. Downhill lies are also hard to pull off under pressure.

2. Going for P.B. That stands for *personal best,* and nothing makes amateurs choke faster. Most golfers will choke for their all-time best score much faster than they will for money. Nothing makes you depart your "comfort zone"—the mental state where you glide along without fear—more quickly than playing better than you think you can. This one never bothered me, and one mark of a professional is that they aren't afraid to shoot as low a score as they can. It doesn't matter if they make seven birdies in a row, on the next tee they're totally jacked about making birdie number eight.

3. Playing for the team. It's one thing trying to perform for yourself. The consequences of choking are limited, because the only person who is upset is you. When your performance affects someone else, it's a different story. That's why the Ryder Cup brings out the worst in some golfers, as it did with Jay Haas and Mark Calcavecchia.

4. Fear of success. When you're on the verge of winning a tournament, or shooting a career round, a few realizations take hold. It means more will be expected of you. People will be watching you more closely. You'll have something to live up to. That's more than some golfers can bear. They take one look inside the big dark room of fame and start to lose their cool.

5. Fear of failure. No one likes to look like a fool. The possibility of being embarrassed, humiliated, or ashamed makes you think of the consequences of the shot instead of how to play it. The PGA Tour is loaded with players who are consistent money winners but don't win tournaments. They have the ability to succeed, but something inside makes them walk the other way. This isn't choking, really. It's one of the rare examples of cowardice at the professional level.

6. Confronting the weakest link. Under pressure, your golf game is exactly like a chain hoisting several tons of bricks. Whatever your weakest link is, that's where you'll choke. Every tour pro will tell you there is one part of their game that is not as good as the rest. Under pressure, that part will jump up and bite you, because you lack confidence in it to begin with and under stress your shortcomings tend to be magnified. At the 1990 U.S. Senior Open years ago, Lee Trevino finished the final round and went up to the TV booth to see if Jack Nicklaus would catch him on the last few holes. Jack had a very holeable putt on the 17th hole that would get him to within one stroke of Lee. Never one to mince words, Lee pointed out that under pressure, Jack had a tendency to lift his head too soon when he putted. Sure enough, Jack lifted his head and missed the putt. It really bothered Jack that Lee had identified his weakest link. He didn't like the fact that another player recognized his tendency and that he wasn't more aware of it himself.

7. That thing called putting. Most choking occurs with the putter. Usually it happens on putts inside four feet. Short putts look so easy and the player knows it. You're aware of how silly you'll look if you miss and how that three-foot putt is every bit as important as a 280-yard drive. There also is the fact that it is a function of the small muscles, which, like I said, is where choking manifests first.

Short putting was always the weakest part of my game. I was in good company. Ben Hogan, Byron Nelson, Sam Snead, Tom Watson, Arnold Palmer, and Bobby Jones all developed the yips. But it's hardly an old-timers' disease. When you see a tour player on television putting cross-handed, using a long putter, or employing anything other than a conventional grip and putter, you can bet they've had at least a mild case of the yips. If their nerves had held up putting conventionally, they never would have tried an alternative. Most of the time the weakest link is in short putts, because you've convinced yourself that under pressure that's what you do wrong. It's a mindset. So you say, well, gee, I'm nervous, maybe I'm going to miss a short putt like my buddy did last year and you remember that that's where a lot of guys do it. Maybe it's the most obvious one.

Keeping the Beast at Bay

I have great admiration for the player who is labeled a choker and overcomes it. It's one of the most impressive things a golfer can do, because they've succeeded while playing under even more pressure than they had when they got the choking tag to begin with. Tom Watson did that; he had led the 1974 U.S. Open at Winged Foot by one stroke going into the last day and shot 79. In 1975 he set what was then the 36-hole scoring record for the U.S. Open at Medinah before closing 78–77 to lose to Lou Graham. But Watson came right back and won the 1975 British Open a month later, and nobody called him choker anymore. It took a lot of guts to do that.

Watson overcame the battle with himself with sheer determination. Not everybody has the capacity to do that. I think Tom met the problem head-on and simply said to himself, "I will not choke." There was no psychobabble about it, although Watson had majored in psychology at Stanford. That approach never quite worked for me. Over time, though, I learned some other techniques that helped negate the toll my nerves were taking on my game. I feel like sharing them, because it's one thing to point out all the occasions when players choked, another not to provide some constructive solutions. A few of my mind games may seem a little bizarre, or out of the realm of something a sports psychologist might recommend. But they worked for me, and they can work for anyone, pro or amateur.

1. The truth will set you free. The first thing a player should do is admit they're choking. Like an alcoholic, the first step to getting better is to acknowledge you've got a problem. For some reason it seems to alleviate some of the pressure. At the 1974 PGA Championship, Lee Trevino needed two putts at the last hole to win. He'd been fighting the yips something fierce. He lagged his first putt up to within a couple of feet and was closer to the hole than Jack Nicklaus, who was in second place. It's customary for the guy who is farthest from the hole to putt first, but Lee said, "Jack, if you don't let me finish, I'm going to pass out right here." Jack said, "Go ahead," and Lee somehow shook in the putt. Lee is one of the smartest players who ever lived, and at that moment he was aware of two things. First, he knew that if he marked his ball and waited, the pressure just would have gotten worse. Second, by being honest with himself, he mentally was able to move on and think, "OK, so how do I deal with it?"

I have always admired Hale Irwin, not only for winning three U.S. Opens and a bunch of other tournaments, but for how honest he always was with himself. When he won the 1979 U.S. Open at Inverness, the last several holes were a trial for him, his game held together by a thread. He managed to win, but he told the press afterward, "I felt like the barn was on fire and I got out just in time." It was a clean admission he was choking.

If you don't admit you're swallowing the apple, you're in deep trouble. You'll try to play the type of shots you planned on hitting, but they won't come off because your nerves won't allow it. On the other hand, if you openly admit that the pressure is getting to you, you'll acquire a Plan B that will enable you to get the job done. When I won the AT&T Pebble Beach National Pro-Am in 1994, you can bet I was nervous coming down the stretch. I hadn't won a PGA Tour event in seven years. I sure was aware that my nerves were acting up, so I didn't do anything foolish. I played as conservatively as possible, so that my bad shots wouldn't turn into disasters.

When Jack Nicklaus won the 1986 Masters with that great back nine charge, one of the guys he beat was Seve Ballesteros. Seve's big mistake that day came on the 15th hole. He'd led the tournament virtually the whole day, but now, with Jack hot on his heels, Seve choked. He had only a middle-iron shot into the green, but instead of hitting a firm 5-iron, he tried to hit a smooth 4-iron. He came over the top and hit the ball in the pond. I think Seve was too proud to admit he was choking. If he'd come clean about it, he would have realized that trying to smooth shots under pressure doesn't work very well, because you're trying to swing slow while your brain is churning a million miles an hour. He just didn't have a handle on his thought processes or his emotions.

2. Get angry. Payne Stewart was one of the gutsiest players of the 1990s. But his nickname in the early part of his career was "Avis" because, like the car rental company slogan at the time, he seemed destined to always finish second. Much of it was his own doing; he had a hard time closing the deal. He let a lot of tournaments slip through his fingers. It about drove him crazy. After I birdied three of the last six holes to beat him at the 1987 AT&T—Stewart choked by bogeying 17 and failing to birdie 18—he walked over to me and said, "You were lucky. That will never happen again." Not an especially nice thing to say, but he was just plain mad. Later he channeled his anger in a better direction, and won two U.S. Opens and a lot of other tournaments.

The late Dave Marr, a great TV analyst and fine player, won one major championship. He often talked about playing the final holes at the 1965 PGA Championship with Jack Nicklaus breathing down his neck, and how hard it was to function under that kind of pressure. He was choking and was fearful of what might happen over the last few holes. After playing scared for a while, he decided enough was enough. He got angry at himself for being timid in a situation that called for decisiveness and control. "Just close him out!" he said to himself, and that's what he did. Marr won with some tough, rock-solid play. When you're choking, talking sweetly to yourself doesn't work. It takes tough love.

Anger can be manufactured. When I was playing well and had made a string of birdies, the way I avoided a letdown was to pretend I'd actually just made a string of bogeys. On the next tee, I'd contrive a sense of being hacked off, and just kill a drive down the middle.

3. **Eschew the X factor.** The modern swing is not conducive to playing well under pressure. One reason we've seen so few consistent challengers to Tiger Woods is the technique of the fellows trying to beat him. I'm talking about the type of swing where players turn the shoulders as far as possible while moderating the turn of the hips. The idea is to create resistance between the hips and shoulders so there is a lot of tautness, like a stretched rubber band. This type of swing produces a ton of power, but isn't conducive to control. When a player is under pressure and the adrenaline is flowing, he loses some semblance of feel to begin with. When you wind up that rubber band, it can go off like an atomic bomb. A 7-iron the player

intends to hit 170 yards may go 185. I think the speed at which players unwind their upper bodies today is close to double what it was in the 1970s. It's obvious by looking at the follow-throughs of the players. They're wound up like Gumby dolls; my back hurts just looking at them.

The best pressure players I saw had long, loose, languid swings. Fellows like Julius Boros and Sam Snead had a very relaxed coil, and were able to regulate the speed on their downswing with ease. Ernie Els swings like that today, and so does Phil Mickelson. Tiger Woods has an explosive swing, but he's learned to make a softer swing when he needs to. If players added a softer type of swing to their repertoires, they wouldn't be as susceptible to choking. And they'd have longer careers, because it's less stressful on the body.

4. Learn the punch shot. When the heat is on, you need a shot you can absolutely put into play off the tee and onto the green from the fairway. It doesn't need to be a pretty shot, a powerful one, or one you can work the ball with. Every great player has had an antichoke shot they can resort to when their swing is deteriorating or they're having a hard time closing the deal on Sunday.

The best antichoke shot is a punch made with less than a full swing. The ball flies low, but dead straight, and won't roll into trouble. It sounds like a no-brainer, but I'm surprised by the number of players who don't have it. Greg Norman never did learn to use a punch shot effectively; he hit a high, towering shot regardless of the circumstance. Tiger Woods did learn the punch. At one tournament in early 2003, he hit a 7-iron from 135 yards and it was the talk of the tour. For a long time he also had an effective punch shot off the tee, his famous 2-iron "stinger" that went 260 yards without getting much higher off the ground than his head. For whatever reason,

Tiger stopped hitting his stinger in 2003, opting for his driver or 3-wood instead. The loss of accuracy killed him; it's one reason he didn't win a major that year.

5. **Listen to your hunches.** Linear thinkers don't make the best tour players. If you've got a mechanical, one-dimensional swing, what do you do on a day when your timing is off? What do you do when your natural shot is a high fade, and the high fade isn't working? That happens, because the golf swing changes a bit from day to day. Your body never feels quite the same; your strength and muscle flexibility vary a great deal. You need to be able to make small adjustments, and have enough faith in your intuition to trust it. If you can't do it, it's like trying to put a square peg in a round hole.

On the final day of the 1973 U.S. Open, I came to the course without much chance of winning. I'd been playing well, but on Saturday I'd forgotten to bring my yardage book to the course and wound up shooting a fat 76. As I stood on the practice tee warming up on Sunday, a little voice in my head told me to fan my left foot open toward the target. I'd never tried it before, but I decided to try it. It led to one of my best ball-striking rounds ever; I missed a bunch of putts and still shot 63. From then on, I trusted my intuition and my heart. Just as everyone has a conscience, a little Jiminy Cricket telling you what's right and wrong, you also have a little voice that makes suggestions for little swing adjustments. That little voice rarely leads you astray.

I really went to extremes with this. When I got to the 1976 British Open, my putting was giving me a lot of trouble. The more pressure I was under, the jerkier my stroke became. On the eve of the tournament, I had a thought: *Don't look at the ball when you're putting.* So, I got a bottle of red fingernail polish and painted a red dot on the handle of my putter.

Throughout the British Open, I'd line up the head of the putter behind the ball and then rivet my eyes on the red dot. All I tried to do was swing the putter so the red dot moved at the same speed, back and through the ball. I putted just fine. And I won.

Another hunch paid off at the 1987 AT&T. Again, my putting was a wreck. I was hitting the ball great and was only a couple of shots off the lead, but on the 15th hole I yipped a putt so badly I knew there was no way I could make any birdies coming in. Walking to the 16th tee, I heard that little voice again. It said: *Try looking at the hole while you putt.* I thought, what a weird idea. But I tried it. I made putts of fourteen and twenty-two feet coming in, and beat Payne Stewart by a shot. I even putted with my eyes closed once, against Seve Ballesteros at the Million Dollar Challenge in 1982. I won that one, too.

Understand, these bursts of inspiration are only temporary. The techniques you derive from them don't last. You've heard about golfers sitting on the couch at home thinking about the golf swing and suddenly exclaiming, "I've got it!" The little secret they've dreamed up often works—for one round. I call these swing Band-Aids W.O.O.D. keys. That stands for Works Only One Day.

7. Bring in a pinch hitter. For most of my career, I was fine playing golf like Johnny Miller. I had my own swing, my own technique and swing keys. At times, though, when I needed to pull off a shot that wasn't in my wheelhouse, I adopted the swings of other players. When I needed to hit a draw, I pretended I was Chi Chi Rodriguez and swung from the inside, throwing my right side aggressively through the ball. I won the 1994 AT&T at Pebble Beach with Chi Chi's swing. My follow-through was like Chi Chi's, which is to say not very pretty. But it consistently produced a draw. When I needed to hit a fade, I became Lee Trevino, stabilizing the clubface through impact so I got a left-to-right ball flight. When I needed a straight shot, I imitated Tony Lema.

My favorite alter ego was my oldest son, John Jr. At age ten or so he was like a lot of talented kids in golf, in that he made every putt he looked at. He hardly even looked at the line, he just got up and drilled every putt into the middle of the cup. Facing a difficult putt on the 18th hole, feeling the pressure and knowing my own stroke was crap, I said to myself, "I'll just give this one to John." I pretended I was him and, ignoring any thought as to how difficult the putt was, just rapped the ball into the cup.

8. This course owes me. If you choke going for P.B.—personal best—you somehow have to disassociate yourself from the score. The way I did this was to think of all the times the course ripped me off with bad bounces or at least not giving me the score I felt I deserved. I imagined the course as a living, breathing thing that was in debt to me. It *owed* me, and it was time to collect the bill. This gave me a confident, no-fear mind-set where the pressure was on the course to defend itself instead of on me not to choke.

I think Ben Hogan did that when he won the 1951 U.S. Open at Oakland Hills. He said he had "brought the monster to its knees," which to me means he personalized his assault on the golf course. Tom Weiskopf did much the same thing when he beat me at Troon to win the 1973 British Open. Tom didn't like the golf course very much the first time he saw it, which is not a good sign. He moaned about it a lot, until golf writer Dan Jenkins told him to get mad at the golf course, to just go out and "kill it." That's what Tom did. In the performance of his career, he made the course his enemy. I was paired with Tom on Sunday. He holed every putt and tore the place apart. I tied for second, three shots back. I wish Dan had kept quiet.

Choking shows up in strange ways. Sometimes you feel like you can't breathe. Some golfers tremble. Others find they can't speak. Sometimes your hands sweat. My caddie at the Masters for several years, Mark Eubanks, had that problem. During the 1975 Masters, the most exciting in history with the possible exception of Jack Nicklaus winning in 1986, Mark was a mess. His hands literally dripped perspiration, like he was standing in a shower or something. When I got in contention, I had to tell Mark not to touch the grips on my clubs, because they were so slippery I couldn't hold on to them. Watching Mark choke made me think, "I've got to take care of this guy, he might have a heart attack or something." It had the odd effect of relieving my own choking.

With case studies like Mark and dozens of tour players who have choked more times than I can count, I just have to talk about it. The players shouldn't worry about how I discuss it, though. When I pull their pants down, I promise to leave their underwear on.

CHAPTER 3

Calling the Shots

Adventures in Broadcasting

BY 1989, MY PLAY on the PGA Tour had become so erratic that I considered chucking the whole thing. From tee to green I was never better, but on the greens I would flinch as though I had some kind of nervous disorder. My yips were so bad I'd feel embarrassed even when I was alone on the practice green. I'd tried every type of putter and technique you could imagine, but nothing worked for long. It wasn't unusual for me to hit fifteen greens in regulation and make only two birdies, along with a bunch of three-putts and blown four-footers. I shook in a few putts to win the AT&T in 1987, but that was an exception. Golf just wasn't much fun anymore, and after twenty years as tour pro, I'd had enough. I secretly told my wife, Linda, that I was going to retire. I intended to ride off into the sunset and only do a few corporate outings and expand my golf course design business.

An exception to my woes happened late in the year at the Chrysler Team Championship, where I acted as host and was partnered with Peter Jacobsen. I ended my round on Sunday by going birdie, par, hole-in-one, birdie, birdie—5 under par for the last five holes. ABC was televising the event and asked me to come up to the booth for a postround interview. I was in a good mood and made some glib comments about my game and the tournament in general. It so happened that the producer of golf for NBC at the time, Larry Cirillo, was tuning in. And that's where my career as an announcer really began.

NBC was looking for someone to replace their resident analyst, Lee Trevino. Lee had done a good job for NBC and they were happy with him, but he had just turned fifty and let the network know he intended to play on the Senior PGA Tour full-time. NBC was considering a number of possible replacements. Hale Irwin's name came up and so did Raymond Floyd's. Then somebody mentioned me and the interview I'd given ABC.

Cirillo phoned me and said the job was available—and all mine if I wanted it.

I was stunned. They didn't even know if I could do the job. And I wasn't interested even one little bit. But Cirillo was persistent.

"I hear you, John," he said. "But why don't you think about it for a week, talk it over with your wife, and I'll get back to you."

So, in keeping with our protocol, I told Linda about the offer, which, incidentally, was quite generous from a financial standpoint. But I also said that on a scale of one to 100, my interest in this job was somewhere between zero and one.

"It doesn't sound like the worst offer in the world," she said, in a way that told me she liked it.

I reminded her how much I hated public speaking—that it terrified me.

"Yeah, but you're good at it." And then she added, "It would be nice getting a regular paycheck."

That was it. When Linda prods me like that, there's only one thing to do: Take her advice. I phoned NBC and told them we had a deal.

At first I had no clue what I was doing. I had no media training at all and even the little things were a mystery. When do you go to the bathroom? (During a commercial, though you're usually absent for a couple of minutes when we're back on the air.) Could I eat? (You can snack, again during commercials.) Did I have to wear makeup? (Very sparingly, because I have pale skin and that pancake stuff makes me look like a corpse.)

There are no dry runs in front of a live microphone. My performance at my first tournament—the Bob Hope Chrysler Classic—was not good. I said a lot of inane things like, "Gee, I hope he hits a nice chip," and "The leader board sure is crowded today," things that didn't tell the viewer anything he couldn't see for himself. I felt awkward and useless.

Cirillo, bless his heart, was patient with me, almost paternal. He focused on the positive things I did and encouraged me to talk about the golf course and explain the challenges confronting the player without being too wordy. He urged me to use the telestrator, in which the announcer draws features on the screen the audience at home can see. I grew more confident and assertive by the day. By the end of the day Sunday, I was feeling my oats. That's when I made the remark about that tough shot Jacobsen had and introduced the word *choke* into TV golf's vocabulary.

I was off and running, though for several months I had a very hard time accepting my new role. I felt diminished. A lot of top athletes will tell you that it's hard letting go of the perception of themselves as competitors. Anything else they do seems like a step down. They aren't comfortable being on the outside looking in, which is a major reason why so many attempt comebacks after retiring. Fortunately, I quickly got over my discomfort.

In time, I developed a style. I take a lot of chances and don't hesitate to criticize players or their decisions. I talk in a no-holds-barred manner that has consequences, good and bad. When you speak the truth, you make a lot of birdies, so to speak. But you also make a few double bogeys.

My job, believe it or not, requires stamina. I've talked live, on the air, for up to twenty-five hours in a given week, and after I come down from the adrenaline rush, I feel exhausted. People with "real jobs" have a hard time sympathizing with that, but it's true. I get whipped. Announcing takes a lot out of me. I've considered retiring from television every year.

Fortunately, I've always had a lot of help. Not long after I started, they put Bryant Gumbel, who already was one of the top people in TV, in the booth alongside me as an anchor. Bryant didn't bring a lot of golf expertise to the table, but he brought a lot of knowledge of television and that was at least as important. His presence helped me in a lot of ways. His diction, his demeanor, the way he let the cameras tell the story, and his ability to encapsulate everything that had transpired in a tournament and summarize it skillfully in thirty seconds impressed me. I learned from it. His stardom also took a lot of heat off of me, deflecting attention away from a lot of rookie and sophomore mistakes I made. Bryant would become a good friend and ally, and also my amateur partner when I won the AT&T in 1994.

Guys like Bryant are as good at broadcasting as I was at golf in my prime. Charlie Jones demonstrated the importance of raw enthusiasm, and his thrilled-to-be-here personality taught me to get pumped up before we went on the air. Dick Enberg, the consummate pro, amazed me with his diction, flare, and color. Jim Lampley was a smooth, if not very golf savvy, companion. And the team of guys I work with today are the best: Dan Hicks is a fine anchor; Gary Koch and Bob Murphy really keep viewers informed; and Roger Maltbie and Mark Rolfing are fabulous as our chief on-course correspondents.

Dan, Gary, Bob, Mark, Roger, and myself are known as *the talent*, but in broadcasting live golf you quickly learn that the producer and director are even more important. They lay the foundation that enables us to do our thing. For example, Tommy Roy, the executive producer for NBC Sports and the man in charge of our telecasts, insists that we tape a good chunk of live action three hours before we go on the air, just to have on hand in case there's a rain delay. Tommy is a perfectionist. He puts together the production meetings where we critique our most recent show and confer over every detail of the next show. Gil Capps and John Goldstein make sure everything in the booth is organized and they also give us mountains of pertinent information to incorporate on the air. Gil is particularly good; if you hear me say that Ernie Els hasn't made a bogey in fifty-six holes and that he's hit twenty-one consecutive greens in regulation, that stuff comes from Gil.

The quality of the NBC broadcast team in general is why NBC's golf coverage is consistently rated the best among the three major networks. When I say it's a team effort, I'm not just throwing around platitudes. My exposure to these guys has given me the underpinnings necessary to do a decent job. Which leads me to the dos and don'ts of good golf announcing. TV critics tend to praise commentators for the clever, insightful things they say on the air. I believe it's more important to know what *not* to say—and when not to say it. Although I often talk freely and sometimes at length, I perform under an informal set of rules.

Golf Announcing 101: Ten Sacred Rules

Rule No. 1: Learn to talk and listen at the same time. Those headsets we wear in the booth get a workout. In the organized confusion that reigns during a broadcast—particularly if it's Sunday afternoon and there's a crowded leader board—voices are chattering in your ear constantly. And it isn't idle chatter. You're informed of what's going on out on the course, asked to comment on something, or told where the action is going next. The trick is to talk intelligently while listening to the producer at the same time. Some experts say the mind can only concentrate on one thing at a time, but I don't believe it. You can learn to describe verbally what you're seeing while at the same time gathering the important fragments of what someone else is saying.

There's a knack to doing this, and some people never do get it. Years ago, when Deane Beman was PGA Tour Commissioner, he came to the booth as a guest and was fitted with a headset. When someone interrupted him in mid-sentence with the words, "five seconds left, Deane," Beman just stopped talking altogether. It made for an awkward moment, for Deane, for us, and certainly the viewers. He later told us that he was taught as a boy never to talk while someone else was talking.

Rule No. 2: Install a firewall between the brain and mouth. There are certain subjects that should trigger a blinking yellow caution light in the announcer's brain. You never joke about race, sex, or the fact someone is going through a divorce. In fact, you think twice before saying anything funny at all. Don't allude to gender in any way, at least not on a comparative basis. If Se Ri Pak hits the green with a 3-wood from 235 out, you don't say, "She compresses the ball like a man." By the same token, if Jim Furyk misses the green with a 4-iron from 235 yards, you shouldn't say, "He should take a lesson from Se Ri Pak, who hit the green with a 3-wood from the same distance last week."

Sometimes there are issues that are inescapable. When Martha Burk started her campaign to change Augusta National's men-only membership policy, I was very interested to see how CBS would handle the story during the tournament. They were in a tough spot; if they editorialized against Augusta National, they jeopardized their relationship with the club and their TV contract, which is renewed annually. If they came out in favor of the club, women everywhere might have been up in arms. If they elected to remain neutral and cover the story as a news event during the tournament, it would have deflected attention away from the golf action, which the club and many viewers would have resented. Their decision not to cover it at all during the tournament and deal with it only on its news broadcasts was roundly criticized, but on the whole I thought it was a good decision on the part of CBS Sports.

Ideally, you want a filter between your brain and mouth that is small as possible. Because if it's too big, you won't be lively or hard-hitting. If it's too small, you run the risk of offending people. For good or ill, my filter is smaller than most. I've made my share of mistakes, but although I'm fairly blunt, I'm not mean-spirited. I'm very comfortable calling things the way I see them with very little hesitation, because I don't really dislike anyone. I believe that what I have to say will seldom be construed as cruel or that I'm making fun of somebody, because I don't feel that way in my heart. I'm able to talk freely without placing too big a firewall between my brain and my mouth.

I'm lucky that way. I don't think it's something you can teach.

Rule No. 3: Never talk over the shot. This rule was originated by Henry Longhurst, the late, great BBC announcer who later worked for CBS. It's one I've borrowed without hesitation. Our job as announcers is to set the scene. If Annika Sorenstam is looking over a difficult twenty-foot putt for birdie that will put her in the lead, I'll describe the importance of the putt, how it breaks, and allude to the fact she's made two others like it on the back nine. But once she takes her stance over the ball, I shut up. The idea is to let the action speak for itself. There isn't one thing I can say that will add to the drama of the ball rolling toward the hole.

I've never understood why some announcers start talking the second the ball takes flight, saying things like, "That looks good . . . he caught it flush . . . it's right on line," when the viewer is going to find out for himself in three seconds whether the player caught it flush, whether it was right on line, and how good it really looks. If the announcer is right, so what? He didn't add anything. If he's wrong, he looks like a fool. So the smart thing to do is just be quiet.

Rule No. 4: Avoid the cliché of the day. Catchphrases go in and out of style. Depending on the year and month, the same putt can be described as "center cut," "right in the heart," or "dead center." I try to avoid the clichés, because they don't convey independent thinking. They come across as vapid, give-up expressions the announcer uses because he can't think of anything else.

These expressions are contagious, like a disease. As I speak, the cliché of the day is "nice play." When someone hits to the fat part of the green or lays up safely on a par 5, you hear a lot of announcers say, "That was a nice play."

You have to be careful with phrasing. First, know what these expressions mean to begin with. For example, when two players are paired together, one should be referred to as the "fellow competitor" of the other. This one gets butchered badly. I've heard individuals described as "fellow partner," "playing competitor," and one time even as "playmate." I can stand the expression "playing partner," but the others are beyond the pale.

Rule No. 5: Turn twenty seconds into ten seconds. Time is always of the essence. The camera jumps from one scene to another very quickly. You don't always have much time to describe a shot at length, so the good announcer learns to condense his thoughts into short, meaningful bursts of language. They don't have to be grammatically perfect, but they must contain as much information as possible.

Say Tiger Woods has just missed a key putt for a par and his lead over Phil Mickelson has shrunk to one shot. The camera suddenly darts over to another hole, where Mickelson is preparing to go for the green of a par 5 in two. The shot is over water and risky, and he's addressing the ball. You know you've got only ten seconds to encapsulate what this shot means.

The good announcer will say something to the effect of: "Mickelson's second on the par 5 . . . 230 over water, 3-iron to a front pin . . . Ball is sitting down . . . Phil hits it high but this is dangerous . . . Here goes nothing."

That doesn't read very smoothly, but it sounds OK and gives all of the pertinent information. Get the voice inflection right, and under the time frame this is all the viewer needs or wants.

Rule No. 6: Keep your eyes on the monitor. Years ago, the broadcast booth was commonly located near the 18th green. Today it's in a protected location—Tommy Roy doesn't want the booth where anyone can see it. The booth is made of plywood, sits on scaffolding, and is painted a dark green so it blends in with the trees and shadows.

The interior of the booth is fairly Spartan. There's a camera aimed at Dan Hicks and me. Behind us is a Plexiglas screen, beyond which is an attractive part of the course—a pond with a fountain in the middle, say, or a rock wall and waterfall. Near the cameras is a monitor that shows us the same thing you see at home. In that sense, I might as well be at home in my living room, because I'm merely elaborating on the view you have.

That monitor is all-important. It's crucial that the announcer not take his eyes off it. Something can transpire that needs addressing. It may be something fairly insignificant, like a squirrel running across one of the greens. But you must keep your eyes riveted on the same thing the viewer and the anchor are watching and fall into a rhythm describing it. If you get distracted and start describing a statistic you see in your notes, or look at the clouds through the Plexiglas behind you, you run the risk of missing something important.

Rule No. 7: Be quick on the uptake. Early in my career I discovered I possessed a few traits that were conducive to good television. I found that television was kind to my face, which I'm grateful for because you never can tell whether someone will be telegenic or not. My voice was somewhat distinctive. Most important of all, I was blessed with the ability to be fast and straightforward. Many people just don't have the capacity to see an event and grasp its bottom line, the chief cause and consequence. Some people see all things as mitigated—their filter is turned up too high. It makes for good politics, but it doesn't make for very good television.

I also am fairly quick-witted, which isn't a gift at all. It can be developed. Growing up around the Olympic Club, where the atmosphere was one where kids and even adults needled each other constantly, you developed a fast wit or else perished. It was all in good fun—for the most part—but a person was judged by how they could take it and give it back.

I was lucky to have been exposed to that. Right after I joined the PGA Tour, I played with Lee Trevino for the first time. We didn't know each other very well, and when Lee looked at the pale, thin, blond-haired kid fresh out of Brigham Young University, he saw a piece of fresh meat. He threw a few zingers at me, and then we went to the first tee. There were lots of people around, and Lee decided to keep hammering away at the rookie. I came right back at him, and fast. He jabbed, and I countered even harder. I remember the surprised expression on his face, and his ambling over to me and whispering, "Man, you're one tough dude."

Another thing about wit: Humor is a dangerous thing because it's subjective. I'm very careful about saying something that strikes me as funny, especially if it applies to a human being, because you end up running over people. You may think you're being lighthearted, but in truth you still leave tire marks. Gary McCord is the best at injecting humor because he rarely pokes fun at people directly. He tends to joke about inanimate objects or events, and is given a wide berth because that's his shtick. Even then, it's a bit of a high-wire act. When he alluded to the greens at Augusta National being so fast that someone had applied "bikini wax," and hinted that some of the mounds concealed "body bags," it cost him his position at Augusta.

Rule 8: Invent some original nomenclature. Golf on television is relatively new and in many ways the craft of announcing is still in the formative stages. There have been a handful of terrific announcers, but there's still room for people to come along and make contributions to the craft. I've broken new ground in several ways, most notably by introducing the word *choke* into the lexicon. When I hang up my microphone, that will probably be my legacy.

There are other words and phrases I've introduced that don't rate as contributions to the profession, but have made me distinctive. I'm the first to refer to "backboards," "fault lines," and "sideboards" to describe slopes and tiers on the greens. I refer to shots as "lean-in-squeeze-fades," "trap-ups," "shoot fades," and "Campbell's Chunky." A certain hole might be a "reverse bank dogleg." I've invented twenty other expressions like them. Some of them are technical, others are whimsical, and some are just plain silly. But they do add color and a personal touch. If you don't come up with an original saying or two, you're just another talking head.

Rule 9: Do your homework. The importance of boning up before a tournament seems obvious, but not everyone does it. There's no substitute for preparation. A good announcer can't survive on style alone. There has to be substance. And you have to be prepared every week.

For the first seven years of my career, I got to the course early every day and walked the holes I'd be covering. I checked the hole locations and putted the greens, so I knew which way the ball would break when a player had a putt later on. I wanted to know how firm they were and how fast they were running. I measured the width of the fairways, charted yardages from the fairway bunkers to the greens, and took note of the prevailing wind. I put all this information down on charts I carry with me on tour.

I don't do that to the same extent today, because I know the courses so well. We tend to cover the same tournaments year after year, and I know courses like Bay Hill and Doral as well as anyone. I still show up a couple of hours before we go on the air and watch a few groups play some holes. I still talk to the gallery marshals for any special insight they might have, such as fairway bunkers that players consistently are finding with their tee shots. It's important that I update my charts, but nowadays I do it in an abbreviated fashion. At the major championships as well as the Solheim Cup and Ryder Cup, I research the courses as carefully as ever. I keep abreast of the players, too, but I still rely on that extra boost from Gil Capps.

Rule 10: Go easy on the competition. I refuse to pick on announcers at the other networks. Criticism makes you look small. I've been asked a thousand times about the styles and abilities of Curtis Strange and Lanny Wadkins, and before he retired, Ken Venturi. No one's ever quoted me on those guys, because I give the standard, "no comment." I will say this: They each have their own style, and each brings something unique to the table.

Because I've been ranked the number one TV analyst in golf so many times by *Golf Digest*, I'm under the microscope more than my competitors. They've certainly taken some shots at me. Doug Tewell criticized me once, and Frank Chirkinian once dismissed me by saying, "Anyone could get publicity if they took shots at players like Johnny Miller does." I'm not fazed by that criticism from them; the only feedback I'm interested in is that offered by Tommy Roy, NBC Sports president Dick Ebersol, or my on-air colleagues.

Major Moments

By my count, I've worked more than 120 events for NBC. That includes eighteen men's and women's U.S. Opens, six Ryder Cups, thirteen Players Championships, and eight U.S. Amateurs. It's the big events that always provide the most dramatic moments. The fields are the strongest, the players are always on edge, and the courses are terrific. These competitions usually turn out to be self-fulfilling prophecies; the players, public, and media want something dramatic to happen and something usually does.

From an announcing standpoint, certain championships rate especially high. Invariably there's more pressure on us TV guys to perform well, and it shows. On five occasions I've walked down the ladder from the booth early Sunday evening feeling completely spent emotionally, as though I had just played myself. Like any other fan, when a competition is close I've lived vicariously through the players. I've sweated, become nauseous, and sometimes even felt at a loss for words. Whenever I've contemplated retiring from announcing, it's the thought of being at the next U.S. Open or Ryder Cup that keeps me coming back.

I played in some of the most dramatic tournaments of all time. The 1975 Masters, in which I played and finished second, may have been the greatest Masters of all time, though most people give the 1986 tournament—also won by Jack Nicklaus—a slight nod. I was at Turnberry for the Nicklaus–Tom Watson duel in 1977 and played at Muirfield in

1972 when Lee Trevino edged Tony Jacklin. I played in a bunch of great U.S. Opens.

Here are the best five competitions I've seen in my career as announcer, dating back to 1990. I can't put them in order; they all were sensational.

1994 Players Championship. In all my years as a player and announcer, three individual performances stand out. Two were by Tiger Woods, the first when he shot 18 under par to win the 1997 Masters, the second when he won the 2000 U.S. Open by fifteen strokes. The third, and maybe the best, was Greg Norman shooting 24 under par at the Tournament Players Club at Sawgrass in Ponte Vedra, Florida, to win The Players Championship in 1994.

Norman was always explosive, but he rarely put it all together for all four rounds on a tough course. Almost nobody can. But that week was something very special. I don't think anyone, Tiger included, could have beaten him. The TPC can be exploited by a good player who is on his game, but the design is so quirky that it's almost impossible to avoid mistakes. There's a lot of water. The wind blows. The mounds around the greens—and on the greens for that matter—demand a precise style of play.

It made for great television. Greg led the first day after shooting 63. He followed with two 67s to set a 54-hole scoring record, but Fuzzy Zoeller was also playing well and was only two shots back headed into the last round. Almost ten years after losing to Zoeller in a playoff at the 1984 U.S. Open, the stage was set for a great head-to-head matchup. It had the feel of a major championship about it, although contrary to the PGA Tour's fervent wish, The Players isn't officially a major. In that final round, Norman played the kind of round everyone knew he was capable of producing. He birdied three of the first four holes to lead Zoeller by six strokes, and despite all the danger that lurks on the TPC's back nine, you got the idea the tournament was over.

When Norman bogeyed the 13th hole, I had a nice statistic ready to present to the audience. It was his first bogey in sixty-seven holes, a phenomenal accomplishment. The bogey didn't faze Norman. On the 16th hole, a dangerous par 5 with water behind the green, Greg pulled his drive to the left. A cart path there came into play and he wound up with a very bare lie. He then played an extraordinary shot, a long iron that stopped just short of the water behind the green. Another birdie.

After Greg holed out on 18, Fuzzy, ever the showman, strolled over, removed Greg's hat, and mopped his brow with a towel. The idea was to indicate that Norman had shot 24 under par without breaking a sweat. And he hadn't.

2000 U.S. Open. Tiger Woods had it going early at Pebble Beach and late on Thursday was 5 under par on the back nine. A bunch of guys were under par, so to most people the championship seemed to be up for grabs. The camera drew in close on Tiger and Dan Hicks asked what I thought of his play. I said, "I talked with him yesterday and watched him play a practice round. My feeling is, he's not only going to win this thing, he's going to win with a record score."

I'm not much of a prophet and in fact he only tied the 72-hole record for a winning score at the U.S. Open, at 272. But if I'd said, "By a record margin" I would have been dead-on, because Woods won that U.S. Open by fifteen strokes. It was a phenomenal performance, one I appreciated even more because I know Pebble so well. The course was not easy that week; the guys who tied for second, Ernie Els and Miguel Angel Jimenez, finished at 3 *over* par. Tiger hit the ball phenomenally well from tee to green, but his putting was supernatural, the best I've ever seen. He didn't lip out one putt all week. Everything went in the middle of the hole. Tiger would rap the ball and just start walking toward the hole because he knew it was going in. At Pebble Beach that's unbelievable, because the greens there are bumpy even when conditioned to hold the Open. He putted so well that he shot 12 under for the tournament even while making a triple bogey on Saturday.

I was awed by what I saw in Tiger that week, but even more impressed by the effect it had on the other players. From that moment on, guys couldn't look Tiger in the eye. I'll borrow an expression that is applied by a lot of writers in describing confrontations in a lot of other sports: They all knew Tiger was the best, Tiger knew it, and he knew that they knew. And that's pretty much how things have stood ever since.

1995 Ryder Cup. The importance of strategy, the power of momentum, and the effects of pressure were never underscored more emphatically than at Oak Hill in the fall of 1995. Corey Pavin had wound up Saturday's four-ball matches with a spectacular chip-in for a win on the 18th hole. That gave the U.S. a two-point lead heading into Sunday's singles matches. But the lead seemed even bigger than that. There was a feeling in the air that there was no possible way the Americans could lose. Not on home soil on a course set up like it was hosting a U.S. Open, which a European hadn't won in twenty-five years.

Then the American team fell apart. The Europeans won six and a half out of a possible nine points midway through the final day, and took the lead with only two matches remaining. That's when the pressure really set in. Jay Haas, 1 down to Philip Walton coming to the 18th hole, hit that crooked pop-up off the tee—Stage Three Choking at its best—and bogeyed the hole when par would have retained the cup for the United States.

As the Europeans began their comeback, you could see the blood draining from the faces of the American players. Their loss of confidence was palpable. The Europeans must have holed six shots from off the green, including a hole-in-one by Howard Clark. It was like someone had thrown cold water into the faces of the entire U.S. team.

It was at that moment that the importance of captaining strategy came into play. Lanny Wadkins, the U.S. captain, had chosen a fellow Virginian, Curtis Strange, as one of his two captain's picks. On one hand it was a sensible choice. Strange had won the 1989 U.S. Open on the same course, was known for being tough under pressure, and had a great appreciation for the Ryder Cup. On the other hand, it doesn't matter what course a guy is playing, he still has to hit the shots. Strange was 1 up with three holes to play and bogeyed all three holes to lose to his old nemesis, Nick Faldo. It was a stunning collapse, the worst of Strange's career. The Ryder Cup was lost for the Americans. The 18th hole was particularly memorable. Strange had a 4-iron shot to the green for his second shot. Just after the ball took flight, Paul Azinger, who was on the ground for NBC, said, "It's a great shot . . . headed right for the pin." I interjected, "No, I can tell by the sound that he caught it a groove or two down on the clubface." The ball fell short into heavy rough, Strange made bogey, and lost his match. I felt then, and had said so previously, that Lee Janzen, a tough competitor who'd won the 1993 U.S. Open but hadn't qualified for the team, deserved the spot more than Curtis. It's hindsight, I guess, and I felt badly for both Wadkins and Strange.

That wasn't the only mistake Wadkins made. His lineup the final day showed no real strategy at all. He sent two of his weaker players, Peter Jacobsen and Jeff Maggert, out early and they both lost, which contributed to the Europeans' momentum. I'm a big believer in "front loading," of putting your best players out early and just slamming the door on the other team. I think that's the way to do it whether you're ahead, behind, or tied. That's what the Europeans did in 2002 (remarkably, against a U.S. team captained by Curtis Strange), and the early momentum helped them to a big comeback and victory against the Americans. And the Americans did it in 1999, the year the United States trailed by a mile heading into the last day and Ben Crenshaw seemed to cross the line mentally at the Saturday postround press conference. Front loading works.

1999 U.S. Open. This championship was remarkable on several counts. First, the USGA had broken away from its standard rotation of U.S. Open courses and went to Pinehurst No. 2, a great course if ever there was one. As a player, I was never fond of inverted greens that slope away at the edges and repel shots. As an announcer, however, I loved how even good shots paused and then trickled off the sides of the greens, leaving the players frustrated and facing a difficult recovery. Not to sound sadistic, but some of the fun of watching the U.S. Open is seeing players have their patience tested.

The cast of contenders was compelling. Tiger Woods, Phil Mickelson, and David Duval all were shooting for their first U.S. Open victories and were contending heading into Sunday's final round. Mickelson provided the running sidebar to the championship because his wife, Amy, was on the verge of delivering their first child and Phil had made it known that he was going to walk off the course the second the birth became imminent. Payne Stewart, who'd collapsed at the Olympic Club one year earlier, was trying for his second Open. When you have a lineup like that, you can't help but have great theater and a big viewing audience.

Woods missed short putts on the back nine and fell away. Duval blew up early in the round and was never a factor. It came down to Mickelson, who was putting beautifully and had his long game under control, and Stewart. A steady drizzle beat down on the players, giving the scene a haunting, surreal look. Stewart was wearing a rain jacket with no sleeves—we showed him cutting them off with scissors before he teed off, so the sleeves wouldn't distract him.

Mickelson was using a heel-shafted putter with a wide, thin head. It had a ton of loft. It was an odd-looking thing, but he made a boatload of putts. Then, on number 17, it let him down. He pulled a six-footer and Stewart made his, giving him a one-stroke lead going to the 18th hole. There, Payne pushed his drive to the right and had to punch out, while Mickelson hit the fairway. They wound up with putts of similar distance. I thought there was no way Payne could make that putt. It was nineteen feet and up a crest to the hole, the kind of putt you never make. You couldn't see the slope on television because the cameras tend to flatten topography, but it was one brutal putt. Stewart's reaction when the putt went in was unforgettable. He crouched in that wildman manner of his, screamed, then approached Mickelson and cradled his face in his hands and told him to be happy, that having a baby meant more than golf. Mickelson was thankful for that, but he still registered shock at seeing Payne's putt go in. "Nice putt" was all you could hear him say on the television.

Providence had something to do with that putt going in, I think, because a few months later Payne Stewart would die in that awful plane accident. Stewart was a great Hall of Fame player and more important a ticket seller if ever there was one. I'm glad we still have the video of him winning that Pinehurst U.S. Open, because I never tire of watching it.

1991 Ryder Cup. If I *did* rank the competitions in order, this would be number one. The "War at the Shore" at Kiawah Island began months in advance with an unprecedented jingoistic buildup. The United States hadn't won a Ryder Cup since 1983. Patriotism was running high because we had just expelled Iraq from Kuwait. The Europeans were defiant and flying high, thanks to the leadership of Bernard Gallacher. Everyone seemed to fan the flames. Paul Azinger said something to the effect of "We thumped the Iraqis and now we'll thump Europe." And then the Americans showed up wearing camouflage caps, an over-the-top move that had the Europeans rolling their eyes. The American team's wives wore screaming red, white, and blue outfits. The gallery waved huge flags. The roars emitted after every hole won or lost were huge.

The format of the Ryder Cup is especially well-suited for television. The viewer knows the players are battling for their country and for each other, rather than for money. I've always suspected that prize money is a turnoff to many viewers. The average person who works his or her tail off for a weekly paycheck has to be just a little envious of the pro golfer who makes millions of dollars a year playing a game in exotic locations in perfect weather. Another draw is the match play format. People like to see golfers compete against flesh and bone—other golfers—rather than the golf course, which is dirt and grass. Every day of the Ryder Cup is like a dozen tournaments happening simultaneously. And the pressure is so obvious that the viewer is almost sucked through the screen and placed on the course. Every red-blooded American golf fan feels they are part of it.

The 1991 Ryder Cup brought all these aspects to life. It was a sensational battle from start to finish. The Americans led by a point after the first day but the Europeans battled back to tie it heading into the final day's singles matches. Early on there was a hot dispute between Azinger and Seve Ballesteros—it wasn't their first—over Azinger and Chip Beck switching types of balls during the foursomes matches. By and large, the chemistry between the two teams was like oil and water. I've never seen guys more combative or trying harder to win.

That last day was as dramatic as any in golf history. The Europeans took the lead early when two of America's best players, Payne Stewart and Raymond Floyd, both got beat. When Mark Calcavecchia lost the last five holes to halve his match with Colin Montgomerie, it looked dim for the United States. But on came the Americans, winning four of five matches near the end to gain a one-point lead with only one match still alive. It came down to Hale Irwin versus Bernhard Langer, two of the toughest players ever. On the 18th tee, their match was all square, and Irwin needed to keep it that way in order for the United States to win the cup.

There was more pressure put on those two players than ever was exerted on anyone on a golf course, ever. Irwin's nerves may have been good enough for him to win three U.S. Opens, but this was too much even for him. He seemed to be having trouble breathing. It took him three shots to reach the green, and he left his par putt short. Langer, meanwhile, had also reached the green in three and faced a seven-foot putt for a par and the whole ball of wax. He missed and the United States erupted into the biggest celebration I've ever seen. Players and fans on both sides were weeping. Irwin's face was a mask; he could barely talk.

Away from the cameras, Langer cried. The next week he would win the German Masters.

Can I Have a Do-Over?

Most TV announcers will tell you they are at their best when they are relaxed and talking as though they're chatting with friends in their living room. That's true and I always try to acquire that state of mind. But there's a downside to it. You can become so relaxed that you blurt out something you don't mean or that is taken out of context. I've learned this the hard way. I can point to a couple of instances where I'd have paid money to have been given a verbal mulligan.

Do-over number one. On Saturday at the 1991 Ryder Cup (like I said, the best competition I've ever seen), Paul Azinger hit a terrible pull on the 17th hole, a long, tough par 3 over water. It was a bad shot and I said so on the air. Paul's wife, Toni, got word of it and informed him. When a reporter approached Azinger and asked him to respond to my comment, he said, "Aw, that Miller is the biggest moron." When I saw the headline on Sunday morning, I felt blindsided. I hadn't been announcing very long and didn't take it well. The truth is, it hung in the back of my mind all the last day. It didn't help when I read the papers on Monday and read that Azinger had "retracted" the comment by saying, "I was misquoted. What I said was, he is the biggest *Mormon*."

I was even more offended by that. People thought the joke about my religion was funny and newspapers and magazines continued to print the quote even months later, just to get laughs. My favorite golf magazine thought it was hysterical and put it in their year-end issue. I learned something about the media's sensitivities about religion: The extent to which they use blasphemy to get laughs depends on the religion they're poking fun at. As for Paul, I forgave him. We're good friends, and I think he has the potential to be a better TV announcer than any other golfer, active or retired.

Do-over number two. I got seriously caught up in the 1999 Ryder Cup at Brookline. I try to be objective and not root for a particular player or team, but the fact is, I'm an American and a part of me is pulling for the red, white, and blue. So when the Americans played terribly in the early going, I started feeling frustrated. During the Saturday morning foursome matches, Justin Leonard faced an 8-iron shot to a front pin, and pulled it so badly the ball wound up to the left of the left greenside bunker. Leonard and Payne Stewart ended up losing their match to Sergio Garcia and Jesper Parnevik, and the United States fell behind by four points, a huge deficit.

For the afternoon four-ball matches, captain Ben Crenshaw had arranged for Jeff Maggert and Hal Sutton to tackle Miguel Angel Jimenez and Jose Maria Olazabal. Maggert and Sutton had both played well in the morning and I saw them as likely to win their match. Then we got word that Maggert had told Crenshaw he wanted to sit out the match, that he was tired. I thought, *Tired? At a time like this*? It was unbelievable. If you can't get enough adrenaline flowing to make it through Saturday of the Ryder Cup, you must not care very much about it. I was probably more tired than Maggert was; we'd been on the air twenty-eight hours already that week. In any case, Crenshaw replaced Maggert with Justin Leonard, who in six Ryder Cup matches over a two-year period had yet to win a point outright. My comment was, "My hunch is that Justin needs to go home and watch it on television."

On Sunday, when Leonard holed a bomb of a putt to square his match with Jose Maria Olazabal and clinch the Ryder Cup for the United States, he suddenly was a hero. And man, did I take some heat for my comment. Leonard smacked me around for a while, saying, "I guess it's a good thing I didn't go home." Then Jim Furyk, whom I'd classified as an underdog in his match against Sergio Garcia (this was 1999, remember, before Furyk was truly a world-class player), took me to the woodshed by saying it was my comment that motivated him to beat Garcia.

Like I said, my announcing style is high risk. I'm going to make some double bogeys, and this was one of those times. Leonard to this day still hasn't won a match in Ryder Cup competition, and I wasn't wrong by pointing out he wasn't playing well. But it's not what you say that counts, it's how you say it. And I wish I could turn back the clock and say it in a way that wasn't smart-alecky or insulting.

Do-over number three. Juli Inkster is one of the best women players of her generation and probably the most durable. She's won seven majors, including the 1999 and 2002 U.S. Women's Opens. She was past forty when she won her second Women's Open, a fact that blew me away. "Most women her age are home cooking dinner," I remarked to a national audience. Ouch. I got cooked like I *was* a dinner after that remark. Now, if I were really a sexist person I would have said that Juli *should* have been home cooking dinner, but no matter. I didn't mean to hurt anyone, Juli especially. She belongs in two Halls of Fame: one for being a great player, the other for being one of the great moms of all time.

Do-over number four. The Bob Hope has almost as many celebrities as the AT&T. One year, country singer Vince Gill—a fantastic player, by the way—was wearing his visor, which sported a big Cobra logo, way back on his head to accommodate his pompadour hair. I said, "Vince has a smooth swing and is a good player, but he's got to learn to wear his visor right." A fan, watching the episode on a small television in his fairway condo, shouted down, "Hey Vince, Johnny Miller says you don't know how to wear your visor!" So Vince took his visor off and put it back on his head upside down. Fast on the uptake, I said, "Well, they've been trying to turn that company around for a long time."

Most people in golf are aware I have a contract with Callaway Golf. The people at Cobra certainly were aware of it, and were not amused. They fired off a letter to NBC and me, and I saw their point.

But if those instances are as bad as it's going to get for me as an announcer, then I'm in decent shape.

CHAPTER 4

Can Tiger Catch Jack?

The Case for an Emphatic "No"

AS TIGER WOODS CONTINUES to cut a wide swath through professional golf, the questions regarding his ability are diminishing. There will always be the tabloid topics—his personal life, how much money does he have, is he happy with his caddie, and so on. When you move to the subject of his game, the questions are moot. He has been the best player in the world for six years now and there is no question that the game he plays is the best the world has ever seen. To me, there is only one question left: Will he break Jack Nicklaus's record of winning eighteen professional major championships? The subject is tantalizing, because it opens an entire new area of discussion, speculation, and more questions.

Over the years I've vacillated. When Tiger turned pro in 1996, I didn't think he had a chance. I predicted he would win twelve majors and fifty tournaments, which most people thought was grandiose. But after Tiger started picking off majors like ducks on a pond and won the Tiger Slam in 2000 and 2001, I felt there was no stopping him. I assumed he'd surely win twenty professional majors at least. His golf was so sublime, his way of going so intoxicating, I saw him averaging two majors a year until he reached age thirty-three. I figured he'd sprinkle in seven more majors before the age of forty-five. That would give him roughly twenty-five major championships, and he wouldn't break a heavy sweat doing it.

My opinion today is that he won't get the record. Although he's the best player the world has ever seen and is almost halfway home with eight majors, I think the challenge of winning eleven more will be brutally difficult. I see a host of potential roadblocks which, cumulatively, will make the second half of his quest one of the most difficult challenges in sports history. In the end, I see him winning sixteen professional majors. If you want to count his three U.S. Amateur victories as majors (why not? we count Bobby Jones's U.S. Amateurs and British Amateur victories as majors), that gives Tiger nineteen—still shy of Jack's record of twenty.

In this era of Tiger mania, when every human being on the planet is pulling for him to break Jack's incredible standard for winning majors, it's almost politically incorrect to say Tiger will come up short. There is a certain irrationality to the extent the world has become pro Tiger. For example, when he won the U.S. Open, British Open, and PGA Championship in 2000, and followed that up by winning the 2001 Masters, he held all four major championship titles at one time. Arguments were set forth that he had won the Grand Slam, which to me didn't have the ring of truth. What he accomplished was the equivalent of pulling a straight flush in poker, 9-10-Jack-Queen-King. But he was missing the ace. If what he accomplished was the Grand Slam, what would you call it if he won all four majors in a calendar year? The "Grand Tiger Royal Slam"? Come on. The accomplishment was spectacular and may never be equaled again. But it was not the Grand Slam, and saying so is only an evaluation of the achievement, not an affront to Tiger.

In any case, there's a pervasive wave of hope that Tiger will surpass Jack. Tiger is viewed almost as an underdog in his quest, and if Americans love anything, they love an underdog. Records are made to be broken, and we all want to live in a time of extraordinary achievement. If Tiger does break the record, it will be the sports equivalent of man walking on the moon. I'd like to see him get there, but I can't help but side with the factors that inveigh against Tiger.

The primary pitfall is the tendency to look at Tiger as though time will stand still for the next twenty years. They see his youth, his ability, and his competition as parts of a continuum that will stand without interruption. Of course, golf doesn't work that way any more than life itself does. Things change. It's a long and winding road with lots of variables, not all of them conducive to success. For Tiger to squeak past Jack and win eighteen professional majors, he'll have to sidestep a lot of little land mines. The path he's walking is fragile, and if he negotiates everything just right, he's got a shot. But if one of those land mines explodes, he won't get there.

Before I make my case against Tiger breaking Jack's record, I should point out the factors going in his favor. There is no question that Tiger has played the best golf ever seen in history. If you take Tiger's best against Jack's best, Tiger wins. If the race were a sprint instead of a marathon, Tiger would leave Jack in the dust. Some of Tiger's achievements are mind-blowing and he's set some formidable records that Jack never approached. If you're pro Tiger, here's how you make your case:

Tiger's performance knows no bounds. When Tiger is at his best, anything is possible. In winning the 1997 Masters, he was 22 under par over the last 63 holes. Tiger's winning total of 270—18 under par—was a tournament record that may never be equaled because the course has since been lengthened and is more difficult than ever. Remember, Tiger shot 40 on the first nine holes of the opening round. The display that followed was the second best of his career and is unequaled by anyone else. I always thought my closing rounds of 65–66 at the 1975 Masters—a thirty-six-hole record that still stands, by the way—was special, because I was 13 under par for that stretch. But Tiger playing the last sixty-three holes in 22 under par makes that look pretty skimpy by comparison.

That wasn't even his best golf. His fifteen-stroke margin of victory in the 2000 U.S. Open will never be matched, except by Tiger himself. Pebble Beach is always one of the toughest U.S. Open venues. When Tom Kite won in 1992, the conditions on Sunday afternoon may have been the most difficult in championship history. It was very nearly as tough in 2000. The rough was more thick and savage than usual, the wind was blowing and the greens were like bricks. Tiger took the course by the throat and killed everybody, winning by a record fifteen strokes. It was the best golf he's ever played, and probably ever will play. One thing is for sure: Only Tiger has the horsepower to win a U.S. Open so convincingly.

This type of golf from Tiger was apparent even when he was a kid. He won three consecutive U.S. Junior championships, three straight U.S. Amateur championships, and two U.S. Open championships, all by the age of twenty-six. I don't think anyone will ever match that record. He won his first U.S. Junior at age fifteen, beating a bunch of kids two years older than him and who were headed off to college. That was impressive, but winning the same event the next two years was incredible because he did it at match play. Match play is a flukier, more temperamental format than stroke play. The best player in the field doesn't always win. One so-so round by Tiger or an extraordinary one by one of his opponents, and he loses. But it never happened.

The same was true at the U.S. Amateur. Tiger lost one match and was eliminated in 1993, but he followed up by winning eighteen consecutive matches, many against players who were much more seasoned. His 1994 victory was especially impressive and gave the world its first look at Tiger's magic and genius. Down 6 holes to Trip Kuehne during the morning round of the championship final, Tiger looked whipped. He had no energy and looked annoyed and unhappy. In the afternoon, he turned his game around 180 degrees and won on the 36th hole. A similar thing happened at the '96 Amateur. Tiger looked beaten against Steve Scott, but began willing putts into the hole and eventually won in extra holes.

Tiger can make par (or birdie) from anywhere. Tiger can draw the ball, fade it, knock it down, hit it high and low, upshoot it, skip it, float it, knuckle it, and sting it. There isn't a shot he doesn't own. But his command of the golf ball only partly explains why he rarely shoots high scores. Tiger makes the golf course wider and shorter than anyone in history. He makes very few bogeys, a ton of easy pars, and a lot of impossible birdies because *he almost never is in jail*. That isn't to say he doesn't hit the ball plenty crooked at times, with his driver especially. Tiger can spray it with the best of them. He's never ranked higher than 49th in the PGA Tour's Driving Accuracy stats category his entire career, and he finished 2003 ranked an awful 142nd. But it doesn't seem to affect him much, because he escapes trouble so well. He is strong enough to plow the ball out of deep rough and his fantastic speed enables him to hit the ball extraordinarily high. He doesn't go around trees, he goes over them. He also is an astounding fairway bunker player. The shot he hit on the final hole at the 2000 Canadian Open—a 218-yard 6-iron over water from a nasty fairway bunker—brought me out of my living-room chair. Poor Grant Waite, the guy Tiger beat that day, had a "why me?" look on his face when the ball hit the green.

Tiger has power to burn, of course, even though he's lost some distance due to a so-so driver and a desire to be more accurate. His strength comes into play in unlikely ways, especially around the greens. His knack for playing shots out of thick greenside rough is abetted by his ability to generate sufficient clubhead speed to hack through the thick stuff, with no loss of feel. This is especially useful on U.S. Open courses. There's a long-standing argument that tall greenside rough evens out the field because no one can play from it, but Tiger has exploded that myth. His imagination, technique, and trust in himself are such that he can play the most daring shots with ease and confidence. This is a trait he'll never lose, though his nerve to play these shots will no doubt deteriorate a bit over time.

Tiger is an intimidator. Make no mistake, Tiger is one of the great class acts in golf. He is always gracious in defeat and modest in victory. On the golf course, however, he is a born killer who uses his presence, reputation, and skill to unnerve the opposition. Tiger is very conscious of his aura and is comfortable letting his playing partners—at least those who threaten to beat him—feel ill at ease. I have no problem with that, by the way. Tiger obeys all the basic rules of etiquette and even the advanced ones that apply only to him. For example, when Tiger holes a putt, he waits patiently by the side of the green until his playing partner also holes out. If Tiger nonchalantly walked to the next tee after picking his ball out of the hole, he'd bring half the gallery with him, and all the noise and commotion would make it difficult for his fellow competitors to concentrate on the putt. There's no rule stating Tiger has to do that.

Tiger's persona and bearing come into play, too. He doesn't talk much to his fellow competitors, especially on Sunday. Again, this is fine. Ben Hogan hardly said two words to the opposition, and nobody knocked him. Tiger can also be proactive in asserting his dominance. He's admitted he strides by his opponents' drives, which customarily are shorter than his, and all but sneers at their ball.

There's also a psychic power constantly being exerted in Tiger's favor. The sheer number of people who follow Tiger can be jarring to a player who isn't used to large crowds. Tiger doesn't do much to cuddle the fellows who feel out of place. It also doesn't hurt that the galleries are usually rooting for Tiger. In major championships, where the pressure is already more intense than most players can handle, the feeling that people are rooting against them en masse rarely helps them play better. There is a marked subliminal message, transmitted by ten thousand people standing near you, telling you they want the other guy to win. All I'm saying is, Tiger uses the intangibles to his advantage, and as his legend grows it will always be an effective weapon. Jack Nicklaus still makes players a little nervous, and he's a sixty-four-year-old man.

Tiger's swing is almost perfect. He is the most technically perfect golfer I've ever seen, and that includes Ben Hogan. It has absolutely no nuances to it. Jack Nicklaus had the flying right elbow, Hogan had that fast tempo and flat swing, and Bobby Jones had the long swing with a languid, over-the-top move. Great players tend to have swings that are slightly peculiar. But Tiger's swing is a computer model for precision and conformity. It is styled perfectly for the majors, not only because of its strengths but because it has no marked weaknesses. Low-ball hitters such as Lee Trevino and Paul Azinger never did particularly well at the Masters because the course demands a relatively high ball flight. Jack Nicklaus had an upright swing, which was tooled very well for the longer clubs but wasn't so good on pitches and from sand.

His motion is awesome in its simplicity. If you were to trace the path of his clubhead from address to the top of the backswing and then back down to the ball, you'd find it describes a near-perfect circle. Other players have swings that are more elliptical in shape. Nicklaus, for example, is very wide going back, then gets narrow coming down. Hogan's backswing was more upright than his downswing. Those guys were forced to adopt makeup moves. Well, Tiger has no makeup moves. His swing is very efficient. He doesn't need to cock his wrists a great deal at the top of the backswing in order to get power. Nor does he need to gather himself and wait for the club to fall into place. He just goes after it from the top, and the speed he generates is incredible. And it's a swing he can repeat.

Tiger's game is made for majors. U.S. Open courses are becoming massively long. The Bethpage Black course, which hosted the Open in 2002, was stretched to 7,214 yards. I've made my points about Tiger's ability from trouble and greenside rough, but he possesses other assets that are tailored for major championship venues. First of all, he hits the ball higher than most players. Greens at the U.S. Open, Masters, and British Open are invariably firm, and the high-ball hitter who can land the ball on the greens with a steep trajectory has a marked advantage over everyone else. Second, he hits exceptionally long, especially with his irons. This is especially helpful at the Masters, where Tiger can go for the par 5s in two and have a much better chance at holding the greens. I've always said that Tiger will win six green jackets before he's through, and this is the primary reason.

Next, he's a very imaginative putter. Not always rock solid, as I'll point out, but very good most of the time. When Tiger won his first Masters in 1997, he didn't three-putt once. That's an amazing accomplishment on those slick, roller-coaster greens. He's at his most effective when the greens are running fast. Like Nicklaus, he's a wonderful lag putter who controls his speed very well. He's also fearless, which cuts both ways. You can't putt fast greens with a defensive, scared-to-death mind-set, and Tiger always putts with confidence.

Tiger wants the record. Enough said. Tiger has accomplished every goal he's set out to accomplish. At least I *think* he has. He has a fatal facility for outlining an objective in his mind, then willing himself to achieve it. Tiger pays an enormous price for this physically and psychologically. He practices more than anyone, he works out more than anyone, and prepares himself for the majors unlike any other pro. The result is a feeling that he *deserves* to win, that the titles are his and if somebody wants them, they're going to have to take them from him. More powerful still—and this can't be quantified, really—is a sort of psychic control he has over the golf ball. It sounds ridiculous, but I truly believe he aligns the stars in his favor. Some of the putts he's made under pressure are just insane. I think the bomb he drained against Steve Scott in that U.S. Amateur victory, the impossible putt he made on number seventeen in winning the 2001 Players Championship, and a whole bunch of others are made with a helping hand from above.

How did all this come about? In many ways, the whole of Tiger is greater than the sum of its parts. He started early, swinging a club at the age of eighteen months. He had a wonderful upbringing; his father, Earl, instilled in him a strong work ethic and deep belief in himself. His dad also found the financial resources to send Tiger to tournaments, so he could gain experience. He had access to good equipment. Tiger was also blessed with a good body for golf—broad shoulders, thin waist, and great flexibility. He began using a sports psychologist at a very early age. He had the benefit of getting a scholarship to Stanford, which had a good golf program and was a fine social and academic environment that permitted him to ripen intellectually and emotionally. The instruction Tiger received from Butch Harmon, beginning at age seventeen, was superb.

None of these factors alone made Tiger great. Individuals have enjoyed some combination of them before. But Tiger was the first to cultivate them all, starting at a very early age. The result was that Tiger became something similar to the Ivan Drago character in *Rocky IV*, a complete dynamo developed in a linear, regimented way, with nothing left to chance. The guys he's gone up against are like a long succession of Rocky Balboas. Except in Tiger's case, he also has more heart than the competition, which was the one thing Rocky had over Drago.

The case for Tiger passing Jack is pretty strong. But as the famed California prosecutor Vincent Bugliosi is fond of saying, "No matter how thin they make the pancakes, there's always two sides." I feel the factors that inveigh against Tiger are too numerous, potentially more dangerous, and in some cases too inevitable, to overcome.

Tiger is older than his birth certificate implies. Don't laugh. I realize he's only twenty-eight, but competitively, he's an *old* twenty-eight. Most golfers reach their prime between the ages of twenty-six and twenty-nine. That was true with Arnold Palmer, Bobby Jones, and Jack Nicklaus. I know it was true with me. There are exceptions; Seve Ballesteros was at his best before the age of twenty-five and Nick Price reached his prime after he turned thirty. Even Nicklaus played some great golf well into his forties. But that twenty-six-to-twenty-nine window is when a player is most dangerous. When you're twenty-five or younger, you have all the tools physically but don't have quite enough wisdom and patience. From age thirty on, you have plenty of wisdom but your body loses that razor edge and your senses start to lose a bit of their acuity.

The rule is different for child prodigies such as Tiger. They age faster. Many people look at Tiger and say, "Imagine how much better he'll be when he gets even more experience." I don't go along with that. Competitively, Tiger is closer to thirty-one than to twenty-eight and over the next few years he'll evolve differently from other players. It won't all be bad; his game from tee to green will probably improve. Already he's playing a much more methodical game than he used to, choosing to play conservatively at times rather than going all out on every swing. His knowledge of swing mechanics continues to grow; he rarely plays two bad rounds in a row because he can fix his swing overnight. But I don't think his chipping and putting can get any better than they are right now. For Tiger's entire career to this point, when he looks at the hole he sees a barrel. The hole looks huge to him and he thinks every putt will go in. He is a fantastic chipper of the ball as well, the best on tour. There is an ephemeral quality to his short game, an inherent sense of feel and imagination that is especially keen in young players.

I have a feeling Tiger is dead in his prime right now, and that it won't be long before the hole shrinks back to its regulation four-and-a-quarter-inch size. Deterioration is normal in athletes and ultimately inevitable. Joe Louis said that late in his career, he could see the punches coming but didn't have the reflexes to block them. Baseball players pick up the spin of a curveball a split second later than they used to. And so it will happen with Tiger, and possibly soon. Like everybody else, he's slowly accumulating bits of scar tissue from small disappointments and putts that burn the edge of the hole and don't fall. I'm lukewarm on the prospect of another stretch of play like he experienced in winning the Tiger Slam.

Will family interfere? Tiger is a wonderful person who appreciates the importance and value of good parenting because he had it himself. He loves children; at his clinics he seems more comfortable around kids than he does adults. How will he react to having a family? Being away from the kids so much may bother him deeply, and when he's home he'll devote a great deal of time, thinking, and energy to them. He won't be sitting on the couch thinking about the golf swing as much, and he isn't likely to practice as much either. Families can be a great stabilizing influence that make some guys better—Raymond Floyd and Jack Nicklaus are great examples of that. But having already achieved tremendous financial security, Tiger's focus on winning major championships may wane a little bit. And that's all it takes—a little bit.

There also is the wife factor. Being the spouse of a celebrity or athlete is not easy (just look at the divorce rates in those areas), and a tough marriage never did anybody any good. I've always felt that an athlete's wife has to be made of special stuff. They have to be content with remaining almost totally in the background, doing the tough work like raising the kids while the athlete goes about making a living. Or in Tiger's case, making history. That is the challenge confronting Elin Woods, Tiger's new bride.

Will he get bored? Tiger is a smart, inquisitive, adventuresome person who enjoys things other than golf. He is a dive master who loves exploring the ocean. He loves other sports and follows them closely. This is good, because it gives his life balance and variety. The downside is that golf is very demanding, and there's always the danger he'll want to devote himself more to those other areas and less to golf. Look at Greg Norman, he makes no apologies for being less interested in golf and more interested in making wine, designing golf courses, and sailing on his yacht. When you do the same thing, day after day, year after year, you can get to feeling like a hamster on a treadmill. The daily grind can make you just want to chuck the whole thing, or at least scale back.

Tiger's not winning the Grand Slam in 2000 or 2002 may have had a significant upside. Had he conquered that mountain, he could very easily have asked himself, "What else is left?" and lost a little motivation. Again, losing a little edge is all it will take to ruin his chance at breaking Jack's record.

Will he stay healthy? As one who has experienced as many injuries as any good player in history, I can tell you that even small injuries can be devastating. It's odd how injuring a small muscle that wouldn't seem to play a role in the swing can be so painful that you can't play at all. Other athletes can muddle through with fairly severe injuries, but golfers are affected even worse. For example, I pulled a groin muscle once, and almost couldn't swing the club. An injury to a finger or wrist can be devastating, and if you suffer a worse injury, such as a torn rotator cuff or a blown disk in your back, forget it. You just can't play at all. Even a case of back spasms, like Hale Irwin suffered during the 2003 U.S. Open, forcing him to withdraw, is serious. In Irwin's case, he then couldn't play in the U.S. Senior Open and didn't have a top-five finish for four months. It ruined his year.

Steve Elkington's career was adversely affected by being allergic to grass. Mickey Wright, maybe the greatest woman player ever, was debilitated by bad feet. Ben Hogan had the car accident. Everyday ailments or a single traumatizing accident can spell doom for a player at Tiger's level.

Tiger is especially prone to injury because of his tremendous body speed. Physically, his entire anatomy gets in on the act, and he exerts tremendous strain on his entire body, his back especially. He works out like a fiend, which is smart because his body is in condition to accept all that twisting, turning, and explosive movement. It also has made him a stronger, more durable, better golfer. But he's been hurt before. He required knee surgery at the end of 2002, he's hurt his wrist, and had a few other aches and pains. He's not a big, raw-boned guy.

If Tiger were to suffer a serious physical problem, such as a bad L5 vertebrae, torn cartilage in his wrist, or a torn rotator cuff, it could change the whole ball game for him. Forget about the surgery and rehabilitation period; it could also force him to modify the way he swings the club. And that could violate the fine line that separates an excellent player from a great one.

Will he burn out? I don't see this as a serious threat in Tiger's case, because he manages his schedule so well and leads as balanced a life as is humanly possible. He also has at his disposal all of the modern amenities that help him stay fresh, including private planes to whisk him to and from tournaments. Still, there are many subtle things that happen over the years which sap your energy, steal your enthusiasm, and make you tired of the whole show.

The media, for example. Nobody is asked more annoying questions, the same ones over and over again, as Tiger. By July of 2003, Tiger had won four PGA Tour events. Anybody would have taken his record and been overjoyed. But reporters had the temerity to imply he was in a slump, because he hadn't won a major since the 2002 U.S. Open. It was nuts. And it clearly got on Tiger's nerves. When you're asked the same idiotic questions by reporters who don't know the game (and some who do), it eats at you.

Tiger doesn't enjoy a lot of the ancillary things that are part and parcel of being famous. He doesn't particularly care to sign autographs, not that you can blame him for the way he is mobbed constantly. He's been stabbed with pens, pushed, jostled, and insulted. He's had people yell on his backswing. It's hard for him to go out to dinner publicly without someone asking for his autograph in the middle of his entrée. It's a level of fame no other pro has experienced, and it isn't easy on his psyche. The trick is to embrace it the way Jack Nicklaus and Arnold Palmer always did, but I'm not sure Tiger does. He puts up with it all, but he doesn't like it. One day, he may just say the heck with it and walk away or else cut way back. It's unlikely, but it happens.

Will the trappings of fame become an issue? A lot of pro athletes and celebrities will attest that wealth and adulation can be a dangerous thing. This is unlikely to be a factor with Tiger, because he has demonstrated a maturity and perspective that probably won't waver. But because he is young, Tiger is also hungry for life. It's one thing to be aware of fame and financial security, another to let it sink in too deeply. Wealth has ruined so many pro athletes. Once the athlete's subconscious tells him he's got it made, he loses his motivation. It's a subliminal realization and a very seductive one. It takes tremendous aspiration to work hard and suffer when, deep inside, you know you don't really have to. Here's a mantra Tiger could repeat every day, with no ill effect: "I don't need every fast, beautiful car on the lot. I don't need houses all over the country. I don't need people around telling me how great I am. What I need is to be on that practice tee and out on that golf course. The only accolade I need at the end of the day is that low score I shot."

Tiger's upbringing should see him through this one. The values instilled in Tiger by his father, Earl, cannot falter. That little list of goals Tiger wrote down a long time ago that he won't show anyone, needs to remain a focal point of strength and motivation for him.

Will he survive the inevitable slump? Without exception, every player experiences a downturn with their golf swing, or at least their ability to win tournaments. Nicklaus, for example, experienced a period from 1966 to 1970 in which he played in seventeen consecutive majors and won only one. In Jack's case, he came close a lot but couldn't quite close the deal. In many other cases, the player experiences serious problems with his golf swing. Psychologically, this can be much more devastating.

I speak from personal experience. In 1975, I began spending a great deal of time on my ranch. I chopped wood, cleared land, built fences, and generally worked my tail off. I went from 170 pounds to 190, all muscle. I became very strong in my upper body. It had a devastating effect on my golf swing. I lost a lot of my natural flexibility, and had a lot of trouble dropping the club into the correct slot on my downswing. My feel suffered; the club felt too light and I had trouble sensing where it was, position wise, during the swing. This was before the days of video and I didn't have a teacher to fall back on. My driving was the first to go. I started spraying the ball everywhere, and that put pressure on the rest of my game. The result was that I didn't win a tournament from 1977 through 1979, and fell way down on the money list.

Tiger may be too well-schooled to suffer a slump of that proportion, but a fallow period is sure to arrive at some point. It could stem from a tiny thing like playing the ball an inch too far forward in his stance. Or he could change equipment companies and alter that great swing to fit his new clubs. In any case, it's bound to happen and there's no telling for sure how he'll react to the frustration, self-doubt, and persistent questions from the media.

Will his putter get balky? Tiger is a very good putter, but he's not a *great* putter. He's not a natural, feel-oriented putter along the lines of Ben Crenshaw, Phil Mickelson, or Bob Charles. If there's a weakness in his game, putting is it. Like Greg Norman, Tiger has become an extremely good putter through hard practice and mastery of sound technique. But it's a stroke that is more prone to difficulty in middle age, and will take a lot of maintenance to keep it sharp.

Poor putting almost drove me off the tour, not to mention out of my mind. Putting troubles got Bobby Jones, Ben Hogan, Byron Nelson, and every other great player you can think of, with the exception of Jack Nicklaus. Tiger would be wise to work on his putting constantly and never try to let his superb ball-striking skills carry him.

Will the competition improve? Tiger has spent the last few years beating up on Phil Mickelson, Ernie Els, David Duval, Colin Montgomerie, Vijay Singh, Davis Love III, Jim Furyk, and several other excellent players. But over the next ten years, the field will change dramatically. There are kids in college—heck, in junior high school—who right now have Tiger in their crosshairs. They are receiving the same sort of training that Tiger had when he was young. They are determined, talented, well-taught, well-funded, and utterly unafraid. By the time they turn pro, it is likely that a few of them will be in Tiger's class in terms of pure ability. Trust me, youth will be served. The players on the horizon will be better than the crop we have right now. And Tiger will be older, albeit more experienced. Winning tournaments will be harder than ever, because in addition to the influx of new players such as Aaron Baddeley, Adam Scott, Charles Howell, and others, some of the "old" guys like Mickelson and Els will still be ticking.

The Most Important Question of All

For as good as his golf swing is, Tiger suffers a recurring problem for which he has yet to find an answer. It has less to do with the positions in his swing and more with the way the positions work in concert with each other. The problem he has mentioned time and again over the years is his tendency to get stuck on the downswing. If he fixes it, the sky is the limit. If he doesn't, then his chances of upsetting my prediction narrow even further.

Let me explain getting stuck in terms the average person can understand. Tiger's method of swinging the club is predicated on his arms staying in front of his body throughout the downswing. If they lag too far behind, his clubface is open at impact and he hits a big block to the right. If he senses the arms are too far behind, he rotates his hands furiously at the last second in an effort to square the clubface. Sometimes he flips them too aggressively, causing the clubface to be in a closed position at impact. That results in a big hook to the left. It's all about timing, and sometimes Tiger's upper body outraces his arms and hands to impact.

Getting stuck is not the kiss of death, however, if you plan for it. Many players—David Duval when he was playing well and Lee Trevino come immediately to mind—let their arms lag behind their bodies on the downswing. The difference is, they had very strong left-hand grips, their left hand rotated well to their right at address. This made it very easy for them to square the clubface; in fact they didn't have to use their hands at all. They just unwound their upper bodies as aggressively as possible, and the strong left-hand grip ensured that the clubface would square itself. It's a very effective way to play golf.

Tiger, however, doesn't have that strong left-hand grip. His grip is in a more neutral position, which means he has to consciously rotate the club to a square position through impact. This is an effective way to play, too, as it provides more flexibility in the type of ball flight you want. But it puts enormous demands on his timing, especially with the driver where he exerts a great deal of speed. Tiger has the ability to unwind his upper body faster than most people, and too often his arms just can't keep up. It's an ongoing battle.

I've long felt that Tiger should strengthen his left-hand grip at address, so he's more like Trevino, Duval, Paul Azinger, and Fred Couples. That way he could unwind his upper body as fast as he wanted without having to worry about his clubface opening or closing to the extreme. He'd hit the ball enormous distances with little loss of accuracy. But for whatever reason, he's resisted making that change.

If Tiger would try to get stuck on purpose with the driver, and maintain his present style with the irons, Jack's record would tumble. As it is, Tiger can still win majors because the rest of his game is so sound, and he does have weeks where his timing is very good. But in regard to his being recognized as the greatest player of all time, hands down, this mechanical problem is a make-or-break thing for him.

Whatever he decides to do, it's going to be a wonderful, exciting ride and it's going to be close. If he reaches major championship number nineteen, I hope I'm in the broadcast booth to see and describe it.

CHAPTER 5

Contenders or Pretenders?

Why Tiger Makes Winning Look Easy

GOLFERS TODAY SHOULD BE BETTER than golfers of thirty years ago by leaps and bounds. Certainly it's true of athletes in other sports. When I hear someone argue that Jack Dempsey, who weighed 185 pounds, could have whipped Muhammad Ali, who weighed 220 and was twice as fast, I start looking for the exit. Johnny Weissmuller's swim times, which in the 1920s won him an Olympic gold medal, couldn't stand up to a fourteen-year-old female high school champion's today. Babe Ruth could probably hit today's pitching, but I can't see him chasing down very many fly balls in the gap. All athletics—including golf—are subject to the laws of evolution. We're bigger, stronger, faster, better conditioned, and better coached.

Equipment is better, golf courses are better conditioned, and travel is easier. With all of that, the best PGA Tour players today would have to be superior to the stars of thirty years ago, right?

Well, no. Comparisons between eras are difficult, but on balance I believe the men I played against were as good as the best guys going today and maybe better. Evolution does not apply, because golf doesn't share a close correlation with other sports. To me, golfers are more like artists. Does anyone today dance better than Fred Astaire? Who writes better songs than the Beatles? Does anyone sculpt better than Michelangelo, or write better novels than Ernest Hemingway?

If you subtract the inherent advantages enjoyed by modern players, the old guys would stack up very favorably. Take away the innovations of modern clubs and balls, perfectly groomed fairways and greens, junior golf programs, easier travel and a host of smaller factors, and players of the 1960s, seventies, and eighties were every bit as good—and so were a select group from fifty to seventy-five years ago, including Byron Nelson, Sam Snead, Ben Hogan, and Bobby Jones. The talent pool is broader today; probably only the top thirty money winners in a given year during the 1970s would be able to make a living against the players on the PGA Tour today. And a guy who is number 5 on the Nationwide Tour money list would easily be in the top thirty on the PGA Tour in 1975. But the very best players then were, on the whole, a shade better than the players I see today. I'll tell you more about these players in chapter 10.

The problem over the last several years is simple: Very few players these days can look across at Tiger Woods without fainting. It's like he's almost had a free ride. When Tiger's toughest challenges in the majors are coming from Bob May, Rich Beem, and journeymen like them, there's a problem. The top players today win a lot of tournaments, but they don't seem to do very well in the majors. If you don't believe it, look at the scores they shoot in the final round when they're in contention. It blows my mind that Colin Montgomerie can win fifty times on the European Tour but fold up like a cheap suitcase when he plays in America. I mean, the guy hasn't won a single tournament here, and has reached a point where he probably never will. Phil Mickelson should have a hatful of majors by now. Same with Davis Love III.

Something, and I'm not sure what, has given Tiger's "supporting cast" feet of clay. Maybe these players have made so much money that their motivation has slackened. Maybe it gets to them that the media rags on them, saying the same thing I'm saying now—that they aren't living up to expectations. Or it could be the old dominant-animal syndrome. Have you watched those nature programs on television where the alpha male rules the roost and the others simply accept it and behave submissively? Challengers to Tiger are a bit like that; it's like they feel they have no chance, and consequently play as if they know defeat is inevitable.

The final round of the 2002 Masters gave us some classic examples of this. Ernie Els began the day four shots behind Tiger but started out with two birdies to close to within two. But Els, feeling he couldn't make any mistakes and feeling like he had to do something heroic, made a triple-bogey 8 on the 13th hole and shot himself out of it. Phil Mickelson also birdied the first two holes but, feeling the same pressure Els did, played 1 over par the rest of the way. Where are the great closing rounds, like the 65 Arnold Palmer shot at Cherry Hills to win the 1960 U.S. Open? Or my 63 at Oakmont that won the 1973 U.S. Open, even though I started the day six shots out of the lead? Invariably, when Tiger is near them on the leader board the young guys play so-so golf.

The back nine on Sunday at a major is like a basketball game where nobody wants the ball with ten seconds left on the clock. Tiger notwithstanding, the PGA Tour lacks the equivalent of a Jerry West, Michael Jordan, or Joe Montana, guys who thrive under pressure. I remember the presentation ceremony after the 1975 Masters, the one where Jack Nicklaus manhandled Tom Weiskopf and me down the stretch on his way to victory. Jack turned to us and said, "Thanks for making it so much fun." I recall the incident late in the final round of the 1977 British Open at Turnberry when Tom Watson turned to Nicklaus and said, "This is what it's all about, isn't it?" And Jack replying, "You bet it is." Those guys relished it. The supporting cast today doesn't look like they're having fun when they're going against Tiger. They look like they can't get out of there fast enough.

Strangely, it's the older guys who seem to be getting the job done. Look what happened in 2003. Players in their forties—Scott Hoch, Kenny Perry, Jay Haas, Vijay Singh, Bob Tway, Fred Couples, Tommy Armour III, and Peter Jacobsen—made the most noise. The young guys pretty much stunk it up. Phil Mickelson didn't win. David Duval, a former leading money winner, fell into one of the worst slumps in the history of the tour. Sergio Garcia spent the year trying to get used to a new swing and didn't win. Nobody in their twenties and thirties, with the exception of Tiger, Mike Weir, Jim Furyk, Justin Leonard, and David Toms, had years worth talking about. Two of the majors were won by guys who were virtually unknown. Ben Curtis and Shaun Micheel, who won the British Open and PGA Championship, respectively, were not household names.

When the young guns fail to step up, fan interest wanes. When Tiger takes a three-stroke lead into Sunday and a feeling prevails that he can't be overtaken, some might say, why even tune in and watch? His play is wonderful, but what the fans want is a dogfight, a close finish. They want a rivalry, a showdown with an edge to it. Just as Muhammad Ali needed Joe Frazier to be considered the greatest fighter of all time, Tiger needs somebody—anybody—to put his feet to the fire.

If I'm coming off as being unduly critical of the supporting cast, I should add that lately there has been a glimmer of hope. Tiger didn't win a major in 2003 and played poorly (for him) the last half of the season. We saw in him a vulnerability we haven't seen before, and which the supporting cast had to have noticed. They saw Tiger struggle with his driver, hitting the ball shorter and less accurately than ever before. They saw that he doesn't necessarily make every putt from ten feet and in. They saw a Tiger whose confidence has been shaken, a player who can play poorly on Sunday. I'll discuss why this is happening—and why I think it will happen even more—in chapter 13. I'm betting this will increase their own confidence and that we'll see better play from the stars of the future in 2004 and beyond.

Who are these stars and what do they bring to the table? Here are the main threats to Tiger's dominance, the players who can make this decade a golden era of its own.

Ernie Els

The Loudest Whisper in Golf

In an age when no athlete or public figure has escaped indictment or criticism, Ernie's ability to stay under the radar is nothing short of miraculous. The media is endeared to him, his fellow competitors love him, and fans embrace him as though he were an amiable St. Bernard. Ernie's career has been devoid of the stresses that have hammered away at Phil Mickelson, David Duval, John Daly, and Tiger Woods. It is the most important facet of his persona, for it has enabled Ernie to play his best golf without interruption or emotional upsets. At thirty-four, he would appear to be headed to the back nine of his career, but he is aging remarkably well and with his size, skill, and work ethic will remain a force in golf for many years to come.

Think about it: There has never been a controversy, a misquote, an off-course episode, or career disaster for Els to contend with. For a man with two U.S. Open victories, a British Open, and eleven other wins on the PGA Tour, and more than thirty wins internationally, Ernie has received his share of attention, but not so much that it's been a distraction. This is all his own doing. He is happily married with two perfect kids. He accommodates the media. He is graceful, modest, undemonstrative, and sportsmanlike. He never complains. If the PGA Tour were smart, it would write down the details of all that Ernie is about, publish it in book form, and issue a copy to every rookie. The title: *How to Become Rich, Famous, Happy, and a Superstar Without Increasing Your Blood Pressure.*

I believe people draw conclusions about an individual simply by the way they play. When you see Ernie make that big, drowsy swing, then see him lolloping after the ball with his easy, unconcerned gait, you can't help but surmise that he is easygoing, nonconfrontational, friendly, and likable. Such gentleness in a big fellow is very attractive to people. His world is in harmony, and you get the notion that if you were in his world, things would be in harmony for you, too. People like Ernie for the same reason they like Fred Couples. He's like your favorite uncle, but with a lot more talent on the golf course.

Only once have I seen Ernie exasperated. In 2001, after Tiger Woods polished off the Tiger Slam and showed no signs of tailing off, Ernie talked of the frustration of trying to reach his goals with Tiger in the way. He had lost a playoff to Tiger at the 2000 Mercedes Championship, and after a nice start early in 2002, played poorly in the final round of the Masters to let Tiger walk off with his third green jacket. Ernie did stop Tiger's attempt at winning the Grand Slam in 2002 by capturing the British Open. Like a lot of players, however, Ernie seemed to concede the throne to Tiger and rarely played his best golf when the two players were in the hunt together. But with Tiger having a majorless and relatively average (for him) 2003, Ernie seems to have the gleam back in his eye. He finally sees that Tiger is human, and I believe he's likely to get back to the business of winning major championships.

Ernie's game is to die for. He has that wonderful temperament, of course, an internal rhythm that is impossible to rush. He thinks at the same pace he swings—deliberately and matter-of-factly. He can make bad swings due to his tempo getting out of sync, but he's never far off. And mechanically, he has the best first move down in all of golf. When you reach the top of the backswing, the way you initiate the downswing is critical. It has to be soft and slow, to allow the body parts to work in concert with one another. The tendency under pressure is to speed things up, but Ernie appears to have an internal governor that slows him down. This is one reason his swing should age well. Guys with long, soft backswings, like Phil Mickelson, Fred Couples, and Sam Snead, usually have long careers. Players who are skinny and high-strung—I fit into that category, along with Bill Rogers and Paul Azinger—often lose it overnight at some point in their forties. So do short hitters who swing pretty aggressively—Justin Leonard and Corey Pavin come to mind. But Ernie's swing seems to put so little stress on that big, flexibile physique of his, he should be able to just play and play for a good long time.

Because he's a big guy, you would expect that Ernie would be prone to problems with accuracy. But that isn't the case at all. His fundamentals are perfect. Like a lot of players from

South Africa and Australia, he is very meticulous. He understands the components of his swing and has a great eye for detail. At address, for example, he always peers down at his hands to check his grip.

So much else is God-given. He has plenty of distance, which is difficult to teach. He bombs it off the tee and has an extra thirty yards in reserve for when he really needs it. Always a control player, Els rarely has been among the top thirty in terms of driving distance. In 2003, however, he cracked the top ten. Yet, for being so tall and having such large hands, he has an extremely deft touch around the greens. He's a beautiful chipper and pitcher. His putting stroke is like a scaled-down version of his full swing, slow and rhythmic, with an exceptionally fine sense of how hard to hit the putt.

His temperament is deceiving. Under the teddy bear exterior lies an extremely tough competitor. Whether it's the U.S. Open or a Shell's Wonderful World of Golf exhibition, he loves to win. He has fire in his belly—watch Ernie thump his driver on the ground after a poor tee shot and you know he isn't merely plodding along out there. He isn't wildly exuberant when he holes a big putt, but the clenched fist shows he relishes pulling off the key shots.

Like Julius Boros, Ernie has the gift of patience. He won his U.S. Opens in 1994 and 1997 not by overpowering the golf course or holing every putt in sight, but by biding his time and picking his spots to be aggressive. Both times he got the better of Colin Montgomerie, who could have won had he not gotten flustered. But Monty is no Ernie. Els's temperament combined with his considerable skill means he could win two more U.S. Opens, whether Tiger is playing well or not.

Where does Ernie go from here? As his kids get older and he begins to age, he needs to keep a close eye on his schedule. Ernie is one of the most active players in the world, which is the reason he's won in Australia, Japan, Europe, America, Dubai, his native South Africa, and elsewhere. Physically, he really puts himself through the grinder, and although he's durable, at times he has shown up at tournaments looking a bit worn out. As he's already set for life financially, he might want to scale back on the number of tournaments he enters. Jack Nicklaus was a master at that; he rarely played more than three tournaments in a row and showed up at each feeling strong and fresh. If Ernie elects to conserve himself better, he just might play forever.

Mike Weir

Little Big Man

One of golf's big concerns is whether the increasing length of courses is going to cause the smaller, slightly built player to become extinct. When Bethpage Black checked in at 7,214 yards for the 2002 U.S. Open, it was pretty much conceded that a player who is physically small wouldn't be winning majors anymore. But then along comes Mike Weir, who stands all of five foot nine and weighs just over 150 pounds. Weir won the 2003 Masters on a revamped Augusta National that had been stretched to 7,290 yards but played even longer because it was wet. Weir proved there will always be a place for the precision player—and a left-handed one at that.

Not that Weir is considered a short hitter. In fact, with the advances in golf club technology, there are no popcorn hitters anymore on the PGA Tour. A 270-yard average will rank you at about 190th in the driving distance stats ranking (though I've never viewed a 270-yard drive as "short"). In 2003, Weir was about in the middle of the pack with a 289-yard average. But he's made up for it by becoming the best short-iron player on tour and the best putter from ten feet and in. He won three times in 2003 and finished third or better seven times in all. To me, he was the PGA Tour player of the year all the way.

Weir's swing is very sound. He has to swing pretty hard to get the distance he does, but he does it without pressing. His swing is so sound fundamentally, his mechanics are so good, that he gets the maximum results from his effort. He's like a high-performance car with a small but efficient engine. I'm proud to say I helped Mike a little with his swing. He's a fellow BYU grad, and some time ago I helped him smooth out his preshot routine. But I *didn't* give him that unusual rehearsal move with the club!

The most impressive thing about Weir is something you can't see: courage. He has more guts than a government mule. When Weir slammed home an eight-foot putt for par to get into that Masters playoff with Len Mattiace, the expression on his face barely changed. It was like the importance of that putt was lost on him. If he missed, it could have had a devastating impact on his career. But, as always, he treated it like any other shot. I'm sure the average fan was a lot more nervous than he was.

Weir is truly a nice guy, which added to the popularity of his victory. It took him several years before his game was ready for the PGA Tour, and that time was good for him. He didn't burn out too soon and has struck a wonderful balance between work and his personal life. I think he'll be a force to be reckoned with for many years. He won't ever be a dominant player because of the fact he doesn't have a big game. But, like I said, it's a game that's big enough to beat a guy like Tiger if Tiger isn't clicking on all cylinders.

Phil Mickelson

Rich Man, Poor Man

I wasn't smart enough to see it at the time, but an episode at the 1995 U.S. Open pretty much spelled what Phil Mickelson's career has been about. The 16th hole at Shinnecock Hills is a tough par 5, one of the great risk–reward holes in all of golf. If you lay up with your second shot, a short pitch to a tricky green sets up a good chance at birdie and a sure par. If you go for the green in two and find the putting surface, you can make a sure birdie and possibly an eagle. Corey Pavin, a short hitter by any standard, laid up all four days. He played the hole in 2 under par. He eventually won the championship by two strokes over Greg Norman.

Mickelson, as he was inclined to do, played the 16th hole much more aggressively. He persisted in bombing away at it with his second shot, and paid a heavy price. Moreover, when Mickelson missed the green with his second shot, he played extremely risky shots in an effort to get close to the hole. They repeatedly backfired on him. On Sunday, one of his greenside flops landed in a bunker, effectively taking him out of contention. He finished fourth. He played the hole in 6 over par for the championship and finished four shots behind Pavin. Had he played the hole in even par, he would have won by two.

What was apparent then is apparent now: Phil can't help but go for broke when there's any chance at all of pulling off a heroic shot. The possibilities thrill him. They thrill the gallery. His success at the daring play has even won him tournaments. But in majors they've killed practically every time, and that is why he's yet to win a major championship. It's become his beast of burden, the millstone around his neck. As backhanded compliments go, "best player never to win a major" is the all-time champion. And it fits Mickelson perfectly.

Phil has been one of the best players in the world for more than ten years now, winning twenty-two times on the PGA Tour and playing on four Ryder Cup and Presidents Cup teams. It's hard to look at his record and say he's underachieved, but based on what was predicted of him, you can't help but say he hasn't lived up to everyone's expectations. This is a guy who won a PGA Tour event, the 1991 Tucson Open, while he was still in college. He was called the "next Nicklaus" (a term the media gave me when I was younger) and many people thought he had a realistic shot at Jack's major championship record. It just hasn't happened, and as the years go by and the pressure on him to win a major increases, it's becoming almost painful to watch.

Mickelson is so good, I'm surprised he hasn't picked off a couple of majors by accident. His talent is amazing, in some ways the equal of Tiger Woods's. His putting stroke is quirky but smooth, and when he's on, nobody in history has putted better. His short game can be a dream; he's enormously creative with his wedges and is blessed with a sense of touch you see only once or twice in a generation. He's big, strong, and flexible and hits the ball a mile. He's fearless and has an almost childlike love of the game, the fans, and the fringe benefits of being famous. From a standpoint of appeal and popularity, he's been a dream come true for the PGA Tour.

When Jack Nicklaus stated that the true measure of a career was based on how many majors you won, it altered the way players looked at the game. It made it much more difficult. The pressure to win at least one major really intensified. I was very fortunate to have won my first major at age twenty-six. It took the monkey off my back and, even though I always felt a little more pressure in the majors, I had the relief of knowing that at least I had one. But when a guy goes three years without winning one, then five, then ten, it does something to his psyche. He begins to feel like he is one of destiny's bad children, like he isn't fated to win. The disappointment begins to build. The media is always there to remind you that you still haven't won the Big One. Tom Kite, Davis Love III, Fred Couples, and many others have been there, and they'll tell you it wasn't a heckuva lot of fun. They'll also tell you what a relief it was to finally win that one major.

Phil hasn't won one yet, and it's clear he's not having much fun. Always accommodating to reporters, he's becoming more sensitive, even snippy at times. He bristles at suggestions that he's too aggressive, or that he misses too many short putts, or that he drives the ball too crooked, or that he's too much in love with his flop shot. When I think about it, I can't think of a player who's been criticized on as many fronts as Mickelson. It's no wonder he is increasingly taking more time off to be with his family and doesn't work on his game as hard as he once did.

He's had almost as many near misses as Greg Norman, though not nearly the number of self-imposed disasters. He lost the 2001 PGA Championship by one stroke when David Toms made a pretty miraculous up and down from 100 yards out. He lost the 1999 U.S. Open by one stroke to Payne Stewart when Stewart made all those putts coming down the stretch, including a long bomb on the last hole. He lost by three to Tiger Woods at the 2002 U.S. Open, but it was closer than the numbers indicated. He's finished third at the Masters three times, not in heartbreaking fashion but enough for him to ponder what might have been. All these things take their toll, sort of like undergoing Chinese water torture for ten years.

If you're a fan of Phil's, like I am, you look hard at choices he's made during his career and wonder why he made them. When he turned pro, he signed an equipment contract with a company that made good clubs, but not great clubs. Very few players used them. He elected to use graphite shafts in his irons, which I think hurt him for years. Graphite is fine for the driver, but there's never been a great iron player who used graphite in their irons, a fact that applies to this day. I'm sure he was remunerated very handsomely, but in the end it may have cost him. He also started switching putters a lot. He never putted better than he did with his remake of an Arnold Palmer blade putter, but for whatever reason he got away from it and began a long game of musical chairs with various putters. Many great players have switched putters, but the true geniuses with the flat stick, like Ben Crenshaw, sometimes stay with the same putter forever.

Then there is his eternal quest for more distance. Already a long hitter, he's seemingly bent on getting even longer. Rarely does a player who adds distance become more accurate at the same time, and Phil definitely has become wilder. Tightening his swing and becoming more physically fit prior to 2002 helped temporarily, but he had a terrible driving year in 2003 and failed to win a tournament for only the second time since he turned professional.

Whether Phil is too aggressive is open to debate. On the one hand, he does take a lot of chances, particularly around the greens. When he loses, it's easy to point to his aggressiveness and spot the plays that cost him. On the other hand, when he's on, he's terrific. More and more, the PGA Tour is about winning. First-place checks are huge. If a player can win two or three tournaments a year, that's all he needs to do for the year to be a big success. The conservative player who grinds out lots of pars will have lots of high finishes, but he won't have those electric weeks of brilliance. Personally, I can understand why he'd rather have the big payoffs than the grinding consistency.

Phil insists he loves to play aggressively, that it excites him and makes the game more fun. He is adamant in saying he won't change his style. I admire his honesty and respect that choice. I've only seen him make a truly dumb play once, at Bay Hill in 2002, when he tried to pull off an impossible shot from the trees over water to a green that wouldn't have held the shot anyway. Most of the time, he's simply aggressive, and he possesses the skill to pull the shots off. A player has to go with a style that is in keeping with their nature, and Phil likes to live on the edge. Good for him.

Pro golf really is a means to an end. You play to make a living and try to enjoy yourself along the way. Mickelson has made $23 million playing golf, has a beautiful wife and children, plenty of outside interests, and good health. He really has it all, everything except that major championship. It's hard not to pull for him to win at least one, and with that big game of his, I'm betting he'll do it.

David Duval

When the Bottom Falls Out

Duval merits mention with the rest of the supporting cast, for what he was and what he still can be. I think he's the most interesting character study in golf today, a reluctant superstar who lost his game completely and now, chastened and humbled, wishes he could have it all back.

What happened to Duval? His slump is the worst since Ian Banker-Finch lost his game in the mid-1990s. It's more than a slump, really, more complicated than a simple downturn. One of the best ball strikers in recent history, he almost can't play at all today. His 2003 season was a nightmare in Technicolor, one missed cut and embarrassment after another. I look at him and see a lost soul. And I look at him and I see myself in 1978. I know what it's like to stand on the tee and have no clue where the ball is going, the awful anticipation of having ten thousand people watching you, the *ooh* that follows when your drive lands in another zip code.

Slumps intrigue me almost as much as choking does. Invariably, they start with poor driving. That old adage "You drive for show and putt for dough" is a crock. I've seen a lot of bad putters make a living on the PGA Tour, but a terrible driver of the ball simply can't make it. The drive sets up everything. If you drive a ball long and straight, it's almost hard to make a bogey. Drive it short and crooked consistently, and you've got a headache. It's also pervasive. When you drive the ball badly, you start pressing on your iron shots. Next, you start putting poorly because you have so many pressure-packed putts for pars. Suddenly, you have no more safety valves, nothing to bail you out. You're a dead man walking.

Slumps often occur when a player says he wants to move to the next level. When I hear that, I think, "Uh-oh, there's going to be trouble." Instead of doing what made them successful to begin with and maybe refining their game here and there, they take drastic action. In Duval's case, he hit the gym and altered his body. He fooled around with his equipment, changed companies a couple of times. He began tinkering with his swing, which was dangerous because it was quirky to begin with. The result of all these changes is that, when something goes wrong, you aren't sure what it is. It could be the clubs—maybe the shafts aren't exactly the same as the ones you liked before. It could be your body; maybe you're a bit thicker through the chest, or the weight you've lost has robbed you of a little mass (which isn't necessarily a bad thing, provided it wasn't helping you generate power). Maybe it was the swing tinkering; by making your swing a little more upright, for example, it changes the way the whole swing should fire. You become a dog chasing its tail, desperate and confused while seeking a solution.

A couple of years ago, I predicted that Duval might one day just pack it in and disappear. I never saw one aspect of PGA Tour life, with the exception of hitting the golf ball, that appealed to him. He doesn't like signing autographs. He doesn't like being asked questions. He doesn't like being surrounded by people, or cutting up in the locker room. I understand that he was aloof even when he was in college, sometimes traveling separately from his teammates. He is clearly a cerebral, private guy with some personal demons. He finds much more joy in snowboarding with a small circle of friends in Idaho than he does chasing a golf ball. To get the most out of your career, you have to find a way to embrace the lifestyle, and I don't think he ever has. He embraced practice and wanted to get better, but he didn't like the life.

When Duval was playing well, he was something to behold. He had a great body for a tour player—big butt and thighs, thick wrists, and fast hands. He was extremely long with all his clubs and was a very good putter. He had that strong left-hand grip, but played a beautiful fade by simply leaving his hands out of the swing. He was a great shot maker and a very tough competitor. There were moments when no player was better; the 59 he shot at the Bob Hope Classic in 1999 was one of the best rounds ever played. He was the world's number-one-ranked player and gave every indication he could hang with Tiger. A couple of setbacks, most notably a poor final round at the 2000 British Open that he could have won, seemed to delay the inevitable. When he won the British Open the following year, the world was at his feet.

But he didn't win in all of 2002, and 2003 was a horror show. He phoned me toward the end of the year, asking for a bit of advice. Having been through the same thing, I did my best to help. I'll keep most of what I said private, but I did suggest that he go back to basics. I hope he finds his way back. Golf needs him, and whether he knows it or not, he needs golf.

Sergio Garcia

Young at Heart, Old for Twenty-four

At age twenty-four, Sergio has accomplished more than a lot of good players who are several years older. Still, he gives me the sense that the clock is ticking. After winning three tournaments and $7 million his first three years on tour, he struggled in 2003, missed the cut seven times, and had his worst year as a pro. Garcia spent the better part of the year getting used to a swing change I feel was ill-advised to begin with. This kid has so much natural ability, you get the feeling he's moving sideways.

"El Niño" is fun to watch. He truly loves what he is doing and it shows. He laughs a lot, talks a lot, and is more expressive than any other player on tour. I like the fact that he acts his age rather than try to behave like he's several years older. There have been some youthful indiscretions, such as when he threw one of his shoes in a fit of pique, and later got into a row with one of his amateur partners in a pro-am. He gets on the nerves of a few other players, and his old habit of gripping and regripping the club incessantly at address even annoyed his fans. But you have to cut Sergio some slack, if only for his age and the fact he means well. He tries so hard and has a good heart. He yearns to please. He's reduced the number of regrips before shots from somewhere in the thirties to only five or so now.

Like his elder countryman, Seve Ballesteros, Sergio's game revolves around feel and inspiration. He always burns hot emotionally. He's a total feel player with a divine touch on the greens and around them. Although he isn't big, he drives the ball extremely long. He makes birdies in bunches. He runs a little hot and cold, sort of like a shooting guard in basketball who can go 12-for-15 from the floor one night and 2-for-15 the next.

Sergio has an unusual swing, one where he lays the club off at the beginning of the downswing and then unloads it as fast as he can through impact. It's a throwback swing, one with a tremendous amount of lag. It's similar to Ben Hogan's downswing in that it's quite flat. It's very distinctive. Apparently he felt that if he corrected it by reducing the amount of downcocking on the downswing, he'd be more consistent. It might have been a mistake, though. I would have left it utterly alone and let the problem take care of itself. As Sergio gets older and he loses some strength, speed, and flexibility, he'll lose the excess lag naturally. By undergoing the swing change, he put his confidence at risk. It helped that Sergio won the Nedbank Golf Challenge in South Africa late in 2003, but the jury is still out. If I were his father, who is a fine teaching pro in their home country of Spain, I wouldn't tinker with that swing from now on.

Because he's so young—four years younger than Tiger—and his potential is so great, he has to be considered the real deal in terms of becoming a threat to Tiger. He beat Woods 1-up at the Battle of Bighorn in 2000, although Woods was exhausted after a long plane flight and also sick. But give Sergio a couple more seasons to mature and gain experience, and you've got the makings of a real rivalry.

First, though, Sergio needs to pick off a couple of majors. We've heard the comparisons to Seve over and over, which is fine. But by the time Seve turned twenty-four, he'd won the British Open and the Masters, and was the number-one player in Europe. The time for Sergio to step up is now.

Jim Furyk

All that Matters Is Impact

Jim Furyk is a fellow who usually speaks only when he's spoken to. But his swing is one loud scream. It is one of the most bizarre actions in the history of professional golf and one of the most functional. Furyk is a testament to everything I like to see in a player. He has tremendous faith in his swing, understands it, and has altered it very little over the years. The same goes for his cross-handed putting grip; he's one of the first players to use that grip from the day he started playing. He is a stoic, tough competitor with a deep desire to be the best he can be.

He's a silent killer. He's won only nine times on the PGA Tour, not an overwhelming number for a guy who turned thirty-four in 2004. But he has racked up more than eighty top-ten finishes and $19 million in prize money. Most important of all, he finally won a U.S. Open, the major that fits his game best. Furyk's game is predicated on accuracy, the one quality that all the majors are now putting greater emphasis on. To tell the truth, it's surprising he's won only one. I look at the record book and see he's finished in the top ten in majors a whopping thirteen times, a testament to his persistence and consistency.

Furyk has evolved slowly but steadily. When he first came on tour, he had a bit of trouble closing the deal. In 1997 and '98, he finished in the top three nine times with only one win to show for it. But he kept at it, and in the last couple of years began modifying his swing a bit, making his backswing a little less upright so its plane more closely matched his plane on the downswing. It improved a swing that was already rock solid; for all of the sword fighting that goes on in his backswing, he keeps his clubface absolutely square through impact. The position of the clubface the instant it strikes the ball is all that matters in golf. I don't care if your backswing has twenty-five loops, the only thing that counts is the position of the clubface the instant it strikes the ball. The ball doesn't care about the backswing.

For Furyk, the result is a lovely fade that doesn't go massively far but is as predictable as sunrise. With that, Furyk also is surprisingly creative and versatile. At Doral in 2003, I noticed that when he wanted to hit his standard fade, he fanned his left foot out toward the target at address. When he wanted to draw the ball, he set his left foot perpendicular to the target. That allowed a fuller hip turn and an ability to rotate the clubface to a slightly closed position at impact.

Jim is one guy who will look Tiger in the eye. He was involved in a thrilling playoff against Tiger at the 2001 NEC Invitational World Golf Championship and was unfazed by going up against the world's best. At one point, Furyk holed a bunker shot just to stay alive, which elicited a rare display of emotion. Tiger won on the seventh extra hole, but Furyk didn't give anything away. He made Tiger earn it, which the rest of the supporting cast often seems incapable of doing.

Charles Howell III

One Last Piece of the Puzzle

I was familiar with Charley long before he turned pro. He beat my son, Todd, in the U.S. Junior, and I saw more of him when he was in college at Oklahoma State. My prediction then was that he would be a superstar, because he possessed certain intangibles the other kids didn't. He had a quiet confidence instilled in him by his father, a doctor in Augusta, Georgia. Although he weighed only 150 pounds, he was exceptionally long. His junior record was excellent, and as I saw it (and see it), a kid who dominates in American Junior Golf Association and college events is pretty much a sure bet to succeed as a pro.

Howell has had a nice career so far, but the crucible of competition on the PGA Tour has exposed one flaw in his game: an inability to get the ball in the hole a little quicker than the next guy. He's a good chipper and putter, but he must find a way to hole the putts that matter most. It's another one of those intangibles that can't be taught, one a player can only find inside himself. Until he acquires a knack for shaving a stroke per round off his game, he'll remain a good player but not a great one.

Charles has one other weakness I feel may be due to his size. He swings pretty hard regardless of the distance of the shot. Whether or not it's a remnant of his having to generate lots of speed with his body, his iron play would improve if he could learn the paint shots Nick Faldo was so good at. Charles is a *golfer* as opposed to a *player*. There's a difference. A golfer is one who relies on good swing mechanics and approaches the swing in a linear way. A player is more artistic, has loads of imagination, and a swing with several gears. When you've become a player, you've found the last piece of the puzzle, the thing that can make you dominant. Charles is only twenty-four and has plenty of time to search for that piece. If he finds it, watch out.

David Toms

Wise in the Ways of Golf

It took Toms a couple of years of grinding on the Nationwide Tour before he made it to the big show. Once he got there, he played four full years before he won his first tournament. After picking off second-tier events for the next few years, he finally won a major in 2001, the PGA Championship at Atlanta Athletic Club. Toms is a classic case of a player who gets better in every way, every year, not just with his golf swing but in the area of learning how to win.

Toms doesn't have a big game. But his patience, experience, and guile under pressure has made him one of the best players in the game today. If I saw Toms gaining on me on the leader board, I'd be plenty nervous. He doesn't give anything away. He's developed an inner toughness that helps him hole the big putts. Under pressure he thinks clearly and rarely makes a foolish play. At all times he is disciplined and hard-nosed.

I find it very difficult to criticize any part of his game. He's very motivated and does the very best he can. I look at some players and question their heart or commitment and sometimes both, but when I look at Toms I see a guy who has almost overachieved. David was a good junior player and an outstanding collegian, but I don't think he was blessed with the raw talent some players on the tour have been. He's hung in there like grim death for years and dug his success out of the dirt. You can't help but admire him.

Toms's laying up on the final hole of that PGA Championship he won said a lot about him. It was a career-defining moment, and with a one-shot lead he desperately needed a par or maybe even a birdie to win. The temptation to go for the green from the hanging lie he'd driven into must have been tremendous. But he laid up, knowing that if he lost the media would crucify him. He followed it with a terrific wedge shot to the green and a pressure-packed par putt to bring home the bacon. I felt sorry for his victim, Phil Mickelson, but I also was happy for Toms because he deserved his major.

At age thirty-six, Toms has never been a superexplosive player, and he misses his share of cuts. But when he's on he makes the most of it. Just as players feel they can't make a mistake when they play against Tiger, I think Tiger would feel that way if he went against Toms.

•

The mission facing the supporting cast in general is to raise their commitment, effort, and choke level. You know, some guys start choking when they see Tiger walking onto the practice tee. Others have a higher choke level—they don't choke until they play a practice round with him. A few get to a point where they can play against Tiger on Thursday and Friday, but choke over the weekend. The next choke level—going head-to-head on a Sunday afternoon with a championship on the line—is one none of them have overcome. Now that Tiger has relaxed his hold on the competition a little by showing he's human, maybe more of the supporting cast will be able to handle Tiger mano a mano. If and when that happens, we're likely to see some of the best showdowns in history.

CHAPTER 6

For Better or Worse

Surviving the "Grand Canyon Syndrome"

THE LONG, WOOLLY SWING of Phil Mickelson is known for blasting the ball prodigious distances, but the direction it flies is often variable. Phil can start the day on one course and finish on another. In 2003 he ranked 189th in the PGA Tour's driving accuracy statistical category. Despite this, he still rates as one of the best shot makers in recent history. Early into the 2004 season, Mickelson had won roughly $28 million on the PGA Tour, with twenty-two victories. His career has been one to die for, with one unfortunate exception: He hasn't won a major championship. That one glaring omission led to a disappointing 2003 season, and points up a problem that is all too familiar among great players.

Mickelson, like so many players before him, decided to revamp his swing. He figured if he could increase his accuracy off the tee without sacrificing distance, his iron play would improve and put him in position to make more birdies. So in late 2001 he enlisted the help of Rick Smith, the famed instructor who'd worked wonders with Lee Janzen and Rocco Mediate. Under Smith's well-trained eye, Mickelson toiled at his swing for five months.

The results were admirable—at first. Mickelson had a good year in 2002, winning twice and coming within an eyelash of capturing the U.S. Open and Masters. But, like a virus that lies dormant before exploding, the swing changes wrought disastrous results the following year. Mickelson's 2003 season started off well enough, then the bottom fell out. His driving became worse than ever and his iron play wasn't much better. Mickelson didn't win a tournament, went 0-5 in the Presidents Cup, and plummeted to 38th on the money list.

Why the new swing didn't work is a mystery. From a technical standpoint, it should have functioned perfectly. But it somehow didn't mesh with his feel and instincts. He stopped trusting it, and when he went back to the old swing, it didn't work very well because the new swing technique had become ingrained.

Mickelson clearly had lost his way. Early in the year he visited Butch Harmon, Tiger Woods's coach, for a second opinion. In the meantime he kept working with Smith. Then he talked about going back to his longer swing. The confusion he experienced is so typical of what happens when a world-class player tries to overhaul their swing. Like Seve Ballesteros, Nick Faldo, Chip Beck, Sergio Garcia, Hal Sutton, and Ian Baker-Finch—and also me—before him, Mickelson's attempts to find that extra edge backfired and ultimately made him worse. Only time will tell whether Mickelson is able to put the train back on the tracks and fulfill his enormous potential.

Mickelson is the most recent victim of what I call the *Grand Canyon Syndrome*. It's as if a very good player is on the left rim of the Grand Canyon, where he prospers but doesn't feel he's the very best he can be. He looks across at the distant rim on the other side and sees a promised land filled with wondrous possibilities. How to get there? There is only one way, through the deep chasm that intervenes—a chasm filled with all kinds of knowledge and secrets. The temptation to dive into the chasm and discover the shortcut that will get them to the other side is tremendous. It is, in fact, irresistible.

But when a player dives into the chasm, he very often doesn't make it out. He gets lost amid the myriad elements that promised to lead him up and out to the other side of the canyon. Teaching pros, exercise regimens, new equipment, diets, sports psychologists, endorsement contracts, and heaven knows what else fill the chasm, and they clutter and confuse the player's mind to the point that they lose sight of what got them to the Grand Canyon to begin with. The player may derive a lot of raw knowledge from diving into the chasm, but the intricate blend of skills they have spent their lifetime acquiring is gone, sometimes forever.

Mickelson's desire to improve is commendable. And I don't mean to imply that Rick Smith gave Phil bad advice. But the fact is, Mickelson taking *any* swing advice is as likely to hurt as help. Phil is the ultimate feel player who swings the club by intuition. He pays detailed attention to basics such as alignment and posture, but as far as swing mechanics go, forget it. He understands his swing and can explain how it works mechanically, but his trying to make his swing conform to something out of a textbook will just mess him up. Mickelson is at his best when he flies by the seat of his pants. He is not a precision player and never will be. He's a high-ball hitter, a Sky King boy, and they rarely are tremendous ball strikers.

Consulting with an instructor does not always constitute taking a plunge into the chasm. They can improve a player's swing, help outline goals, and give them friendship and confidence. The three best examples are David Leadbetter's retooling Nick Faldo's swing, and Butch Harmon's work with Greg Norman and Tiger Woods. In each case, the teacher took a great talent and made it better, which is enormously difficult to do. When a player is as good as Faldo, Norman, and Woods, the teacher must use a lot of restraint and disseminate information very carefully, or it will make the player worse. Leadbetter and Harmon had the intellect to detect problem areas in their games, but they also showed lots of wisdom. Harmon was especially impressive, because he didn't ask Norman or Woods to start from scratch. He merely refined what they had.

I think it's ironic that Faldo, Norman, and Woods all abandoned the very instructors who knew their swings so thoroughly and had the greatest potential to help them even more. Norman left Harmon after his final-round collapse in the 1996 Masters, surmising that Harmon's advice didn't hold up under pressure. As I see it, the fact Norman acquired a six-stroke lead after three rounds proved Harmon's advice was fine. The problem was in Greg's inability to handle the pressure. I was just as puzzled when Faldo left Leadbetter. I mean, how much better did he think he was going to get? As for Woods, he stopped working with Butch prior to the 2003 season, and in the months that followed developed some troubling issues with his game. He had a great year for anyone else, but a poor one by his standard. He should never have stopped working with Butch.

Whether the instructor helps a player or makes him

regress, the fact is, they don't come with a guarantee. Unlike teaching someone piano, calculus, or how to work a computer, there is huge risk involved. Top players often don't realize this—as they see it there is nowhere to go but up. Their talent is so extraordinary they feel they can adapt to any type of swing change and make it work. When you combine that degree of self-assuredness with their ambition to be the best, you have a recipe for disaster.

When the player decides he needs to move his game up a notch, he invariably does it by altering his swing, strengthening his body, or changing equipment. The pitfalls that exist within each area have become clear to me over the years because I've seen them so often. Let's take teaching first, setting aside the excellent work done by Leadbetter and Harmon. Here is where the teacher and player often go wrong.

Physical anomalies are ignored. My vision has always been a bit haywire. When I go to the rifle range, I'm inclined to aim high and to the left. That's what looks straight to me. To compensate I instinctively cock my head a bit. On the golf course I did the same thing, especially on the putting green. Late in 1976, someone told me that my eyes weren't aligned parallel to the target line when I putted. Not being aware of my vision idiosyncrasy, and looking for an edge that would turn me into a super putter, I gave it a try. I immediately went into a terrible putting slump. Up to that point, my brain had done a fine job adjusting to my vision problem, and now I was telling it something that just didn't compute. The new eye alignment tip just killed my putting, even though it makes sense for virtually everybody else.

Anatomical anomalies have to be taken into account in teaching golf. Say the teacher examines a player's swing and notices the student tilts slightly to the left at address. He also sees that the player doesn't transfer his weight to his right side very well on the backswing, so he modifies the player's setup and works on improving the guy's weight shift. Not surprisingly, the player struggles. What the teacher didn't notice is that the player's left leg, like that of Jack Nicklaus, is half an inch shorter than his right. The player instinctively compensated for this by leaning a bit to his left from start to finish. It really is the only way he can play.

To point out another physical characteristic that differs from the norm, it so happens that my arms are inordinately short for a guy my size. I'm six foot two, but wear only a thirty-inch sleeve. Sam Snead, on the other hand, wore a thirty-five-inch sleeve even though he stood only five foot eleven. You better believe that makes a difference in the way we use our arms in the swing. The teacher must consider these things before embarking on a change. If an amateur who is just starting the game has extremely small hands, the teacher shouldn't reflexively recommend that the pupil use an overlapping grip. A ten-finger grip might be better.

They subscribe to a swing model. I distrust system teaching, in which the teacher has a biomechanical model on his computer screen and tries to make the student conform to that model. We see a lot of that today. It enables relatively inexperienced teachers to pinpoint "what's wrong" with a swing and make obvious suggestions as to what needs to be fixed. Very few players who subscribe to such a system become good players, and those that do succeed were good players to begin with. I tend to think it is the player, not the system, that is responsible.

Systems turn players into robots. They swing the club by rote, with no personality or nuance that sets them apart. Systems turn lone wolves—players who learn to play the game by trial and error—into sheep. The players also lose the ability to fix their swing when something goes wrong, because the teacher knows the system better than they do. They lose versatility and the ability to hit different types of shots, because the system invariably favors one ball-flight pattern.

The golf swing is a very intricate motion. One part of the swing is tied inextricably to the next. If one part of the swing is changed it demands that everything else be modified so it fits with that new part. When you make a wholesale change to a new system, the whole machine breaks down and needs to be rebuilt. Take the grip. If you turn your left hand on the grip one inch to the right and change it from a neutral position to a "strong" position, it demands you release the club in an entirely different manner. All of a sudden you find that if you rotate your hands through impact, you hit a vicious hook. To make it work, you not only have to curb action in your hands, you have to change how your whole body moves so the hands are in position to perform their job differently. It totally changes the way you play the game.

They trade art for science. Jackie Burke, the famed Houston pro, tells of a time he went to a downtown office building to pick a friend up for lunch. While he waited for the man to get his coat, he noticed on the man's desk a beautiful ornament, a small dog carved out of wood. The beauty of the thing really got Jack's attention. When the man appeared, Jack asked him where he got the dog.

"I made it myself," the man said.

"How'd you do it?" asked Jackie.

"It was easy," said the man. "I took a block of wood and a knife, and cut away everything that didn't look like a dog."

Jackie believes teaching the golf swing is like that, and I couldn't agree more. A good teacher appreciates nuance in a player's swing, and considers everything carefully before deciding what to carve off and what to add. He's an artist. When he sees Jim Furyk take the club back like a man opening an umbrella, he thinks twice before telling him the move isn't good. Can you imagine what would have happened to Furyk if, at age twenty, a teacher convinced him to try to swing like Ben Hogan? Furyk never would have won the U.S. Open, that's for sure. It's doubtful he even would have made it to the PGA Tour.

I admire teachers who have enough knowledge of the swing, and sufficient mental flexibility, to give advice that is uniquely suited to the individual. I'm partial to teachers who consider a person's height, body type, gender, strength, age, and personality before embarking on a swing change. And one who recognizes that there is no such thing as a perfect swing because the player himself changes from day to day.

They love the big-muscles swing. Swing styles come and go. In my era, most players were *swingers*. They generated clubhead speed primarily with the arms and hands. They directed the clubhead straight down the target line through impact, the momentum of the swing carrying them to the classic reverse C finish, their backs arched backward, their heads farther from the target than their bellies. Me, Tom Weiskopf, Jack Nicklaus, and most other top players swung in this manner.

That changed for good in the mid-1980s when Nick Faldo retooled his swing under the guidance of David Leadbetter. A long but somewhat erratic player, Faldo sought a swing that was more controlled and consistent. Under Leadbetter, Faldo simplified and tightened his swing and made it much more efficient. He kept his arms close to his body throughout the swing, and generated clubhead speed primarily by unwinding his hips and shoulders. Faldo lost some distance, but no player in the last twenty years has been more precise. His success had an enormous influence on other players and teachers. Starting in the early 1990s, everyone adopted the big-muscles swing, with a couple of twists to it that Faldo never implemented. And its weaknesses are becoming apparent.

Before I go further, let me assure you that Leadbetter is not a one-trick pony. He possesses the intellectual flexibility I've talked about, and he styles his teaching according to the strengths and weaknesses of the individual. I respect him a lot, and the swing he gave Faldo was just what the doctor ordered. Their work together put Leadbetter on the map and marked the best teacher–player association in recent history. But despite Faldo's success, the big-muscles swing is not for everybody. Amateurs especially have trouble with it. It requires a lot of flexibility in the hips and shoulders, which older golfers and those with stocky builds just don't have. It also robs the average player of distance, because it removes the flash speed supplied by the arms and hands. I don't think the big-muscles swing has helped the grassroots golfer one bit.

The variation of the big-muscles swing we see today is somewhat different than that used by Faldo. Pros today have tweaked it so it produces incredible power. This is true with players like David Duval and Fred Couples, who combine the big-muscles swing with a strong left-hand grip. Unlike Faldo, they don't square the clubface with at least some degree of arm and hand rotation through impact. With that strong left-hand grip, the clubface pretty much squares itself through impact. The players simply unwind their bodies as fast as they humanly can on the downswing, and merely hold onto the club for dear life. They can do this without fear of hitting the ball crooked, because the modern ball doesn't spin as much and therefore doesn't hook or slice as easily.

With courses getting longer, greens getting firmer, equipment getting hotter, and the competition getting better, there is a huge incentive for players to strive for extra distance. No doubt about it, pros today can hit the ball out of sight. Tour pros today are thirty yards longer, on average, than when I played. In 1980, a 270-yard drive would have ranked seventh on the tour. In 2003, it would have ranked 189th—second to last.

The essential problem with the big-muscle swing is that it lacks finesse. There is so much explosive power through impact, that trying to tone it down is very difficult. It's like driving a car at high speeds down a highway—it's hard to discern the difference between 160 mph and 150 mph. On the other hand, when you swing primarily with your arms and hands, regulating speed to control the distance the ball flies is much easier. Half and three-quarter shots are much easier to pull off. The big-muscle swing isn't quite as versatile in terms of allowing you to intentionally hit draws or fades, knockdown shots or high floaters. It's very dynamic, but not very artistic. So I'm biased against it. I think the swinger method will make a comeback. Styles in golf tend to be cyclical, and it won't be long before you see the reverse C finishes I talked about.

They mistake strengths for weaknesses. When I was a boy, I heard that a flying right elbow was a fatal swing flaw. It was like a commandment—if you let your arm drift too far away from your torso during the backswing, you'd never be any good. Then along came Jack Nicklaus. Jack's right arm separated farther from his body than any champion in history, and he was a tremendous ball striker. As it turns out, that move of Jack's helped him a great deal. It helped widen his swing arc, which contributed to his enormous power. It helped a player who wasn't very tall (Jack is only 5' 11") swing in an upright fashion, which is why he was such a great long iron player.

The point is, just because something looks unusual doesn't

mean that it has a deleterious effect on the swing. Ed (The Grip) Fiori turned his right hand under the handle so far he looked like he was riding a motorcycle, and it didn't hurt him one bit when he won at the 1996 Quad Cities Classic. Charles Owens made a lot of money on the Champions Tour in the 1980s using a cross-handed grip on full-swing shots. Miller Barber, Gay Brewer, the aforementioned Jim Furyk, and many others have played brilliantly despite the so-called weaknesses in their swing. Usually the teachers don't confront alleged flaws as drastic as theirs. It might be something small, like playing the ball too far back in the stance. But the shortcoming, upon closer examination, often turns out to be a strength.

They mistake big things for small things. Things were a little more cutthroat in my early days on tour. Purses weren't huge, there was no Nationwide Tour for guys to fall back on, and not as many club pro jobs were available. Even though players were friendly to each other, some would see a good young player and try to mess with his head. Sam Snead would wander past a talented rookie and chirp, just for fun, "How can you get the ball airborne with it so far back in your stance?" and keep walking. The kid, in awe of Snead, would ponder the remark. Then he'd move the ball forward in his stance. And that would be the end of him. Or Tommy Bolt would watch a guy for two minutes, wrinkle his face, and say, "You can't play with that grip," and move on. This happened more than once—a tiny suggestion would wreak pure havoc.

The moral of the story is, the small things in a golf swing often are big things. Snead's ball position caper is a terrific example. Of all the fundamentals, to me ball position is the most overlooked. The consequences of moving the ball forward or back in your stance even an inch can be tremendous.

It's especially dangerous to move the ball up in your stance if you're accustomed to playing it toward the middle. When a teacher looks at ball position and sees it isn't "off the left heel" the way the textbooks say, and tries to correct it, he can ruin the player right there. The teacher should be aware of this and be very careful about suggesting a change.

They don't teach the short game. The best short game teacher in the world today is Dave Pelz. He's a good hands-on instructor, but his strong suit is studying and interpreting the science behind chipping and putting. He knows technique, and understands cause and effect. A player can read Pelz's books or watch him on television and glean an enormous amount of knowledge.

Pelz doesn't have much competition. Most famous instructors, including Hank Haney, David Leadbetter, Jimmy Ballard, and Rick Smith, specialize in full-swing teaching. I'm sure they see themselves as versatile, but I'd be willing to bet the ratio of time they spend with tour players on the full swing versus short game runs something like 80–20 in favor of the full swing. It seems to be that good short game teachers are a dying breed. It's not where the money and excitement are.

Make no mistake, teachers have a place in world-class golf. But I find it interesting that Ben Hogan, Byron Nelson, and Sam Snead became great without ever taking a lesson. Old-timers aren't the only examples: Fred Couples, Bruce Lietzke, and Lanny Wadkins became successful despite knowing hardly anything technical about their swings.

But gurus aren't the only pitfall that golfers face when trying to take their game to a higher level.

The Trouble with Equipment

The best players on the PGA Tour tend to overrate their skills and underrate their equipment. They think they are so good that they could play with a bamboo fishing pole if they had to. That just isn't the case. The arbitrary way some players have switched equipment companies and staked their careers on a totally unfamiliar set of clubs, all for endorsement money and a vague hope of playing better, just blows me away. Often as not, their games go south for at least a year. Corey Pavin, Lee Janzen, Payne Stewart, Mark Brooks, and Steve Stricker are examples of players who switched manufacturers then plummeted out of sight.

I wish I could have told them my story before they made the switch. In 1975, my manager convinced me I had to leave MacGregor. His reasoning was that MacGregor already had Jack Nicklaus and Tom Weiskopf in its fold, and that as long as I was alongside them I would never get top billing. So I switched to Wilson. Now, Wilson made good clubs at the time, but not great ones. Try as they might, they just couldn't duplicate the playing characteristics of my MacGregors, which I had spent years tweaking with lead tape, different shafts, and so forth.

The difference wasn't apparent at first. From a level, perfect lie on the range, I hit my new Wilsons about as well as I did my old MacGregors. But from sidehill lies, rough, and other real-life situations, they didn't perform very well at all. The clubheads didn't penetrate the grass the same way. The shafts behaved differently when I had to choke down on the grip. My game slipped two notches immediately, and I came to regret switching manufacturers.

My advice to everyone, from tour stars to rank amateurs, is to stick with a set of clubs you like until they fall apart. That's true more with irons than woods, because there are new and better drivers, fairway woods, and hybrid woods coming out all the time. Never switch to a new set of irons just because your friend plays well with them or you get bored and want to make a change just for the heck of it.

The Trouble with Physical Conditioning

Players have become manic about getting in shape. On one hand, it makes sense. Golf takes more stamina than people think, and it's also important to maintain the strength and flexibility you had when you were young. I'm also glad to see that fewer players smoke and drink and that more pay attention to what they eat. What concerns me, or at least fails to impress me, is lifting weights. I don't think it does much good for a golfer, and I know it can hurt.

One danger of the big-muscle swing I haven't alluded to is the enormous stress it places on your lower back. The sudden twisting and turning of the torso takes its toll. The feeling among players is that they have to strengthen their bodies in order to withstand the stress the modern swing puts on their bodies. That's one reason David Duval and Tiger Woods decided to hit the weights. But both players hurt their backs in the gym, and they aren't the only ones. There are more injuries taking place in the gym these days than are made public. It's a dirty little secret on the PGA Tour.

In the 1980s, when I took time off the tour and spent all the time around my ranch, I got very strong and put on twenty pounds of muscle. It killed my game. The clubs felt like feathers. My chest was so big it affected my flexibility and ability to swing my arms on the proper swing plane. I hadn't realized yet that golf is more a game of speed than raw strength. Strength helps, but it never spells the difference between success and failure. From that time on, I knew that lifting weights would be about the worst thing I could do.

The trouble with weights is that they put your body out of balance. When one part of your anatomy gets strong, it affects its relationship with another. It upsets your mechanics and timing. It's very difficult to build up every part of the body equally so you maintain that balance. That's why natural sports that improve overall conditioning, such as basketball, racquetball, and hunting, are ten times better for golfers than lifting weights.

The best example of a body being balanced was Billy Casper. Don't laugh—although he didn't have a very athletic build, in his prime Billy's muscles were very nicely attuned. He was consciously aware of this. When you shook hands with him, he never gave you his entire hand. He'd extend a few fingers and give you a gentle little squeeze. He didn't want you to upset his body balance, and he didn't want to squeeze anything more tightly than he did a golf club. There's a lesson in that. Casper hit the ball far enough. He had plenty of stamina. He won fifty-one tournaments and did it without acquiring extra muscle mass. He was a golfer, not an offensive lineman, and he approached conditioning sensibly: the way a pro golfer should.

The Trouble with Money

For one year, Bill Rogers was the best player in the world. In 1981, the year he turned thirty, he won the British Open at Royal St. George's and three other tournaments on the PGA Tour, including the World Series of Golf. He also won three more tournaments outside America and played in the Ryder Cup.

Outside America are the operative words, because the company that managed him, IMG, wanted to cash in on his success by having Rogers travel nonstop all over the world. Rogers complied and, by his own admission, burned himself out. By June 1982, something was seriously wrong with his game. He contended for the U.S. Open at Pebble Beach, but his fellow competitor the final day, Tom Watson, inexplicably was outdriving him by as much as fifty yards. Watson went on to win. For Rogers, things got even worse. He won one more tournament in 1983, but only a few years later, he was gone from the tour forever.

When a player finds success, there is an urge to make as much money as possible because you don't know how long the fame is going to last. There is no shortage of opportunities, what with endorsements, corporate outings, golf course design fees, exhibitions, and appearance fees for showing up in foreign countries, but they all take time and a big toll on your mind and body. In the end, it all is done at the expense of what got you those things in the first place—your golf game.

The smart player knows that if he focuses primarily on golf and says *no* to most of the offers that come down the pike, the off-course income will be there later. And the player needs to learn to say *no*, not only to the companies making the offers, but to his manager. Even though the manager is supposedly looking after the player's well-being, his primary goal is to make money, because the more the player makes the more *he* makes. One thing that amazes me about Tiger Woods is that, as many deals as he has going, it somehow doesn't encroach on his ability to play his best golf. He always shows up to play well-rested and with a clear mind. It's yet another way he's an example to other tour players.

The bottom line to all these pitfalls can be found in the words of Ben Hogan. He said, "The secret is in the dirt." He didn't mean at the equipment rack, in tournaments in Dubai, or in the weight room. He meant the practice range, all by your lonesome, where you figure out your game for yourself.

CHAPTER 7

Courses for Horses

Examining Our Fields of Dreams

THE GREATEST PHOTOGRAPH in golf history is Hy Peskin's image of Ben Hogan hitting a 1-iron to the 18th green at Merion in the final round of the 1950 U.S. Open. The photo is striking, beautiful, and balanced, the outline of the bunkers and gallery in the distance framing Hogan, who is at the top of his follow-through. But what really sets the picture apart is the story behind it. As you gaze at Peskin's photograph, you are witness to a rich and compelling saga. Hogan came to the final hole needing a par 4 to get into a playoff with Lloyd Mangrum and George Fazio. The 18th hole at Merion was a monster par 4, long and uphill to a fast, firm green. After a fine drive, Hogan had to hit the most difficult shot there is, a 1-iron from a tight lie. And he *had* to find the green to have a reasonable chance at that par. It was the supreme test of skill, guts, and daring, the defining moment of Hogan's career.

We'll never see a photograph with that extra killer dimension again, for one simple reason: Professionals don't hit 1-irons into par 4s anymore. Not one player in fifty even *carries* a 1-iron, let alone would attempt hitting one from the fairway. Tour pros are hitting the ball so outrageously far with modern clubs and balls that even the short hitters among them rarely have more than a 5-iron left to the green. I miss the long iron dimension of the game. I miss seeing Hale Irwin hitting a 2-iron to the final green at Winged Foot in the 1974 U.S. Open, or Jack Nicklaus hitting a 1-iron to the 15th green at Augusta National in the 1975 Masters.

The PGA Tour and USGA apparently miss it, too, because they're stretching courses to the limit to ensure the pros hit every club in the bag. Bethpage Black, Olympia Fields, and Augusta National are just a few of the courses that have been revised to measure in the neighborhood of 7,200 yards. Augusta National's course revisions got the most attention, because they lengthened the layout immediately after Tiger Woods shot a record score of 18 under par to win the 1997 Masters. Their attempts to Tigerproof the course by making it longer actually played right into Tiger's hands. Tiger still hit medium and short irons into the greens, while average-length hitters had to bomb away with long irons and even fairway woods. I've always felt the way to Tigerproof a golf course is to slow down the greens. Tiger is a fabulous putter and if you make the greens slower and grainier, it will rob him of one of his stealth weapons.

In general I applaud the trend toward lengthening courses for PGA Tour players, because there's a broad-based sentiment that we need to preserve the challenge of the game. Length is a sure way to accomplish that. What alarms me is that *all* courses are being lengthened, not just the ones we see tour pros play on television. The poor 18-handicapper is going up against courses they can scarcely play because they're too long. New clubs and balls enable everyone to hit the ball farther, but for the amateur the promises are a bit misleading. Whereas the average golfer can squeeze an extra five or ten yards out of a new titanium-faced driver and aerodynamically perfect multipiece ball, tour pros who turn one loose get an extra twenty to thirty-five yards at least. A swing speed of eighty-five miles per hour, which is typical for a hacker, isn't enough to take advantage of the technology. Only when you get up to around 110 mph does the equipment kick into what can best be described as *overdrive*. When that happens, there's an exponential payoff to each mile per hour you add to your swing speed. The upshot is that modern courses for the average golfer are being designed with high swing speeds in mind rather than the speed generated by the typical hacker.

So, even though I like the idea of seeing more 1-iron shots into par 4s, it should be the professionals who have to play them, not the everyday player. Remember Merion? It no longer can host a U.S. Open because its overall length is too short and it doesn't have the infrastructure to house the concessions, TV trucks, corporate tents, and so on. But they've added length where they can. The 18th hole, where Hogan pulled off that 1-iron shot, was recently lengthened. I don't get it. They're planning ahead for Davis Love III to hit a 1-iron to the green, when Love isn't even going to play there. Meanwhile, the club members who use that back tee are going to need a 3-wood for their second—followed by a pitch shot.

It's outrageous. The Pines Course at The International in Massachusetts tips out at 8,325 yards. One of the par 4s there measures 567 yards! A course in China called Jade Dragon is even longer: 8,548 yards. A course currently being designed in Las Vegas will tip out at 8,600 yards. I don't get it. For one thing, these ultralong courses eat up more real estate, and that means higher maintenance costs. You're paying more for water, overseeding, mowing, everything. For another, almost nobody can play them, or would want to. I guess there's a certain cachet in saying you played an 8,500-yard course, but after playing the back tees one time, most if not all golfers will never try it again. What's fun about shooting a high score?

You can argue that players can always move forward to an easier set of tees, but that to me is impractical. It's demoralizing to have to move up to the white tees when you've been playing the black or blue tees. You feel less than what you were. Some people may shrug and say, "Well, that's just tough," but it isn't very productive. Nobody's approaching the problem creatively—by making the old white markers blue, the blue ones black and so on, to help the average golfer preserve their dignity.

The bottom line is that golf is becoming too difficult for the average player. At a time when we're trying to expand the game, recent statistics show that as many people are leaving the game as there are new people coming into it. It has to be because they aren't enjoying it as much. The decrease in enjoyment can be attributed to courses becoming too difficult, sort of like every ski resort having nothing but black diamond runs. In golf parlance, people are tired of falling down, especially when they pay eighty dollars or more to do it.

Some people disagree with me. They point out that the average handicap for a man is approximately eighteen, the same as it was forty years ago. They assume golfers are coping with the long courses just fine. Think about it: With new clubs and balls, better course conditioning, advances in instruction, and more leisure time available, the average handicap should be lower, not the same as it was four decades ago. That means golfers are having to work harder just to stay afloat.

The trend is hurting some segments of the golf population more than others. Women and seniors have it the worst by far. For one thing, women only have one set of tees while men can choose from several. What's up with that? Moreover, improvements in agronomy have made fairways firmer. Always challenged by getting the ball in the air and being able to carry it a satisfying distance, women can't get the club under the ball on those firm fairways. It helps that newer clubs have lower centers of gravity, which make it easier to get the ball airborne. But for the ladies and old men, it isn't enough. Here you have a demographic with more money to spend and more free time to play the game, and you make them miserable. Great.

So, the increasing yardages of golf courses is a problem. The next question is, who is to blame? Surprisingly, it isn't always the designer. Very often, the owner demands that you build an extremely difficult course, and as an "employee," what can you do but follow the boss's orders? But too often, the ego of the designer comes into play. They don't want their name associated with a course that is duck-soup easy.

The distance issue notwithstanding, there are other features of modern architecture that aren't conducive to golf the way it should be. Some faults are glaring, others more subtle. But if you've ever disliked a hole (or an entire course) and weren't sure why, you may find the reason on this list.

The shutoff fairway. The 1997 Ryder Cup was held at Valderrama in Spain, a pretty good test that has produced a lot of drama. The 17th hole there is a controversial par 5, one the long hitters can reach in two with a powerful drive and strong second shot. The green borders on unfair, but it's still a great match play hole, one where there usually is a resolution. Prior to the 1997 Ryder Cup, however, the Europeans, noting that the American team had a preponderance of long hitters, wanted to negate that advantage. They ordered up a band of rough to be stretched across the fairway at a point where the longest hitters wanted to position their drive. The fairway was shut off, and everyone was forced to lay up. It was clever of the Europeans to do that, sort of like a major league baseball team watering down the basepaths before the game to nullify the speed of an opposing team.

It ruined the hole, though, turning it into just another par 5. The sad thing is, the shutoff fairway is a fairly common feature in American golf. You see it more on short par 4s than on par 5s. Clubs don't want long hitters driving the green, so they install a patch of thick rough just short of the putting surface. If long hitters go for the green, the tall grass snags the tee shot and forces them to play an awkward pitch from thick rough. It takes the driver out of the players' hands and makes them choose a long iron or middle iron—a nothing shot.

Internal out-of-bounds. When the first golf courses were built in Scotland, *out-of-bounds* basically meant off the property. The stroke-and-distance (two-stroke) penalty was created to punish the really bad shot, one that flew into neighboring cow pastures. When the golf course boom got under way in the United States, many designers weren't given a lot of real estate to work with. Many times fairways closely adjoined each other. So, to protect golfers in adjacent fairways and discourage players from cutting the corners on short holes, they placed out-of-bounds stakes within the golf course. It's a necessity, but an unfortunate one. With very few exceptions, I don't think a course with internal out-of-bounds can really qualify as a design masterpiece.

Artificial affectations. If you're building a desert course, you don't want too many pine trees or manmade waterfalls. If the terrain is dead flat, you don't want too many artificial mounds. You also don't want too many railroad ties with terraced landscaping or rock walls anywhere. A bit of artificiality is almost unavoidable, but it's easy to overdo it.

Cart paths visible from the tee. Golf carts are a part of life and I've come to accept and even appreciate them. Carts enable you to bring an extra sweater and beverages. They turn the round into a picnic, which is nice on occasion. And let's face it, carts are fun to drive. If they had them at an amusement park, you could sell tickets to drive them. I can't tell you how many times I've asked someone if they play golf and get the answer, "No, but I like to drive the cart." Carts are the biggest source of revenue for country clubs. I think they're fine—provided you have a choice of walking or riding.

Carts, however, run contrary to the natural setting of a golf course. I dislike standing on the tee and seeing a vast field of beautiful green disrupted by a black cart path winding through it. It makes the course look like a Go-Kart park. Good designers know how to hide the cart paths, tuck them behind hills or on the opposite sides of trees, so you can't see them. Flat courses that get heavy traffic can't avert this problem entirely, which is understandable. But it does make the overall quality of the course slip a few notches.

Bunkers and water fronting greens. The older I get, the more empathy I have for older golfers, juniors, and women. One of the things that takes the fun out of the game are forced carries, not just from the tee but from the fairway. When you plop a bunker in front of the green, the weaker player has no option but to mindlessly plop their approach shot into the sand, or else lay up so close to it they can't spin their pitch shot close to the hole. Regardless of your ability, you shouldn't be forced to lay up from 150 yards. There always should be an opening to the green that gives players the option of running their ball onto the green. Golf can be played along the ground or through the air, but sand—and water, too—in front of the green removes one of those important options.

There is a place, I suppose, for the forced carry. But it should be constrained to the best players under tournament conditions. The par-3 17th green at the TPC at Sawgrass is surrounded by water on all sides, which provides wonderful theater during the Players Championship. But you have to wonder what goes on there the other 361 days a year. I'd sure love to have the golf ball concession there, I'll tell you that. I'm curious to know the quality of balls they pull from the water. Are they old balls, a sign that the player surrendered to the water before hitting? Or are most of them brand-new shiners, which says the player refused to admit that a soaking was just ahead?

Forced carries from the tee. The 492-yard 10th hole at Bethpage Black during the 2002 U.S. Open was one of the hardest holes in championship history—for the wrong reason. To reach the fairway, players had to boom their tee shot 270 yards through the air, an impossible carry for many players. Hale Irwin, whose skills are still such that he could contend in a U.S. Open, couldn't reach the fairway. Even younger players saw their balls come up short in rough so thick they may as well have hit their balls in a lake. My feeling is, a straight shot should never be penalized. I don't care if it goes only 100 yards, you shouldn't pay the same price as someone who hit a titanic slice from the tee. The game just wasn't meant to be played that way. A good hole should test both power and accuracy, but just because you lack the power part shouldn't mean you accept the equivalent of a one-stroke penalty.

Trees in the fairway. The 10th hole at Spyglass Hill (one of my favorite courses) has one silly, distinct flaw: There's a tree growing in the middle of the fairway. Nearby is Pebble Beach, where there used to be a tree growing on the right side of the 18th fairway, too, though good players tended to drive their ball past it. But it definitely came into play for players with a weak slice, who unfortunately constitute about 70 percent of the golf population.

There's a place for trees in golf, but the fairway isn't it. Any shot that goes in the fairway should be rewarded with an unobstructed line to at least part of the green. Imagine reviewing your round with a friend and telling him, "I hit it in the middle of the fairway and played out sideways." It doesn't make sense. I'm not against trees forcing you to alter your strategy a little. At Colonial Country Club in Fort Worth, oak trees near many of the greens come into play when you're in the fairway. Although they may block your play to the hole, you at least can hit the ball on the green.

Trouble within trouble. The fairway bunker shot is one of the toughest in golf. It's made even tougher when your ball is up against pampas grass or something else growing within the bunker. I appreciate decorative touches, but they shouldn't come into play in any way.

A similar thing I dislike is what insiders call "double negatives." Positioning a bunker right next to a water hazard is an example; you might have to stand in water to play a shot out of sand. That's like being penalized twice for one infraction. Trouble should never be set up against other trouble.

A premium on putting. Even as a kid I was amazed at how short grass could be cut and still stay alive. I'm even more surprised today. New strains of grass can be cut to 3/32" and thrive. The result is that greens can be made so fast as to be unreasonably difficult, if not unplayable. On one hand that's a good thing. Greens are as smooth and true as a billiard table, and very little is left to chance when the ball leaves the face of the putter. The downside is that extremely fast green speeds are placing too much of an emphasis on putting. This is especially true on older courses with severe contouring. Take a sloping green and combine it with a reading of 11 on the *stimpmeter* (the device that determines how fast a green is running), and you have the makings of a very long afternoon. To give you an idea how fast the 11 reading is, greens at an average public course run at about 8.5 on the stimpmeter.

As much as I love Augusta National and the Masters, I've felt for some time that its roller-coaster greens give the good putter too much of an advantage. Ben Crenshaw, a fabulous putter, won the Masters twice and they were his only majors. Jose Maria Olazabal and Mike Weir are two more examples of recent winners whose greatest strength is putting. Putting has always been a great equalizer, but giving it too much weight doesn't make sense. The fact that a beginning golfer can be a good putter but can't be a good ball striker tells me something. At every course there should always be an emphasis on the game from tee to green.

Not factoring in the wind. Every geographic setting has a prevailing wind direction. Designers sometimes consider this when designing a hole. For example, the 9th hole at the Ocean Course at Kiawah has a shallow green that slopes front to back and has a bank in front of it. The hole usually plays downwind and when it does you have almost no chance of stopping the ball in the green because the ball comes in too hot. If a hole plays downwind, the green should be long and narrow, not wide and shallow.

I don't want to hold the cudgels up to course designers in general. Having designed more than thirty courses myself, I'm well aware of the constraints and demands put on the designer. Sometimes the parcel of land you're given is too small or the terrain is bad. Sometimes the designer and architect are forced to work around an environmentally sensitive area. Often your budget doesn't allow for large-scale earth-moving to shape holes the way you want. So I sympathize. But it's hard to find excuses for some of these design gaffes.

Golf and the Environment

About fifteen years ago, the environmental movement began taking a hard look at golf courses. They didn't like what they saw—at first. They assumed golf course architects were like other proponents of commercial and residential expansion, reckless and insensitive to the land they encroached on. They saw in golf the stripping of wooded areas, pesticide use, invasion of wetlands, and extravagant use of water resources.

Over time, environmentalists have come to view golf courses in a different light. Though still suspicious of the motives of the men behind the courses, and vigilant in monitoring their every move, they now have a better appreciation of what golf does for the environment, and how well-intentioned the vast majority of golf course builders truly are. Golf courses generally get a huge property tax break for "preservation of open spaces," and it's deserved. Golf courses invariably enhance and preserve an environmental setting as opposed to harming it.

Pete Dye, the legendary course designer, points out that pesticides used in golf today are much less toxic than those used for farming. One ingenious pest-control substance isn't toxic at all. It consists of a gel filled with the eggs of parasitic worms called *nematodes*. Superintendents spread the gel, the eggs hatch, and the nematodes seek out harmful insects, bore into their bodies, and devour them from the inside. As for fertilizers, virtually all in use today are organic and have little or no ill effect on humans.

The other ecological complaints don't merit much consideration because they are no less consequential than those in other forms of development. Do golf courses expend energy? Yes, the clubhouse does need interior lighting. Do courses emit foul gases into the atmosphere? They do when they use gas-powered carts, but most courses now use electric carts. Do courses emit waste? No doubt about it, where you find people, you'll find garbage cans. Do they endanger rare species of animals? No, not one.

In fact, golf courses do the environment a great deal of good. They serve as a habitat for birds and animals. There's no end to the critters you see on golf courses; it's almost like visiting a nature preserve. Well-maintained grass and trees prevent soil erosion. As for the water they require, very often it's effluent water one can't drink anyway, or fresh water collected from ponds on site. There is some concern that the increasing number of golf courses in arid areas such as Palm Springs, California, can upset the climate because of the evaporation of water into the atmosphere, but it's difficult to substantiate.

Courses are required to obtain local approval before they begin building and must adhere to some pretty strict guidelines. At Stonetree, a course south of Napa, California, that I designed along with former USGA president Sandy Tatum, we had to remove a number of oak trees. For every one we removed, we were required to plant ten in its place. We also had to be sensitive to parts of San Francisco Bay. I'm not sure people realize to what extent builders are required to respect the land they're building on.

As Bobby Jones said, you don't thank a person for not robbing a bank—when you build a golf course, there's an inherent responsibility to do it with regard to the natural habitat. But I'll say this: The vast majority of golf course builders work with the environment not because they have to, but because they want to. In every sense, golf makes our planet better.

Fields of Dreams: My Top Ten Courses

I suppose I've played more than a thousand courses in my lifetime. I've enjoyed every one of them, and I've never gotten spoiled by playing great courses. Great golf is where you find it, and all golf is good regardless of the quality. Still, some courses are much better than others. And when I think of the best courses I've ever seen, I'm sometimes guilty of being partial to venues where something extraordinary happened to me personally. With that said, here's my list of favorite courses, the ten places I'd choose to play above all others.

10. Royal Birkdale Golf Club (Southport, England).

Of all the courses on the British Open rota, Royal Birkdale is the most underrated. Though located in England, it is a seaside course that plays more like those in Scotland. With its crisp turf, creative bunkering, treeless expanse, and wind always blowing, it has the feel of a links course. The only difference is that its fairways are relatively flat. I never was better rewarded for course management and strategy than I was at Royal Birkdale when I won the 1976 British Open.

Like all British Open courses, the weather dictates how difficult it plays. When it's dry, as it was in 1976, the ball rolls forever and the course isn't particularly long. When it rains and the wind shifts, it can be a bear. What makes it unusually hard is that it now plays to a par of 70 in the Open Championship, as opposed to par 72 for club members. The front nine is a par 34, and you don't see a par 5 until the 15th hole. The 17th is another par 5, but it's a long time to wait for those birdie holes. And you finish on one of the more challenging closing holes in golf, a par 4 that requires a long iron to a green that is very well bunkered.

Odd things tend to happen at Birkdale. In '76, the course was so dry it actually caught fire twice during the championship. I've never seen a stranger sight than those fire engines, their sirens howling, racing out onto the golf course to put out the fire. In 1961, a gale blew down most of the tented village.

Birkdale is where Hale Irwin whiffed a three-inch putt in 1983 and wound up losing to Tom Watson by one stroke. It's where Lu Liang-Huan, better known as Mr. Lu, almost stole the Open from Lee Trevino in 1971 before hooking his second shot on the last hole into the gallery, where the ball struck a woman spectator in the head, knocking her out and causing a big gash. It's where Arnold Palmer muscled a 6-iron out of the scrub and buckthorn and onto the green at the 16th hole on his way to winning the 1961 Open. The club built a plaque at the spot where Arnie played from, and it's still there today. Birkdale is where Jack Nicklaus conceded a short putt to Tony Jacklin that halved the 1969 Ryder Cup.

For all the caterwauling about sexism in American golf, women have had a much more difficult time of it in Great

Britain. But Birkdale is unique that way, too—women have had access to the course for more than a century, and the club is proud of that.

I miss Birkdale and haven't seen it lately because ABC airs the British Open. I want to go back. British Open champions age sixty-five and under are still exempt, although it's unlikely I'll compete again. But next time I'm on vacation in England, I intend to pay a visit to the course where one of my dreams came true. I'm bringing my clubs, and hope Royal Birkdale will allow me to play one more round there—this time playing the course at a par 72 instead of 70. On that course, I'll need all the help I can get.

9. Cypress Point Club (Pebble Beach, California).

It's tragic in a way that Cypress Point is no longer one of the courses played during the AT&T Pebble Beach National Pro-Am. Were it still there, fans, players, and a national TV audience would annually witness one of the most beautiful courses in the world, and certainly one of the best. Although it's never hosted a major, Cypress Point also has a fantastic history, one rich with wonderful and comical tales of disaster.

Like Pebble Beach, Cypress Point warms up slowly. Its front nine qualifies as very good but not great, with the 8th and 9th holes a little quirky for my taste. But, like most great courses, this Alister Mackenzie masterpiece builds as it goes along. The back nine gets better, more challenging, and prettier as you go along, until you arrive at three of the very best finishing holes in golf. The 16th hole is simply the greatest par 3 in the world. It requires a 220-yard carry over the ocean to a green surrounded by bunkers, ice plants, and the ocean itself. If the wind is blowing, the smart play is to choose a 5-iron and bail out toward a patch of fairway on the left, where you can chip up to try to make par. The 17th is one of those beguiling holes you puzzle over every time you play it. Do you bump a safe shot into the fairway to avoid the big cypress trees that lie farther ahead, and bring the ocean into play on your second shot? Or do you bust the drive and afford yourself a shorter approach, and risk a bout with the trees? I never can figure it out—that's the mark of a great hole.

The 18th hole is indicative of what Cypress is all about. A challenging little par 4, in calm weather I usually hit a 2-iron off the tee followed by an 8-iron approach. During the 1974 Bing Crosby, the wind came up and I hit a driver off the tee, followed by a full 3-wood, followed by a full 5-iron. Imagine that! The weather dictates how hard Cypress plays, and it can be a kitten or a dragon.

I played perhaps the greatest round of my career there during that 1974 Crosby. Unfortunately, it didn't count. In that horrific wind, rain, and cold, I turned in a 72. The next best score was 80—no kidding. Maybe someone would have scored better, but we never had a chance to find out because the round was cancelled. I won the tournament anyway, but it was that 72 in a round that was washed out that I remember the most.

A lot of disaster stories have come out of Cypress Point. One year, Raymond Floyd was leading the Crosby when he came to the dreaded par-3 16th. Raymond decided to go for the green, but his drive found the ocean. He teed up again, and hit it in the ocean again. On his third try he found the ocean yet again. Steaming, he refused to give up. On his fourth try he found the green—and made the putt for a "birdie" that went down on the scorecard as an 8. Raymond didn't win that year.

It's been said that Cypress Point could no longer be a part

of the AT&T because, at just under 6,600 yards, the course is too short. With the typical PGA Tour layout stretching to 7,000 yards or more, there's an assumption that the pros would tear Cypress apart. I disagree. It's a beautiful, bewitching course, one that requires pinpoint precision, especially when the weather takes a turn for the worse—which it often does during the AT&T in February. Here's hoping a new generation of pros someday get to face that 16th hole with something on the line. They'll likely add Cypress Point to their list of favorite courses, too.

8. *Oakmont Country Club (Oakmont, Pennsylvania).*

The fact my greatest golf achievement took place at Oakmont adds a certain bias to my consideration. Take away my victory at the 1973 U.S. Open, however, and Oakmont still would rate high on my list and is in everybody's top ten. Aside from its distinctive design and great history, it's the most difficult test of golf in America.

Oakmont's strength is its legendary greens. They are the largest, firmest, fastest putting surfaces on Earth. I believe they're even tougher than Augusta National's. There are places on them where it's all but impossible to two-putt from, and where even three-putting is a challenge. I remember when Larry Nelson won the U.S. Open there in 1983. On one hole Nelson just touched a downhill putt, and then followed the ball down to the hole as though he were walking a dog. It took forever for the ball to reach the hole. The putt fell and Nelson went on to win.

Whereas superintendents pull their hair out trying to keep their greens healthy and growing, the supers at Oakmont pretty much let nature take its course. I don't believe the greens at Oakmont have ever been rebuilt. The subsoil is tremendous—rich red clay that repels rain almost like plastic. When they change the cups at Oakmont, very often some of that red clay comes up when the holes are cut. They drain very nicely. And boy, are those greens fast! Prior to some competitions, they bring out heavy rollers and run them across the greens, making them even firmer and faster than normal. It's intimidating just watching them prepare the course. Even though it rained early in the week of the 1973 Open, they still were scary fast.

The course is a killer from the get-go. The first hole is the most difficult opening hole I've ever played. The green is down over a hill and the terrain falls away to the left. The most famous feature is the "church pew" bunkers that straddle the third and fourth fairways. It's essentially one huge bunker laced with successive rows of grass. If you stray into the church pews, you can either hit back to the fairway or else go for the green—saying a quick prayer before you swing. The bunkers notwithstanding, Oakmont is a long, punishing course with very good balance and variety of holes. It's always at its toughest for the U.S. Open, not only because of the way the USGA prepares it, but because of the influence of its membership. They demand that the course play even more difficult for the pros than it does for them, and that means tough.

Like St. Andrews and Pebble Beach, Oakmont has produced a long list of great champions. Tommy Armour, Ben Hogan, Jack Nicklaus, Larry Nelson, and Ernie Els won U.S. Open titles there, and its PGA Championship winners include Gene Sarazen and Sam Snead. I'm extremely proud to see my name among theirs. I also admire Oakmont for having hosted so many national championships. It's hosted seven U.S. Opens, five U.S. Amateurs, three PGAs, and a U.S. Women's Open.

7. *Pine Valley Golf Club (Pine Valley, New Jersey).*

Pine Valley is similar to Augusta National and Pinehurst in that it just screams golf. The clubhouse and pro shop are well-appointed yet modest. The gravel parking lot is tiny. The scorecards are small and simple; pencils come with no erasers. More golfers walk than ride and the caddies are superb. Forget a swimming pool and tennis courts; the membership would sooner blow up the property than befoul it with any nongolf accoutrement.

People don't raise their voices at Pine Valley. It's like being in a big cathedral. There's a feeling of privilege there. Not the privilege of money and power, but the privilege of being able to experience golf in its purest state. Playing golf there is like padding around on an Indian burial ground. You don't want to upset the spirit that presides over the place. People tend to look at each other with their eyes slightly wide open, as if thinking, "Is this awesome or what?" Everyone is a kindred spirit there. It's wonderful.

It doesn't surprise me that Pine Valley is perennially ranked the number one golf course in America by *Golf Digest*. It was knocked out for one voting period a couple of years ago and replaced by Pebble Beach, but regained its top spot the next time around. I can see why. The setting amid the sand and pines of southern New Jersey is specially suited for golf. There are no weak holes. Every single one is a masterpiece. There is a surprise around every corner, eighteen unique and beautiful challenges. Each of the holes is self-contained; you can't see anything except the hole you are playing. There's a sense of seclusion there even on a busy day.

There are design signatures there you don't see very often. The fairways are very generous, but heaven help you if your driver is acting up. A really crooked drive usually means a lost ball. On some holes there are unkempt waste areas running between or alongside parcels of fairway that can fluff up your scorecard should you venture into one. "Hell's Half Acre," the waste area running across the par-5 7th hole, is especially nasty. Pine Valley also has one of the great par 5s in golf in its 15th hole. It's uphill all the way and gets narrower as you go along. The drive is difficult, the second shot is harder than the drive, and the third shot is more demanding than the second shot.

Pine Valley probably has the best collection of par 3s on the planet. The unforgiving 3rd hole is completely surrounded by sand. The 5th hole is 220 yards or so, with a falloff into pines on the right and bunker-strewn hillside to the left. The par-3 10th hole is unique; it's little more than a 9-iron shot but if you hit it thin or fat, you can wind up in the Devil's Asshole, the nastiest sand trap this side of St. Andrews' Road Bunker. (The only time I use a profanity, incidentally, is when I refer to that bunker—and if you ever play it, you'll know why.) Then there's the downhill 14th, which plays over water to yet another well-guarded green. For length and variety, there's no better set of par 3s anywhere.

It says something that Pine Valley's reputation has been formed despite not having a lustrous tournament history. It's never hosted a major championship or PGA Tour event, though on occasion it gladly welcomes a Walker Cup. It doesn't want a big event, doesn't need one, and couldn't handle the galleries anyway. It doesn't matter. Without ambition or pretense, Pine Valley is as good as it gets.

6. *Winged Foot Golf Club (Mamaroneck, New York).*

If you asked me how I would design an easy golf course, my orders would be simple. First of all, no surprises. Put the greens and fairways right in front of you, with no blind shots.

Make the landing areas flat so you don't have severe sidehill, uphill, and downhill lies. There will be no water except a tiny stream or two for beauty's sake. Next, there will be no elevated greens. Every green should have an opening up front so there are no forced carries over bunkers. Finally, I want large greens. Got it?

Winged Foot fills that description exactly. Except that it is one of the most difficult courses I've ever played, with only Oakmont ranking tougher. The A.W. Tillinghast–designed layout just north of New York City is a beast. Through the use of subtle design features that are markedly his, Tillinghast's West Course at Winged Foot is one of the most demanding courses you can imagine. Every aspiring course designer should walk Winged Foot and take notes. Its features belong in Course Design 101.

Winged Foot is a second-shot golf course. The emphasis is on hitting the greens, and it isn't easy. The green complexes are consistently maddening. Most of them don't appear to be elevated when you look at them from the fairway, but they are perched higher than the terrain immediately surrounding them. Most of them are flanked by deep bunkers. The greens run slightly away from the bunkers, so if you miss the green on the side where the flagstick is located, it's very hard to get the ball close to the hole.

That's just for starters. The greens also tend to be narrow in the front and wide in the back. They slope fairly severely from back to front, so if you end up above the hole, two-putting is one tough job. Winged Foot's greens aren't filled with crazy undulations, but they are lightning quick. They are extremely difficult to chip to if you're barely off the green. Then there's the fact they are surrounded by tall, thick trees. That gives them the appearance of being closer to you than they are. Even with a yardage book, you tend to underclub a lot.

Winged Foot can humble you. Coming into the 1974 U.S. Open there, my game was flying high. I'd won five times that season and came to Winged Foot as the defending U.S. Open champ. I couldn't have been more confident. Then Winged Foot proceeded to chew me up and spit me out, along with everybody else in the field. The winning score that year was Hale Irwin's 287, which was *7 over par*. There hasn't been a higher winning score in an Open since, and I don't believe there ever will be. It was partly because of the conditioning. The rough was simply impossible; rumor had it that the course superintendent had defied a USGA order to lower the rough. And the greens were like polished bricks. Downhill putts were murder—on the first hole, gently struck putts gained speed and ran completely off the green. It was murder. In the second round, I remember catching a bunker with my tee shot on the 7th hole, a par 3, and going back and forth, from bunker to bunker, before making a 7.

Winged Foot has a tremendous history. Bobby Jones won the 1929 U.S. Open there, making a great sidehill putt on the 18th hole to get into a playoff with Al Espinosa. Members today know the exact location of the hole that day, and when it happens to be in that spot, they always challenge their guests to try to make that putt. Few of them do. I have no hard feelings for Winged Foot, just grudging respect. You have to know what you're doing. Billy Casper won the U.S. Open there in 1959 because he was a great technician and course manager. On the par-3 3rd hole, which plays at about 190 yards, Billy refused to go for the green from the tee. All four days, he deliberately laid up. He chipped up and made his par every time. Imagine, laying up on a par 3!

The U.S. Open is coming back to Winged Foot in 2006, and I can't wait to call the action. If the USGA sets up the course properly, you can bet that Winged Foot will more than hold its own.

5. *The Old Course at St. Andrews (Scotland).*

I've never met a knowledgeable golfer who loved St. Andrews the first time he played it. He may be smitten by its atmosphere, awed by its history, or charmed by its quirks, but in terms of classic course design, even the most sincere lover of the game comes away trying to grasp what was so wonderful about the Old Course.

On the other hand, I've never met a golfer who didn't absolutely love St. Andrews after they got to know the course and played it in various wind and weather conditions. The fact is, the Old Course is a masterpiece, a one-of-a-kind marvel that will never be surpassed. You look at the roster of great British Open champions who won there—Bobby Jones, Sam Snead, Jack Nicklaus, Seve Ballesteros, and Tiger Woods—and you can't help but hold it in awe. Aside from being a great test of golf, St. Andrews is unique. No course in the world is remotely similar to it. Like a Michelangelo painting, St. Andrews is timeless. But when you play the Old Course, you're not just admiring a historical masterpiece. You become part of it.

You can't judge St. Andrews by a normal set of criteria. It's rarely in good condition, at least by American standards. You have no idea where to aim your drive or, having hit it exactly where your caddie pointed, where to aim your second shot. "Good" shots don't always turn out that way; they might carom wildly into a terrible place, or else catch a downslope and skitter well past the hole or even off the green. It seems, at first glance, that the course was laid out willy-nilly, as though the person who created the course didn't even play golf.

The course has seven double greens. There is one bunker, aptly named Hell Bunker, with a face that is taller than your head. Hit your ball there and you have to play out sideways. There is the Valley of Sin, a deep hollow in front of the 18th green which you can play over, through, or around, but which is awful to have to play *from*. There's the Road Hole, where a road runs directly alongside the green—from which you must play if your ball comes to rest on it.

When you play St. Andrews, it's like traveling to golf's equivalent of Alice in Wonderland. Only you find that the world beyond the Looking Glass is real. You must either rise and confront its surreal qualities, or else get your head chopped off by the Queen of Hearts. You can't scoff at its craziness. You have to deal with it. And the strange thing is, the more you see of it, the more sense it makes.

I played St. Andrews for the first time in 1965, when I was a student at Brigham Young. We traveled there to play against St. Andrews University, Cambridge, and a few other amateur teams. At the time I thought the course was all right, but I certainly didn't think it was anything special. Bobby Jones had the same impression the first time he played it, and when Snead saw it from a railway car, he thought the course had been abandoned.

It was when I came back for the 1978 British Open that I gained a fuller appreciation of the Old Course. Like Jones, I would fall in love with it. I had always been a precise player who relied on yardages, and for that British Open I had them down pat. But I almost threw my yardage book away. During the championship the wind switched directions and instead of blowing steadily came in big gusts. Holes I was hitting 6-irons on before now required a 2-iron. Bunkers I hadn't even noticed the day before suddenly were in play. I was in awe. That year Nicklaus won his third British Open.

The 17th hole, the famous Road Hole, is the best hole in the world, hands down. The drive there is blind and plays to a diagonal fairway. The second shot is the hardest in golf. You play a long or middle iron to a green that also runs diagonally, and which is guarded by the infamous Road Bunker, the most dangerous hazard in the game. In the old days, the bunker was in play even if you were on the green. If you putted too firmly, your ball would catch a slope and roll into the bunker, which really is a deep pit. Woe to the player who goes in there. Tommy Nakajima took five swings to get out in 1978. It took David Duval four in 2000. J. H. Taylor, who won five British Opens around the turn of the twentieth century, once took thirteen strokes to escape. It's murder—or at least *was* murder, until the bunker was softened somewhat in 2002. We'll see how it plays in 2005, when the Open Championship returns to the Old Course.

4. *Augusta National Golf Club (Augusta, Georgia).*

Some people feel Augusta National is overrated. They say the greens are tricked up, that the fairways are too wide and—with all the flowers and superdetailed grooming—too artificial. To a degree they're right, but it's still the greatest tournament course in the world and the one that John Q. Public would most want to play if given the chance. Augusta drives me crazy, but I sure do love it. It's a slice of heaven on earth.

Augusta's design is pure genius, though you might say it was genius by accident. Dr. Alister Mackenzie and Bobby Jones originally designed the course with the present nines reversed, so the terrific back nine that invites such drama today was actually the front nine until 1935. Even then, the course was distinctive. There was no rough. The greens were large but undulating. There was a lot of risk–reward, with reachable par 5s guarded by water. Birdies were to be "dearly bought" as Jones put it, though the lack of rough made it fairly easy for Jones's and Cliff Roberts's hacker buddies.

What makes the course great is the sequencing of the holes, especially on the back nine. The 10th is a challenging par 4, the 11th is a bear of a par 4, and the par-3 12th can be a nightmare, especially on Masters Sunday when the flagstick is planted on the right side of the green. The par-5 13th always forces the action because it's reachable in two shots. You get a little breather on the 14th hole, then you have the 15th, a short par 5 where the possibility of an eagle can shake up the leader board. The par-3 16th is extremely dangerous, especially when someone comes there needing a birdie. The 17th isn't particularly special, but if you hit the left side of the green when the hole is cut on the right, two-putting is a supreme test of nerves. Then there's the 18th hole, which I've never thought was inherently great but which does feature one of the most dramatic and intimate settings in the game. It's a course that forces the player to gamble and gives him the opportunity to do it successfully.

The course has evolved a great deal since I played my first Masters in 1967. Back then, the greens had Bermuda grass and were much slower and grainier than they are today. The bunkers didn't quite have those jigsaw puzzle edges. The ponds had grass growing around the edges. It was sensational for the time, though the grooming wasn't extraordinary by today's standards.

From a difficulty standpoint, the course gradually lost its fangs. Always a long hitter's paradise, it began favoring guys like Tiger Woods and Greg Norman, who needed only middle irons to reach the 13th green and short irons to get home on the 15th. You only needed a short iron for your approach on number seventeen, and the fairway bunker on the 18th hole became obsolete because the big hitters just blew their drives over it. When Tiger won with a record score of 18 under par in 1997, it was clear something had to be done.

Today the course is much longer and moderate rough flanks the fairways. The fairways are faster, firmer, and more difficult to hit from, almost like hitting off hardpan. Those factors have made it a harder test from tee to green, but the sloping nature of those lightning-fast greens place too much emphasis on putting. They're ridiculously fast for the amount of undulation and slope, and an iron shot that misses the mark by as little as five feet can give you an impossible two-putt. But what could they do? The greens are the last line of defense, and if they weren't as severe as they are, players would tear the place apart.

I've always wished NBC could televise the Masters. I'd love to call the shots there. I know every nook and cranny of the course, and definitely can relate to what goes on in a player's mind when he's in contention there on Sunday. CBS has a death grip on the TV contract, but you never know what will happen. I'm finished there as a player, but lately I've had a hunch I'll get to drive up Magnolia Lane one more time before I hang up my microphone.

3. *The Olympic Club (San Francisco, California).*

I'm very partial to Olympic because the club was so kind to me when I was growing up. I started playing there when I was twelve as a guest of some members. When I turned fourteen, the club made me its first junior member whose father was not a member, which was quite an honor. The cost: seven dollars per month. Until I turned sixteen and was old enough to drive, I'd take a streetcar and bus after school to the bottom of the hill below the club. I'd hitchhike the rest of the way. It was a special time. I'll always be grateful to the members of Olympic for all they did for me.

It was a wonderful place to build a game. When I played away from Olympic, every other course seemed easy. Lee Trevino has talked about growing up putting on bad greens, and how when he played on smooth greens for the first time it was almost like cheating. Olympic's greens are fine, but the hole designs are so challenging that everyday courses are a breeze by comparison.

On the surface, Olympic would seem to be a pushover for the world-class player. At just under 6,800 yards from the tips, it isn't long by any standard. There's no out-of-bounds, no water hazards, and not many bunkers—in fact, there's only one fairway bunker, on the 6th hole. It's far enough inland, and shrouded by enough trees, to diminish the effect of the wind. Yet Olympic can be a beast. That's why it hosted the U.S. Open in 1955, '66, '87, and '98. Like all truly great courses, its difficulties are subtle. It beats you by testing your patience, persistence, courage, concentration, course management, and creativity. You finish a round at Olympic feeling like you've just donated three pints of blood.

Olympic has a lot of what I call *reverse doglegs*. The par-4 9th hole is typical. The hole bends gently to the right, but the fairway is sloped to the left. If you put your drive into the fairway, you find that the ball is above your feet. That's called a *hook lie*, because when you address the ball the clubface is angled to your left, plus you're encouraged to make a flatter, hook swing. The prevailing wind calls for a draw, too. The trouble is, the shot into the green calls for a fade. It's very difficult to hit a fade from a hook lie. That happens over and over again at Olympic. It's awkward. It's very difficult to find your rhythm.

The seaside air is usually thick, cool, and very damp, even in summer. Shots that would fly 170 yards everywhere else only go 160 yards at Olympic. When you combine that with small greens, it's very difficult to be pinpoint accurate—and there's a lot of pressure to hit those greens, especially in a U.S. Open, because the greenside rough can be brutal. It follows that to have a decent shot into the greens, you must be in the fairway. The moist rough along the fairways is nasty. On the last hole of the 1955 U.S. Open playoff, Ben Hogan missed the fairway to the left. It took him three swings to get the ball back to the fairway.

There also are a lot of trees to contend with. Many are pine trees with long boughs that make the fairways play narrower than they are. Balls have a way of getting stuck in those trees. I reckon some of those trees hold one hundred golf balls. When Lee Janzen won the '98 Open at Olympic, one of his tee shots lodged in one of those big trees. Janzen had given up on the ball dropping from the tree and had started walking back to the tee when the ball inexplicably fell to the ground. He escaped the two-stroke penalty and ended up beating Payne Stewart by one shot.

When things start going bad at Olympic, the course can strangle you. Arnold Palmer found that out in 1966. With nine holes to play, it looked like he was going to set a new U.S. Open scoring record. But Arnold started hitting big hooks, and shot 39 on the back nine to fall into a tie with Billy Casper. Billy won the eighteen-hole playoff the next day.

Olympic is beautiful, bewitching, and full of great history. It's where Jack Fleck beat Hogan and Palmer lost to Casper. Baseball great Ty Cobb was a member there. Its rich past has a way of sweetening the experience of playing there.

2. *Pebble Beach Golf Links (Pebble Beach, California).*

Ranking Pebble Beach behind Shinnecock isn't easy. It's like voting against your sister in a beauty contest. I have a deep personal connection with Pebble Beach and the entire Monterey Peninsula—it's almost spiritual, like I've lived there in a previous life. I feel tranquil there, utterly at peace. I built a home there a few years ago. When life gets a little hairy, I escape there with my family. Pebble beckons to them, too.

Even in the throes of my deepest slump, I was transformed when I went to Pebble Beach. I seemed to play well there in spite of myself. I won at Pebble Beach in 1987 for my first victory in four years. I wouldn't win on the PGA Tour again until 1994, when by a minor miracle I won the AT&T Pro-Am—at Pebble.

Pebble Beach is the ultimate courses-for-horses layout. Mark O'Meara won there five times, in addition to a California State Amateur. Tom Watson won the U.S. Open at Pebble in 1982 and a pair of AT&Ts there. It's partly because the course suits their games, but both guys have spoken about feeling energized when they step onto the property. O'Meara, Watson, and I all have a strong California connection. O'Meara and I grew up not too far from Pebble. Watson went to college at Stanford, just north of there. Pebble is loyal to its family.

It sure was loyal to me. My win in 1994 was pure magic. I played wonderfully, hitting lots of inspired shots I didn't play very often but which the course called for at the time. The best example was my tee shot on the 17th hole on Sunday. I had no iron in my bag stronger than a 4-iron, but that day I really needed a 3-iron. I had a 7-wood but that was definitely not the club to hit. So I hooded the 4-iron, closing the face to program a low, hard hook. Pretending I was Chi Chi Rodriguez, I put a big in-to-out swing on the ball, rotating my hands aggressively through impact. The ball bored through the wind and stopped on the right side of the green. It was all I could have asked for. I two-putted for a clutch par.

It was a strange tournament in other ways. The final round featured the most awful display of putting ever seen on live television. I mean, *everybody* putted terribly. Tom Watson, his yips at their most pathetic, three-putted the last three holes. Watson's amateur partner, Sandy Tatum, watched glumly as Tom faltered—and then three-putted a lot like Tom did, or else just picked up his ball, his score for the hole too high to matter. Tom Kite, using his trusty cross-handed putting grip, couldn't hole anything either. Dudley Hart, who was contending, actually *four-putted* the 18th hole from eight feet. My stroke wasn't much better; someone said watching me swing the putter back and through that day was like watching someone trying to start a lawn mower. But somehow, I shook in short putt after short putt, and won.

How surreal was it that day? On the par-3 17th, Bryant Gumbel, my amateur partner, hit a seagull with his tee shot.

From a design standpoint, the whole of Pebble Beach is greater than the sum of its parts. It's the confluence of the ocean, the sunsets, the seals, the celebrities, and naturally, the golf course, that combine to make it unique. Some of the holes are fairly ordinary, especially as you set off on the front nine. But it gathers momentum in a hurry. The 7th is a perplexing little par 3 of 110 yards that can require a flip sand wedge when the wind is at your back, or a 5-iron if it's howling in your face. It builds gradually but steadily to a great finish. The 8th hole is a tremendous par 4 that requires a long approach over the Pacific Ocean. The 16th is a wonderful par 4 to a tricky, sloping green. The long par-3 17th is a beast, especially when the hole is cut on the tiny shelf on the left side of the green. The wind howls there, making the tee shot and then the putting, very dicey. Then there's the 18th, the most beautiful hole in golf, with the treachery of the ocean along the entire left side.

Conditions-wise, you never know what you're going to get. During the Bing Crosby National Pro-Am in 1962, it actually snowed, delaying the final round. In recent years there's been horrific amounts of rain, so much that people lobbied for the dates of the tournament to be moved a few weeks ahead, closer to spring. I like it right where it is, in February. The wind, cold, and rain are part of the charm. I don't drink, but I enjoy watching people reach for their hip flasks for a nip of something to keep them warm. You don't see as many hip flasks anywhere else in America. When I think of Pebble, I often envision comedian Phil Harris sitting on a bench, his vocal cords very well oiled, singing "The Bare Necessities" with Glen Campbell in 1994. Phil was a mainstay at the Crosby for decades, and that was his last appearance.

The course also varies tremendously depending on the time of year. During the AT&T in February, it isn't particularly backbreaking. A lot of guys can shoot in the 60s without much trouble. But when June arrives and the course is prepped for hosting the U.S. Open, it becomes the hardest course in the world. The 1992 U.S. Open featured the course at its most vicious. On Thursday, Friday, and Saturday the course was fairly benign. Gil Morgan got to 12 under par through 43 holes, making putts from everywhere. When the final round began Sunday morning, it didn't seem to be much harder. Then the wind came up. The greens, already firm and fast, became like concrete. Players couldn't reach some of the par 4s in two. Everybody crashed and burned that day except for Tom Kite, who played one of the best rounds I've ever seen in shooting an even-par 72. He won by two.

If there were a cemetery nearby, I wouldn't mind being buried there. It would make for a shorter trip back if there's another life after this one.

1. *Shinnecock Hills Golf Club (Southampton, New York).*

For a long time I thought no course could ever surpass Pebble Beach. Then came the 1986 U.S. Open at Shinnecock Hills on the eastern end of Long Island. After that week, Shinnecock nudged out Pebble and became my favorite course in the world, and I fell in love with it, even though I didn't play very well there.

Shinnecock embodies everything I love in a golf course. From the simple but elegant old clubhouse designed by Stanford White to the rugged terrain that hasn't changed since God created it, the setting is spectacular in every way. The place is devoid of the extraneous, manmade features so common in course design today. There are very few trees, and you can bet the ones you see weren't planted. There are no flower beds, rock walls, waterfalls, or windmills—I'm surprised it even has a sprinkler system. The native fescue rough on the sides of the fairways turns the color of oatmeal and is a raw counterpoint to the winding, knobby firm green fairways.

It's that gnarly, browned-out look that I love the most. Golfers today demand a course that is wall-to-wall green. They want—or at least *think* they want—everything to be perfectly lush. Greenkeeping in American golf has become a grass-growing contest. To me, it's a misguided, shallow interpretation of what's beautiful. Like the Miss America pageant, the emphasis is on cosmetics more than inner substance. Well,

Shinnecock has never been liposuctioned and never will be. It's all about substance over style.

And what substance! Shinnecock could host the U.S. Open on a week's notice. All you'd have to do is shave the greens a bit, and the course is good to go. It's vicious but fair. It's has tremendous variety, with holes bending left and right to greens that are elevated and below you. It has a natural flow to it, the holes sequenced perfectly. There's no jarring surprises at Shinnecock, just one great hole after another that says "come and get me" and dares you to do it. It's exhilarating.

The finishing stretch is much better than even Augusta National's. The 14th hole, a par 4 that sweeps down from the tee and then up to the right to an elusive green, may be the best hole in America. I know Ben Crenshaw thinks it is. And the finishing holes are the best in golf. The 16th hole, a well-bunkered par 5 that narrows as you near the green is an exasperating hole that will kiss or kill you. The 17th is a long par 3 with the prevailing wind blowing from the left, but with the green's opening set to the right. The 18th is five miles of lonesome road, an uphill par 4 where pars are dearly bought.

Shinnecock is golf's Holy Grail, a place where you can feel spirits in the air. I could play it every day the rest of my life and never tire of it.

CHAPTER 8

Is the PGA Tour a Closed Shop?

Why Talent Is Not Being Served

JAY DON BLAKE is a PGA Tour journeyman best known for winning the Shearson Lehman Brothers Open in 1991. A card-carrying member of the tour since 1987, Blake's victory at San Diego remains his only tour triumph, though over the years he's had a number of top finishes. If you've followed the PGA Tour, you've probably heard of Jay Don.

The problem is, we haven't heard from Jay Don lately. In a five-year period dating back to 1999, his highest finish on the PGA Tour money list was eighty-second. He dropped as low as 128th in 2002, which by itself wasn't good enough to guarantee a tour card the following year. To avoid a trip back to the PGA Tour Qualifying Tournament, a player must finish among the top 125 on the money list annually. The following twenty-five players can still play, however, if they are needed to fill the field. That's how Jay Don gained access to the 2003 season, which was not a good one for him. He wound up finishing 178th on the money list. He eventually lost his playing privileges.

Jay Don is a friend of mine and I don't mean to embarrass him by calling attention to his mediocre play. Yet his ability to hang on by a thread is symptomatic of a big problem on the PGA Tour. Rather than give eager and talented young players an opportunity to prove themselves, the tour tends to reward guys who hang on by the skin of their teeth, year after year. It seems fellows like Jay Don Blake play just well enough to get by and make a living, as opposed to aiming for the stars and trying to realize their full potential. The bottom line is, the PGA Tour is too difficult to get onto, and too easy to remain in once you get there.

To further bolster my argument, let's take a closer look at two of Jay Don's recent seasons. In 2000, his playing privileges for the following year were pretty much assured by the end of July. From August through the end of the year, he played in only nine tournaments. Conversely, in 2002, with his card for the following year very much in jeopardy, he played in *thirteen* tournaments. What that suggests to me is that Jay Don played only the number of events necessary to get him to next year. A younger player in Jay Don's shoes is more likely to take a different tack. Hungry for experience and eager to take a bite out of those big purses, a twenty-three-year-old player would have played as much as possible.

I don't blame Jay Don for exercising his playing privileges any way he sees fit. He knows the system and makes it work to his advantage. At age forty-five, he may not want to bust his hump any more than he has to. But I believe the system is cracked. Honoring 125 tour players by giving all of them exemptions for the following year is excessive. The number should be closer to 100.

The PGA Tour and its players like to point out that they are the best example of capitalism in all of sports. The players don't get paid unless they perform. There are no guaranteed salaries and there's no such thing as a no-cut contract. If a player gets injured he isn't compensated, although if he's put out of action the tour does have the right to dispense a special medical exemption. Supposedly, this sink-or-swim structure forces players to improve constantly and perform at an extremely high level if they are to stay on tour. In theory, this should make the PGA Tour players constantly get better and more competitive. Players shouldn't be able to afford to simply show up and play. If they get lazy, there are hundreds of talented players from the Nationwide Tour, assorted mini tours, and Q-schools waiting to take their place.

But it really doesn't work that way. In addition to the 125 exempt players from the year-end money list, there are more than thirty other exempt classifications by which a player can get into a field for a given tournament. For example, if a player wins a tournament, he gets a two-year exemption. If you win The Players Championship, you get a five-year exemption. There are so many ways to keep your tour card that you have to play very poorly to lose it. The result is that there is not enough turnover, preventing an infusion of new faces every year.

Trying to get on the PGA Tour is excruciatingly difficult. The primary route is the tour's annual Qualifying Tournament, better known as "Q-School." The player puts up a few thousand dollars, then attempts to survive two stages of local and regional qualifying. If they succeed, they then advance to the final tournament, a 108-hole marathon featuring a field of roughly 170 players. How many players get their cards? A paltry thirty-five. That's out of thousands who entered to begin with. You have a better chance of being one of those thirty-five than winning the lottery, but not much. Another forty-five players or so receive an exemption to play the Nationwide Tour, the PGA Tour's developmental league. Beyond that, if you don't make it, it's just too bad. You come back and try again next year.

David Duval, Curtis Strange, Tom Lehman, and John Daly are just a few of the players who didn't survive the Q-School and had to sweat it out in the minor leagues even though they obviously were good enough for the PGA Tour from the get-go. They just had that one week where they weren't sharp, and it basically ruined their whole year. Meanwhile, Jay Don Blake, who in 2002 missed fifteen cuts and had only two top-twenty-five finishes, was entitled to keep his card by way of his finishing number 128 on the money list.

The Champions Tour is even less democratic. At the 2002 Senior Q-School, only the top eight finishers earned tour cards. They apparently thought this was too many; that number was trimmed to seven at the 2003 Q-School. Worse, only two players are allowed to play their way into a field through "Monday qualifying," a one-day event in which anybody who thinks they're good enough to play a tournament can pay an entry fee, tee it up, and get into the field if they shoot one of the low two scores. Prior to 2004, that number was four. The unfortunate thing is that it makes the rags-to-riches story of a Walt Zembriski, a former steelworker who got onto the Champions Tour and became a star, less plausible. You also are less likely to see a guy like Robert Landers, the colorful yet unknown cattle farmer from Texas who played in tennis shoes and spiced up the tour with his surprising appearance in 1995.

The way the tour is structured today is radically different than when I was a kid trying to get on tour. In 1969, only the top sixty money winners on the PGA Tour kept their cards for the following year. With a limited number of guaranteed spots each week, the field was filled through a number of other avenues. Most notably, a number of spots each week went to the *rabbits*—guys who tried to get in through a one-day Monday qualifier. It was tough. If you played badly on that Monday, you just got a ride to the next town and found a place to practice until the next week, when you took another crack at the Monday qualifier. Those who did make it into the starting field would try like crazy to make the cut so they wouldn't have to qualify the next week. If a guy was close to the cut line, he'd rarely play aggressively because he didn't want to blow his chance of getting into the field the following week. The whole thing was pretty stressful.

The result was the formation of the all-exempt tour, which began in 1983. It was Gary McCord and Joe Porter who thought of it. Both of them were grinders who thought the system was too brutal. The tour brass and the players liked the idea, so the next thing we knew, the top 125 money winners didn't have to worry about qualifying anymore.

The first Q-School I entered, in 1969 at Palm Beach Gardens in Florida, I got one of the fifteen tour cards that were available in a field of ninety-one players. McCord was right about one thing—the pressure to qualify was brutal. I shudder to think what would have happened if I'd played lousy or had a sore thumb or something. For one thing, I'd driven to Florida in a Buick Riviera I'd leased from my sponsor, and the drive back to San Francisco would have been a long one. The bigger issue was, I had no place to play the following year. I had a lot of talent, and it would have been a shame for me to lose out because of one bad week. I would have had to cool my heels for a whole year.

The tour was tough to get on then, and it's even harder now, so I still think the all-exempt tour is ready for an overhaul. McCord pointed out back in 1981 or so that players would play conservatively just to make the cut. I don't think that happens any more. There is enough money available if you do make the cut, or through playing the Nationwide Tour, that a guy who is near the cut line doesn't have to play scared and lay up on every par 5. For one thing, making the cut doesn't get you into the field the following week. For another, with all the money available on the PGA Tour, it lends itself to aggressive play. It's much better to play superaggressively and win two tournaments a year—and miss some cuts—than to play scared and not win any tournaments, but make a bunch of cuts.

Another thing is that the caliber of players we see today on the Nationwide Tour and even smaller tours is much better than the second-tier players of twenty years ago. Ben Curtis, who came out of nowhere to win the 2003 British Open, had only two top twenty-five finishes before that huge week at Royal St. George's and had spent the previous two years grinding away on the Hooters Tour. Shaun Micheel, who won the 2003 PGA Championship, had finished only 105th on the money list in 2002. I think there are a lot of guys like them who are extremely capable and highly motivated. Like Ben and Shaun, they deserve a chance.

Will we see a change anytime soon? I don't think so. The problem is that the guys who are in power are the ones who benefit most by keeping the system the way it is. Of the nine people on the PGA Tour's policy board, four are players. One of them, Olin Browne, finished 130th on the money list in 2003. Another player–board member, Tom Pernice Jr., twice has had years where he finished 127th on the money list. Human nature being what it is, I would think they would prefer keeping things the way they are.

On the Champions Tour, one of the ways a player can become exempt is by being among the top thirty in all-time career money winnings. That's a bogus criteria and always has been. The way purses have escalated in recent years, some pretty good players—or at least some fan favorites—have no way of becoming exempt based on their past performance. For example, I won just over $2,740,000 in my career, with two majors and twenty-five PGA Tour victories. Mark McCumber, who is four years younger than me, won ten tournaments and no majors, but has won roughly twice that. He's exempt, I'm not. Not that I want to play the Champions Tour, but if I did, he'd get in a field ahead of me. At an age (fifty-seven) when I could be considered capable of being a contender, I'm already squeezed out. Money is subjective. It shouldn't count.

So what, precisely, is my solution to the closed-shop status of the PGA Tour? Here's my plan:

- Reduce the number of exempt players from the previous year's money list from 125 players to 100 players.
- Consider expanding Monday qualifying, offering fifteen spots in the field to those with the desire, moxie, and ability to actually *earn* their way into the field. The number at present is four; let's make it more.
- Reduce the exemption granted to a winner of a World Golf Championships event from three years to two years, like any other PGA Tour event. The WGC event in Woodstock, Georgia, has enough added meaning with its $6 million purse. It doesn't need to surpass, by definition, the Memorial or Doral.
- Maintain the exemption given to winners of The Players Championship, British Open, PGA Championship, Masters, and U.S. Open at its present five years.

These ideas are no panacea. But they would add greater equity to an organization that sees itself as being totally democratic, but which in truth is something less than that. One thing is for sure—in a revised system, Jay Don Blake will have as good a chance at making it as anyone else.

CHAPTER 9

Sorenstam and the True Principle Axiom

What We Learned from Her Colonial Experiment

SOME MEN FEARED THAT Annika Sorenstam's playing in the 2003 Bank of America Colonial in Fort Worth, Texas, would be a waking nightmare, an emasculating, no-win, social experiment from which there could be no profit. Some women quietly dreaded that a poor performance by Annika would affirm the worst assumptions about the quality of women's golf at the top professional level and tarnish the LPGA Tour at a time when it could least afford it. Both the men's and women's pro tours hoped the confusing epic would provide an outcome that would benefit their party without damaging the other. Also figuring in the drama were the TV networks, which prayed for a huge commercial success that, given the state of the economy, was much needed. Even the public had a vested interest in the outcome; the average fan anticipated a level of drama, tension, and theater that golf had so rarely delivered lately, and they wanted their expectations to be fulfilled.

What followed was one of the most compelling sagas in golf history. Sorenstam's rounds of 71–74 didn't make the cut and she beat only eleven golfers out of a field of 114, but that didn't seem to matter. The presentation of woman versus man and Sorenstam versus herself added dimensions that transcended golf. It was like John Henry taking on the steam drill and winning. In the end, everyone came away happy, or at least satisfied. Both sides were able to claim a kind of victory. The people who said Sorenstam had no chance of making the cut turned out to be right, while those who wanted her to succeed found enough evidence in her opening 71 to say she could play with anyone.

From the outset, I was all for Annika teeing it up. There were and are negatives should this sort of thing happen on a regular basis, and I'll get to them in a moment. But this one-case episode was unique and turned out to be a home run for the game of golf in virtually every way. The arguments set forth against her right to play came across as insecure whining and outright paranoia. At first a few people argued she was taking a spot that should be occupied by a man who is trying to make a living. The philosophy behind this argument is the same one I looked at in the last chapter: Professional golf is one of the last bastions of pure capitalism and social Darwinism left in America, where its players earn their way and are not guaranteed a paycheck. They earn a living based purely on how they perform. Players who can't cut the mustard are weeded out each weekend. So the notion of Sorenstam playing, the argument goes, runs counter to the basic nature of the tour.

Annika, however didn't take anybody's spot. At the Colonial, as elsewhere, the commercial entity putting up cash for the event is permitted to select a few wild-card entrants into the field. Sometimes the sponsor chooses a nonexempt player who is a local hero. Sometimes it's someone who has demonstrated loyalty to the sponsor. It can be a famous player who can't play very well anymore, but who is guaranteed to bring in some extra fans. In the case at Colonial, the sponsors's exemption went, for the first time in fifty-eight years, to a woman—the best woman player of her time, who happened to be in the prime of her career. The choice was sound, and the possibilities tantalizing.

A complaint was also lodged that inviting her to play was little more than a grandstand stunt designed to sell tickets, and that it tainted the dignified traditions of the tour. No doubt about it, it was a circus move. But so what? When it comes down to it, professional golf is about entertainment. It is not life and death. No bread was taken from anybody's table and nobody's livelihood was put at risk. In no way was the reputation of the PGA Tour diminished by Annika's competing. If her performance would heighten interest in golf in general, put the game on the front page of the national news, and inspire a few kids to take up the game, what was wrong with that? The resentment voiced by Nick Price, the defending champion who said the event "reeked of publicity," came off as sour grapes and sounded sexist. Of *course* it reeked of publicity. That was the idea! No question it deflected attention away from the men for one week (Annika probably got more air time than the rest of the players combined), but it made no lasting negative impression I could detect.

Not that Price was a Neanderthal for voicing his objection. I think any golfer who has played a part in building the PGA Tour into what it is understandably has a right to feel that the tour and its players should be the centerpiece of attention. Unfortunately, he gave the impression that hordes of people were stridently against Annika. In truth, there were fewer critics of the idea than the media suggested there were. A long line of people, fueled by the skewed perceptions arising from the Martha Burk case at Augusta National a month earlier, accused the golf establishment of being biased against Annika, when that wasn't the case at all. After you got past Price and Vijay Singh (who said he would refuse to play if he were paired with Annika), no one voiced any objection to her playing. There was some undercurrent of sexism, but you had to look darned hard to find it. Those in the media who depicted Annika as having to swim uphill against a torrent of people who opposed her should be ashamed. Certainly it was almost impossible to find anyone in the gallery of thirty thousand roaring disapproval that week. I don't think a golfer in history, including Arnold Palmer, ever received more support than Annika did at Colonial.

No doubt, some people were for the idea of her playing, if only for the opportunity to see her fail. Some looked at Colonial Country Club and its 7,080-yard, par-70 layout, and saw Annika as too audacious, almost disrespectful. Americans don't mind seeing someone knocked down a peg, particularly someone who assumes something is easy when it isn't. But if they expected Annika to get her comeuppance, they were looking at the wrong person. Annika Sorenstam is the best player in LPGA Tour history. Like Tiger Woods, who has yet to surpass Jack Nicklaus's record in the majors, Annika does have a long way to go before she beats Patty Berg's record for major championship victories (fifteen) or Kathy Whitworth's record for total wins (eighty-eight). But the golf she has played over the last ten years has been the best golf the LPGA has ever seen. Through dedication, a structured approach to improvement and sheer determination, she has built a game that is better than any woman's, past or present—and one that is better than that of a few PGA Tour players.

That's right. I believe that if Annika competed an entire season on the PGA Tour, she could possibly crack the top 125 on the money list and would become an exempt player. If she got a chance to get to know the courses, and play them in situations where she didn't carry the burden of being the only woman, she definitely could make a living out there. Her golf is just too good. At Colonial, for example, she averaged 268 yards with the driver. That isn't long, but it's long enough. She hit less than 70 percent of greens in regulation, but there are many tour players making a living who hit fewer than she did. Parts of her game would have to improve, particularly her ability to putt fast greens, her chipping, and her pitching, but I think Annika would find a way to do it.

To further illuminate the status of her game, I'd say she could win the men's U.S Amateur if she were clicking on all cylinders. She could be among the top thirty players on the Champions Tour. And she definitely could win the boys' U.S. Junior. It's all speculation, but the comparisons are irresistible.

If that sounds ambitious, keep in mind that when she came on tour, her game wasn't nearly of the caliber it is today. She was easily one of the top players in women's golf, but Karrie Webb may have been better and Se Ri Pak at her best was just as good. Annika's game revolved around consistency. She had a rainbowlike ball flight that was very accurate, but she wasn't particularly long. Her iron play was good, but she couldn't spin the ball as well as Pak, Webb, Joanne Carner, Mickey Wright, and a couple of other great women players. Her putting was only so-so. Annika won often, but in the grinding, persistent, mistake-free way that Hale Irwin and Tom Kite used to win tournaments. She wasn't particularly electric or overpowering.

But something happened to Annika. Always a perfectionist, she suddenly shifted to a higher gear. She began conditioning her body to become stronger and paid even more attention to her diet. She continued her habit of charting every shot of every round so as to identify her weaknesses. She demonstrated a devotion to improving that was the equal of Ben Hogan. Her ball flight suddenly took on a piercing quality, with twenty yards added to her drives. She had her equipment tweaked to fit her swing exactly. She worked hard on her short game and became much more dependable under pressure. Annika will always have a certain frailty about her emotionally; she cried when asked to replay a shot at a Solheim Cup, and cried when she came off the 36th green at Colonial. But emotionally she became much tougher than she was, and more focused.

The upshot is that Annika isn't as far away from competing at a PGA Tour level as people think. The distance she hits the ball will always be a drawback; she is slight physically compared to the men and at age thirty-two she can't get much stronger. She is roughly fifteen yards shorter with the tee shot than the average male tour player, and two clubs shorter with the irons. That equates to her giving up three or four clubs in distance on every hole, which would seem to be overwhelming. But she's so darned accurate with her irons and 7-wood, it almost doesn't matter. People have pointed out that in choosing Colonial, she shrewdly was selecting a course that didn't have a lot of forced carries over water and greenside bunkers, which was necessary if she were to score well. But I truthfully feel she would be even more effective on some of the more difficult PGA Tour courses, such as the TPC at Sawgrass. When accuracy is the name of the game, she would have an advantage over many of the guys.

She isn't there yet, and probably never will be because her career will begin winding down in a couple of years. The facts of her Colonial appearance can't be disputed—she finished near the bottom of the field and at the end of thirty-six holes was thirteen strokes behind the leader and eventual champion, Kenny Perry. She squeezed almost as much out of her game as she humanly could and it still wasn't remotely good enough to even contend. I'm just saying she has the potential, and that what I saw made me view her game in a more positive light.

I mentioned earlier that Annika playing the PGA Tour every week would not necessarily be a good idea. I firmly believe that. There is a school of thought, which I call the *true principle axiom*, which says that to truly test a principle, you multiply it a million times. If the principle is true and without flaw, it will remain as true at the end as it was in the beginning. But if a principle is flawed, that imperfection will become more pronounced each time it is multiplied. By the time you're finished multiplying the flawed principle a million times, you're left with all sorts of problems.

Women playing the PGA Tour doesn't pass the test, in more ways than I can imagine. It isn't hard to see some of the more troubling ramifications. For example, what would happen to the LPGA Tour if its best players were to abandon ship and play the PGA Tour? The answer is that it would turn the LPGA Tour into a minor league of women's golf, or at least give the impression that they were serving up a diluted product. Even while Annika was competing at Colonial, you had to know that fans and players at the coinciding LPGA Tour event were aware that the field that week wasn't as strong as it could have been, and that their main drawing card was missing.

Second, if women were permitted to move into the men's game, why couldn't men move over to the women's game? It's a ridiculous proposition, but it's happened before in sports. Remember Renee Richards, the transsexual tennis player who competed as both a man and a woman? There was a debate about that. And one of the big secrets in golf is that a similar thing happened in USGA competition, when a transgender woman competed in the U.S. Women's Senior Amateur. Not much was made of it (much to the USGA's relief, I'm sure), but it happened.

When I entertain the prospect of men playing the women's game, I'm not talking about young, talented studs moving over to the LPGA Tour for easy pickings. But if women could play the PGA Tour with impunity, wouldn't it be fair to allow a Champions Tour player, who couldn't quite compete with his older fellows anymore, a shot at competing with the women? To disallow it would be to admit that men, even those twenty-five years older than their women counterparts, are athletically superior to women. I don't even want to think of the howling from both sides.

Finally, if the pressure put on Annika was suffocating, imagine what the guys she was playing against were feeling. One of the footnotes to the week was that Annika beat one of her playing partners, Aaron Barber. While Annika basked in triumph, Barber, who was a class act all the way, had to endure a lot of ribbing from other pros. Talk about pressure—the guys near Sorenstam on the leader board had to be miserable. If they were looking for sympathy, I'll tell you where they found it: in the dictionary. In some ways, they had more at stake than Annika did. (Some women snorted a "so what?" at that, which wasn't very becoming.) But I felt sorry for Barber, Mark Brooks, Joel Edwards, Bob Estes, Craig Perks, and Scott

McCarron, some of the guys she beat. They had a poor week, and those who don't know golf well may have been left with the impression that Annika is at least as skilled as they are. If she had played the next week, things could have been different.

On balance, Annika's appearance in a PGA Tour event was a huge success. Her performance and comportment at Colonial were exemplary. The media had something to talk about. CBS and USA Network, the TV networks who covered it, made a mint. Women's golf gained a higher measure of respect, as the perceived margin of ability between men and women was narrowed. Even the PGA Tour benefited, as commissioner Tim Finchem welcomed Sorenstam's participation and the vast majority of players gave her encouragement and support. Kenny Perry may have taken home the trophy, but at the Colonial everybody won.

Imitators followed, of course. Suzy Whaley, a club pro in Connecticut, won her PGA Section title and played in the Greater Hartford Open. Whaley, in fact, had qualified for that tournament before Sorenstam accepted her invitation to play at Colonial. Jan Stephenson played in a Champions Tour event. Michelle Wie played in the Nationwide Tour's Boise Open and later, at the 2004 Sony Open in Hawaii, turned in an even better performance than Sorenstam, missing the cut by only one stroke. And Laura Davies signed up to play in the Korean Open. None of them aroused the sense of wonder and speculation that Annika's adventure did.

Where will Annika go from here? Personally, I wouldn't be surprised if one day soon she just walks away from golf entirely. She's an intelligent person who has sacrificed more than almost anyone to become the best she can be. She has talked about having a family, and knowing her, I can't imagine her giving parenthood anything less than her full attention when the day comes that she decides to have children. As a player, she's conquered every mountain. I imagine her doing what Jim Brown and Rocky Marciano did, retiring at the top of her game with her health intact, her fortune made, her youth preserved, and a big wide world waiting at her feet.

CHAPTER 10

Golf's Greatest Generation

A Front-Row Seat to Greatness

GIVEN A CHOICE as to where I could place my twenty-year career in the long continuum of pro golf, I'd choose the exact time frame where it began and ended. I turned pro in 1969, and played actively through 1987, although I continued competing periodically through 1994. It was a special era. I came along when Jack Nicklaus was at his peak, Lee Trevino was coming on, and Arnold Palmer, Billy Casper, and Gary Player were still winning regularly. Heck, Sam Snead was still playing. In the mid-1970s, a new wave began to arrive, led by Tom Watson, Seve Ballesteros, Greg Norman, Curtis Strange, Lanny Wadkins, Tom Kite, and Ben Crenshaw. With the 1980s came Fred Couples, Payne Stewart, Paul Azinger, Davis Love III, Hal

Sutton, and others. By the time I won my last PGA Tour event in 1994, I was getting glimpses of Phil Mickelson, David Toms, and the rest of the young guard I follow from the broadcast booth today.

The 1970s were particularly exciting. It was a revolutionary era in many ways. Metal woods came on the scene. Graphite shafts were introduced. Perimeter weighted irons became popular. Golf course design underwent a transformation, with a trend toward target golf and amphitheater settings that made attending a tournament easier and more entertaining to watch. Television exploded, with 18-hole coverage of important tournaments. Sideshows such as the National Long Drive Championship spiced up the landscape. Instruction was transformed by the use of video, sports psychology, and biomechanics. The game exploded at the grassroots level, with millions more people taking up the game. The technological innovations we see today, from titanium woods to solid-construction golf balls to lighter golf bags, all are rooted in things that happened in the 1970s.

But it was the players who elevated the game and planted the seeds for what we see today. At no other time could a player have been exposed to so much talent. The sheer number of Hall of Fame players made the PGA Tour a long-running drama that was thick with intrigue. There always were great story lines and subplots, as the careers of young and old players intersected. The competition was consistently close and fierce. Great rivalries such as Nicklaus versus Trevino flourished. Some of the greatest dramas ever—Trevino winning the 1972 British Open, the Nicklaus–Watson showdown at Turnberry in 1977, the epic 1975 Masters and my closing 63 at Oakmont in 1973—took place in the 1970s. Add in Jack's performance at the 1986 Masters and the many dramas involving Norman's and Watson's magnificent runs in the 1980s, and you're talking one prime-time era in sports.

It's human nature to show a bias for the time when you flourished, and I confess to feeling nostalgic when I look back on golf in the 1970s and 1980s. But darn it, the players were just as good if not better than the guys playing today, with the possible exception of Tiger Woods. There's no question they were better competitors. These were guys who knew how to win, and did, regularly. Trevino, Casper, Irwin, Player, Tom Weiskopf, Raymond Floyd, Watson, and Hubert Green were always tough to beat, but what made them really special was you couldn't give them any daylight. They knew how to get the job done on Sunday. If you faltered, they stepped on your neck. They played better under pressure, not worse. They were confrontational.

So who are the best players I've seen since 1969? It's a tough call, but I've come up with a twelve-man roster—a kind of Ryder Cup All-Era team if you will—that could whip any other collection of twelve players you could name.

Jack Nicklaus

Humanizing Golf's Greatest Machine

The person who has suffered most from living in the age of Tiger Woods is Jack Nicklaus. That may sound crazy, seeing how Jack is talked about in a positive way whenever he's compared with Tiger. Nevertheless, I feel for Jack. More and more, he is evaluated on the basis of his playing record rather than the traits that made him the greatest golfer of all time. He is viewed almost impersonally, as though he were a machine that coldly and systematically ground out eighteen professional majors and seventy-three PGA Tour victories. When the current generation of golfers looks at Jack, they tend to see an icon rather than flesh and blood. He is respected in a monolithic way rather than in human terms. That's life, and it's probably inevitable that appreciation of him will dim even further. It's also a crying shame, because to play alongside Jack Nicklaus was to witness athleticism at a level that transcends eras. It's trite to say, but if Jack were in his prime today, Tiger Woods would have his hands full. And the supporting cast would have one huge collective headache.

I've been a fan of Jack's since the summer of 1966, when I was a nineteen-year-old sophomore at Brigham Young University. That year I was fortunate to qualify for the U.S. Open at the Olympic Club in San Francisco, which was the thrill of a lifetime for me. Better still, a friend at the club arranged for me to play a Tuesday practice round with Jack at Olympic. I got a close look at his game that day, and again the next day when Jack invited me to play with him at San Francisco Golf Club. That wasn't all. Inspired in part by those practice rounds, I finished the first thirty-six holes in fifth place, tied with Jack. So we played together on Saturday, where I got a more intimate look at how Jack handled his game and himself as I finished tied for eighth in the championship.

I saw much more of Jack after I turned pro in 1969. I teamed with him in the 1973 World Cup, where we won the team title and I won the medal for low individual. We also won the 1983 Chrysler Team Championship together. He always brought out the best in me. We played a lot of exhibitions together, and for whatever reason I usually beat Jack. (It's been a while since we did a golf gig together, and I've joked that he's quit inviting me because I always beat him.)

Jack opened my eyes in so many ways. He's seven years older than me and from our first meeting he's never hesitated to give me insight into all aspects of the game. He has also inspired me. In 1983, I took time off to have gallbladder surgery. Two weeks after the operation, I was going almost crazy with boredom. So I decided to play in the Canadian Open, which probably was a mistake. My stitches were still in, I was in a great deal of pain and my game was rusty. Lo and behold, I was paired with Jack the first round, which was the sort of pressure I didn't need. Swinging like an old man, I played the first nine holes in 42. I complained of my woes to Jack, which didn't elicit much in the way of sympathy. He gave me a flat-eyed look and said in a matter-of-fact way, "Maybe you should just withdraw. Obviously you aren't ready to be out here." Call it tough love if you will, but it motivated me to prove Jack wrong. Chipping and putting like a fiend, I shot 17 under par the rest of the way and wound up in a sudden-death playoff, losing to John Cook on the sixth extra hole. I don't think any other player could have motivated me the way Jack did.

As a player, Jack's golf swing was something, a blend of power and precision that was just overpowering. But his greatest strengths were more ephemeral and difficult to quantify. Jack's genius lay in the peculiar way he viewed golf and competition. He had a deep understanding of how the game worked that no one could match. I remember a tournament once where Jack started off with three bogeys but finished with a 66. After the round I asked him, "Doesn't it bother you when you get off to a bad start?" He said, "Not one bit. I knew the rest of the round was going to be great because I'm only going to hit a certain number of bad shots. Today I just happened to hit them early in the round." Jack said that so long as he maintained a positive attitude, he would be fine. Jack knew there was an ebb and flow to every round, and he never let his fortunes worry or overexcite him. He had tremendous patience, fueled by confidence, wisdom, and experience.

I never saw Jack hit a shot carelessly. When I first came on tour, I watched his eyes closely. The look in a person's eyes will tell you what they are about, and Jack's eyes never changed. There were moments when Jack seemed more inspired than usual, but it was expressed more in his physical bearing than through the filter of his eyes. Jack's brow had a deep, permanent furrow you could hide the face of your wedge in; it was a semiscowl of deep concentration. He seemed to sense the importance of having clear intent on every swing. Most players shift gears emotionally; you clearly see them concentrating more on some shots than others. Jack instinctively abided that old adage, "You practice like you play, and play like you practice." He never fell into the habit of letting down mentally. Thus, his routine, mannerisms and commitment under pressure was identical to his approach while practicing.

Ben Hogan was once asked by a reporter if he'd rather be one shot ahead going into the final round of a major, or one shot behind. Hogan stared at the reporter for a while and said, "That's a stupid question." I see where Hogan was coming from—strokes are strokes, why spot them to anybody? But Jack said he preferred to be one stroke behind, which, coming from him, somehow made sense. He knew the leader probably wasn't going to sleep very well, being very aware that Jack Nicklaus was hot on his heels, and that if he performed terribly he might be accused of choking. All sorts of thoughts would be going through his mind, not all of them good but each one making him expend a bit of energy. Jack knew that if he was one shot behind, the pressure was all on the guy in front of him. Jack would just chill out, play his game, and watch the leader crumble down the stretch.

Jack was not arrogant, but he definitely carried a mind-set that he was the best golfer in the world. It wasn't contrived.

Jack was a demon for preparation. He practically invented going to a tournament site a week in advance and becoming familiar with the course. He managed his playing schedule so he'd be fresh going into the tournament. He took care of himself physically and played a lot of tennis, which is good for hand–eye coördination. This empowered Jack immensely. Like the Green Bay Packers under Vince Lombardi, he felt he had paid a bigger price in preparation and thus deserved to win. His self-confidence was apparent when someone asked Jack a question. It didn't matter what the subject was—Jack answered it in an emphatic way, as though he couldn't be wrong. He was criticized for this; for a time his nickname around PGA Tour lockers rooms was "Karnac," because he came off as knowing the answer to everything. His certitude was merely a reflection of his ego, which, like every great champion, was considerable. I had no problem with it whatsoever.

Such was Jack's stature that he, and only he, could invent a disease that infected every other golfer. The disease is called *majoritis*, and it broke out when Jack let it be known that his primary focus was winning major championships. If the best player in the game said the majors were what mattered most, you'd better believe the other players were forced to buy into the idea. Jack's statement put tremendous pressure on other players to perform well in the majors, me included. I always was acutely aware of the atmosphere at the Masters and U.S. Open and exerted extra pressure on myself. Jack, on the other hand, was always well within his comfort zone in the big tournaments.

At a British Open some years ago, I asked him offhandedly how he won so many majors. He looked at me as though it were a silly question and said, "John, they are the easiest four tournaments to win."

I told him he must be kidding.

He said, "Look, people want to win so badly, they play themselves right out of the tournament. All I need to do is keep my game under control, pick my spots, and just be around at the end. Everybody else fades away, and I win."

Jack's strategy didn't work every time, of course. He finished second in majors nineteen times, which is incredible in itself. A lot of fellows managed to get their licks in. Still, Jack knew half the field was eliminated before they even teed off, and that most of the others would disappear by Sunday afternoon. More often than not, they would make a huge tactical error or their putter would let them down. When someone pointed out to Lee Trevino that Greg Norman was a good putter on Sunday, he said, "Yeah, but *what time* on Sunday?" His message was, the best players invariably face a make-or-break, tough six-foot putt on the back nine, and they find a way to hole it. Norman and so many others had a tough time getting those crucial putts to drop. And that's where Nicklaus surpassed everyone by leaps and bounds.

It happened that Jack possessed a swing and strategy that married perfectly with the courses and playing conditions that typified the U.S. Open and other three majors. For example, at the U.S. Open the greens are fast and firm, the rough high, the fairways narrow, the course long. That was perfect for Nicklaus. He handled the fast greens by leaving his ball below the hole to avoid three-putting. He handled the firmness of the greens with his natural ball flight—a high, soft-landing fade that could hold almost any surface. He handled the rough simply by avoiding it, and when he did hit the ball in tall grass he had the total-body strength to thrash his way out. His strategic approach was what I call "chicken golf," and I don't mean it in a pejorative way. Jack never gambled unless he thought it was necessary. He was very content to hit to the fat part of the greens and two-putt for par, sometimes making a long putt for a surprise birdie.

Not that he wasn't aggressive in spots. He tore the par-5 holes apart. In the days before equipment got out of hand and guys had to hit long irons or fairway woods to reach long holes, Jack was in a class by himself. He probably is the best long iron player ever because he could hit his 1-iron higher than most guys hit their 5-iron. He made extremely precise contact. The clubheads on long irons in those days were as thin as scalpels, their sweet spots smaller than a dime. I look at them today and wonder how anyone could hit them. Yet Jack would flush them, time after time. He controlled his distances superbly. If Jack needed to hit a 2-iron 215 yards over water to a front hole location, he could do it. He was the best fairway bunker player I ever saw; he could hit a 200-yard 4-iron without moving a grain of sand.

And his length! I played with Jack after he'd lost a bit of distance with his driver, but he still was massively long. He used this to his advantage tactically and psychologically. In the days when Jack and Arnold Palmer ran one–two in the world, Jack would toy with Arnie. Palmer took pride in how far he hit the ball, but Jack always had extra distance on call when he needed it, and when the time was right Jack would just fly it by Palmer. Psychologically, I think that deflated Palmer—and a lot of other guys, too. Nicklaus gave the impression he could hit the ball as far as he needed to.

Jack won four U.S. Opens, but his game was even better suited for Augusta National, where he won a record six Masters. He bullied Augusta's par 5s like no one else before or since, and handled the firm, sloping greens with very precise iron play. Over time his experience came into play as well. He had an uncanny knack for knowing what he needed to shoot to win. In 1986, when he was four shots off the lead going into the final round, he told his son, Jackie, that a 65 would win the tournament. That's what he shot, and he won by one stroke.

His golf swing was unique. I call it a "dinosaur swing," because you don't see his type of technique anymore. At five foot eleven, Jack wasn't particularly tall. His hands were small and his arms were of average length. He derived his power from his legs, the width of his swing arc, and length of his shoulder turn. Jack's right thigh was twenty-nine inches in circumference, his left thigh twenty-eight inches (he attributed the difference to being a kicker on his football team in high school). Jack made a very long backswing for a fellow who was always thick around the middle, letting his left heel rise a couple of inches to facilitate his turn. Through impact, he delivered a very "heavy" hit. Most golfers attain distance by generating tremendous clubhead speed with their hands and arms, and Jack swung as fast as most. But he also exerted lots of mass. Jack applied lead tape both to the clubhead and to the top of the handle, which made his clubs heavier than average. But he had the strength to control the club and generate the necessary speed. When you added in the extra weight, the effect at impact was like a Mack truck colliding with a Volkswagen. The ball stayed on the clubhead an inordinately long time, and just rocketed off the clubface. The result was a high, piercing ball flight that wasn't affected much by the wind.

The high ball flight was one of the great keys to his success. I asked him once about it and he told me, "The guys who hit it low are just players in the field, anybody can do it. Only a few guys can hit it high." There's an old saying that a wise man can imitate a fool but a fool can't imitate a wise man, and in a sense that applied to Jack's philosophy. Low-ball hitters can't hit the ball high effectively even when they try, but a high-ball hitter can hit it low if they need to.

His power was always controlled. Jack's genius for controlling the distance the ball flew was the result of his lengthening or shortening his backswing just enough to make the ball a yard or two shorter, or twenty yards farther. Jack was a "swinger" of the club rather than a "hitter." He didn't swing *at* the ball so much as *through* it. For much of my career, I was very conscious of what the clubhead was doing at impact. I knew that if the shaft of the club was at a ninety-degree angle in relation to the ground when I made contact with the ball, and the clubface was square, that physics demanded that the ball go straight. Jack didn't think about impact. During one of my hot streaks, he asked what I was working on and I told him I thought only about impact. He really was astonished. "Nobody can think about impact!" he said. But impact was what I thought about, whereas Jack thought only about the ball getting in the way of the swinging clubhead.

The most impressive thing about Jack's swing was its nuance. Early in his career, he was criticized often for having a flying right elbow. But Jack was smart enough, and self-confident enough, to let it go in one ear and out the other. He knew what was best for Jack and insisted on doing it his way. In the end, the record proved him right.

He also was the best clutch putter ever. He made more four-footers for par that mattered than any player in history. It seemed like he never choked. I remember Jack missing a short putt on the 17th hole at Turnberry in 1977 to go one stroke behind Tom Watson, but that was the only time his putter let him down when it really counted. He was equally good on fast and slow greens, Bermuda or bent greens. His game traveled well; he won repeatedly on courses all over the world.

Did Jack have weaknesses? Of course, in several areas. He was a relatively poor pitcher of the ball who wasn't comfortable playing run-up shots, and from greenside bunkers he was only average. Poor sand play cost him his U.S. Open playoff against Lee Trevino in 1971, when he left sand shots in the bunker twice. Psychologically, his considerable belief in himself cost him, again against Trevino. Lee liked to yuk it up and make jokes during the round, and against Jack he talked almost nonstop. Rather than shut Trevino out, Jack engaged him. That just wasn't Jack's style, but he was too proud to admit to himself that he couldn't win playing another man's game. The distraction cost him, I think. Jack also didn't always play with the best equipment his whole career, most notably the ball. He played a MacGregor Tourney golf ball for years when it clearly was an inconsistent, inferior ball. It's a testament to Jack's ability that he won so many majors with that ball.

I've noted that Jack never choked, and I stick with that to the extent that he never threw away tournaments. But I do think he wanted to win the Grand Slam very badly, and that when he had his best chance to do it in 1972, he became a little distracted by knowing the accomplishment was within his reach. He won the Masters and U.S. Open that year, and was in close contention during the final round of the British Open at Muirfield. Strangely, though, Jack shifted his strategy on the back nine. Rather than hit his driver, he began hitting irons off the tee to keep his ball in play. He stopped making birdies, and Trevino squeaked by him at the finish.

Jack's shortcomings were few, however, and I remain firm in my belief that he is the best who ever lived. His contributions to the game went well beyond the way he played. He showed it was possible to be a great player and great father and husband. At all times he was an exemplary role model.

Most of all, he elevated the quality of play for generations of golfers. We're all better for having lived in his time, and Jack will always be my greatest golf hero.

Lee Trevino

Genius and Giant Killer

The PGA Tour professes to be happy with its roster of players, but I wonder how many of its stars are actually perceived as "ticket sellers." Do fans pull money from their pocket to come and watch, say, Retief Goosen play, or is he just part of the chorus? Is Stewart Cink ever the deciding factor when a corporation considers putting up millions to sponsor a tournament? Does the guaranteed appearance of Mike Weir induce greater media coverage of a tournament?

The tour tries to suggest that its product as a whole is greater than the sum of its parts, but I don't think that's ever been the case. The PGA Tour, like the NBA, is heavily reliant on a star system. The fact is, only a handful of players actually put butts in the seats. If you erased a core group of six or seven players, the tour would have some serious problems.

Of the current generation, Tiger Woods is the biggest star by far. He's golf's version of Michael Jordan; when he plays you've got a guaranteed sellout. Other "ticket sellers" include Ernie Els, Phil Mickelson, Sergio Garcia, John Daly, Davis Love III, and Fred Couples. They aren't Tiger Woods, but their appeal is considerable and similar to that of a Kobe Bryant or Shaquille O'Neal. The next group, including players such as Stewart Cink, Mike Weir, Brad Faxon, Tom Lehman, and Justin Leonard, has the appeal of a Karl Malone or Kevin Garnett—you'll definitely check them out, but they aren't really the reason you came to the game. The rest of the field is only part of a pleasant afternoon. They provide excitement, but they are not who the fans come to watch.

Which brings me to the subject of Lee Trevino, one of the greatest ticket sellers ever. I don't know what the PGA Tour would give to have a young Lee Trevino in the mix right now, but you can bet they'd take him over anyone else, with the exception of Tiger. Trevino was a great player, of course—he won six majors and twenty-nine tournaments—but he was even better at promoting the game. He was a fabulous, larger-than-life character who understood that hitting a golf ball was only part of a bigger picture. Lee wisecracked to the fans, gave terrific interviews, and in general wore his emotions on his sleeve. He was compelling because his personality had so many dimensions. He could be rude and snappish to people. His famous dislike for Augusta National and the Masters was always an interesting sidebar—he changed his shoes in the parking lot for years, and in the early 1970s refused to play altogether. He thought junior golf programs were a waste of time and disliked the PGA of America, and would tell you why. He wasn't afraid to speak his mind on any subject in a way that was always provocative. In short, he was one of a kind.

Lee probably threw out more memorable quotes than any golfer in history. He suggested you hold a 1-iron aloft during a lightning storm because "Even God can't hit a 1-iron." He said the fairways at Muirfield during the 1972 British Open were so narrow that the greenkeeper "Must have had one eye closed when he mowed them." He said, "When I get enough money, I'm going to become a Spaniard instead of a Mexican." The one-liners never ceased.

I played against Lee in dozens of tournaments. I played a lot of practice rounds with him and also did many corporate outings together. He was a self-taught phenomenon I couldn't resist watching on every swing. His action was complicated and not everyone understood how it worked. Basically, his "four-part harmony" method worked like this: He started by aiming forty yards to the left of the target. He swung the club on a path ten yards to the right of that point, which meant he now was only thirty yards off. He pushed the ball another twenty yards to the right, so now he was only ten yards off. He then curved the ball to the right another ten yards, which brought the equation to 0, or dead straight. And let me tell you, he was the straightest short driver I ever saw. When he won the PGA Championship at Tanglewood in 1974, he didn't miss a fairway the entire week. He was an excellent putter and a terrific short iron player.

Lee had a lot of guts and loved to beat big hitters. He wasn't afraid of anyone. He loved beating Jack Nicklaus especially, and their rivalry was special because they were different in every way imaginable. Their games were opposite; Jack hit it high and far, Lee hit it low and short. Jack was blonde and fair-skinned, Lee was black-haired and dark-complected. Jack was a study in concentration, Lee yakked it up nonstop. As I mentioned earlier, Lee would draw Jack into his world but would never let himself get pulled into Jack's. He did that with everyone. He was a genius competitor that way.

The gallery saw a funnyman, but behind this exterior Lee was dead serious. He totally controlled his environment. He would spew out the wisecracks, but if someone in the gallery tried to join in and Lee didn't like it, he'd let the guy know. In a way, Lee was only entertaining himself. He came off as having a good time, but he would just as soon see his fellow competitors jump in a lake and drown. He wasn't always easy to play with. He wanted to win a lot more than he let on. You don't win all those majors without having a lot of fire inside you, and Lee wanted to beat everybody and everything. He wanted to whip the golf course, he wanted to overcome himself, and he wanted to pummel you in the process.

Greg Norman

A Case of What Might Have Been

Greg Norman is the most compelling golfer of the last forty years. Period. For a substantial period of time he was the most exciting player in the world, the most colorful, and arguably the best. I put him on my team partly because his golf was so special, but mostly because I knew he could be counted on to provide tremendous theater. Greg experienced soaring highs and abject lows throughout his career, and the delicious part about it was you never knew which it would be. In terms of sheer drama, nobody except Arnold Palmer has remotely approached him. Norman was at once strong and fragile, skilled and flawed. He was adored by many, disliked by some, and captivating to all. He was vain and brash, yet always sporting and complimentary. He was blessed with great luck in some ways, and the worst luck possible in others. For a twenty-year period, Norman was a walking soap opera—a package of contradictions who enthralled us with a flair for the dramatic and a human fallibility that showed up when it mattered most.

I speak of Greg as a player in the past tense now, the first time I've done that. But because he's soon reaching fifty and his interest in playing golf professionally has waned dramatically, it's a good time to assess his career. His days of contending in major championships are gone. There was a moment in 2003 when Norman shot an opening 69 to sit one shot off the lead at the British Open, which raised some tantalizing possibilities. But hard as I rooted for him to bring back the old magic, a second-round 79 took him out of contention.

I first met Greg in 1977 when I played an exhibition with him and Seve Ballesteros in Australia. Norman was twenty-two years old and I'd heard only that I'd be playing with a talented kid who had won some pretty good tournaments. The course we played was extremely tight. The landing areas on some of the par 4s were narrow little throats with water on the right and out-of-bounds to the left. The sight of them gave me pause, even with my 1-iron. Greg just pulled the driver from his bag and blasted the ball 300 yards dead in the center of every fairway. In terms of length *and* accuracy, he was the best driver I had ever seen. He knew he was good, too. I came back to America raving about him, and sure enough he quickly became one of the best players in the world. He didn't play a lot on the PGA Tour until 1984, when he won two tournaments—and also suffered the first of many crushing setbacks. At the last hole of the 1984 U.S. Open at Winged Foot, Greg's second shot sailed way right into the gallery. He made a miracle par to tie Fuzzy Zoeller, but lost in a playoff the next day.

At the time, the bad shot seemed like a fluke. But he hit bad shots under pressure time and again after that. The same bad shot to the right cost him at least a playoff at the 1986 Masters. It hurt him again in the 1996 Masters, when he desperately needed a par at the 12th hole but found the water on the right when he was aiming at the left side of the green. He found other ways to lose. He three-putted to lose a playoff to Paul Azinger in the 1993 PGA championship that same year, and dumped a simple wedge shot into a bunker to hand the Tour Championship to Jim Gallagher Jr. In the end, he would finish second thirty-one times on the PGA Tour. He could be a phenomenal underachiever. In 1994, Norman won the Vardon Trophy with a scoring average of 68.81, the lowest in history at the time. Yet he won exactly one tournament that year, the same as an over-the-hill guy named Johnny Miller. It made no sense.

Greg had a tremendous golf swing that was sound and powerful. His short game was a dream. But mentally, he had only one gear—hit it hard and always be aggressive. The mind-set just killed him in major championships. In the majors, the value of a simple par goes way up. Jack Nicklaus knew this better than anyone; he just parred guys to death. He was very careful about choosing his spots to be aggressive. He wore guys out and waited for them to choke or else make some kind of tactical mistake, which they usually did. In Western movie parlance, Nicklaus saw pars as "good guys"—they wear the white hats. Norman saw pars as "bad guys," villains wearing black hats. To him, only birdies wore white hats, and that's what he shot for. Invariably, he'd end up shooting himself. It was impossible for him to play conservatively. He never developed a soft punch shot that would guarantee getting the ball somewhere on the green. He had to hit everything hard. The safe shot just wasn't in his repertoire. If he tried to incorporate it in his mind, it would cause a short circuit because his brain wasn't designed that way. It soon became too late to reprogram the computer.

Not all his failings were his own. If ever a guy were cursed, it was Norman. Robert Gamez holed a 7-iron shot for eagle to beat him by one at Bay Hill in 1990. Bob Tway holed out from a bunker to beat him at the 1986 PGA Championship. Larry Mize holed a long pitch for birdie on the second playoff hole to steal the 1987 Masters. The list of guys who played great final rounds to beat Greg is as long as your left arm.

I admire Greg a great deal, because he never became afraid of putting himself in contention. People tend to remember his failings while forgetting the outstanding golf he played to put himself in a position to fail. For example, at the 1986 Masters,

Greg was well behind Seve Ballesteros and Nicklaus heading into the back nine. But Greg birdied numbers thirteen, fifteen, sixteen, and seventeen to pull himself into a tie playing the 18th hole. That took a lot of guts, and Greg did that sort of thing many, many times. He never did become a great closer of the deal, but with all the failures and scar tissue that resulted, he never was afraid to put himself on center stage.

As good as Greg was, he wasn't the most intimidating golfer around. After players got the better of him a few times, the entire PGA Tour viewed him as vulnerable. A lot of players were especially relaxed playing against Greg and fed off a hunch that if they hung in there, something good would happen to them and things would start going poorly for him. Greg, meanwhile, had to feel a little snakebitten. Setbacks like these take a toll on a person's psyche. The heartbreak, the constant criticism from the media, the hard work that didn't pay off as it should, being denied what he felt like he deserved; these things hurt a man. It took something out of him that couldn't be rekindled. He began to feel that fate, not his own hand, was in control. Like Sam Snead's superstition that he was destined never to win the U.S. Open, Greg's fatalistic mind-set became a self-fulfilling prophecy.

It's no wonder that Greg now finds more pleasure in family and business matters than he does playing golf. In a way, he'll always be a case of what might have been.

Tom Watson

The Man Who Loved Bad Bounces

When Tom Watson turned fifty and joined the Champions Tour full-time, I wondered what he was trying to prove. When you're a Hall of Fame player, are set financially, and reached almost every goal you've set for yourself, what's the point of playing senior golf week in and week out? I've been tempted to play the Champions Tour from time to time, but with my commitments to NBC, my kids, and my course design business—and the fact I'm a balky putter—it's a temptation that's pretty easy to resist. So why would a guy like Watson want to go at it so intensely?

Here's the answer: Anyone who decides to make playing golf their life's work obviously is moved in a profound way by the game's challenges, rewards, cruelties, and vicissitudes. Tom Watson's career in golf transpired like a lot of marriages—after many years of total bliss, trouble started. There were serious arguments with his putter and letdowns in other areas that make one feel disillusioned. But Watson couldn't divorce himself from golf. Despite a long and savage battle with the yips, he never threw in the towel. Watson's love of the game is so intense that he couldn't leave the marriage if he tried. Golf comprises a large part of his soul. Tom Watson *is* golf, and by hanging in there, the marriage is back on good terms and stronger than ever.

I always said that Tom Kite possessed the rarest form of genius, which is the ability to do the same thing every single day without becoming bored or stale. Watson and Lee Trevino are the only other golfers who share Kite's devotion. These are guys who wake up every morning asking, "Where are my clubs?" They have very few interests outside of golf. They love every part of it, from practicing to tweaking their clubs to playing in tournaments. They think about golf all day. I'm sure they dream about it at night.

Watson wears his love for golf on his sleeve. He plays like a Disney character, as though he's in Wonderland. When it comes to his golf game, he's an eternal optimist who sees the cup as half full regardless of how he's playing. He is without question *one of the five greatest players who ever lived.* I rate him just below Jack Nicklaus, Bobby Jones, Byron Nelson, and Ben Hogan. His legacy is that for a period of time in the 1970s, he was the greatest putter who ever lived. That includes Ben Crenshaw and Billy Casper. It's the jumping-off point for any discussion about Watson, because his putting single-handedly made him immortal. In a compelling way, it also wound up killing him.

I hated playing against Watson head-to-head. He always seemed to get the better of me. No matter how good I hit it from tee to green—and invariably I hit it better than he did—he would beat me into the hole. He consistently holed putts from all distances. If I'd knife an iron shot six feet from the hole and he'd be thirty feet away, then he'd snake in the putt. The crowd would roar, and suddenly my six-footer seemed twice that distance. Nothing is more discouraging than having a guy drain putts on you all day, and for that reason he was the worst guy to have to go up against.

Tom won five British Opens and he did it primarily with the flat stick. In America, Tom's style was to putt very aggressively, so that if he missed he'd have four feet coming back. At the British Opens, he didn't have to change speeds like the rest of us. He hit the ball just as hard, but on the slower greens in Scotland, his putts would stop stone dead. Me, I found myself coming up short all day. Many of us just couldn't adjust, but with Watson, there was no adjustment to make.

The other thing was, he was a monster in bad weather or when the course was in lousy condition. He was the best "mudder" I ever played against. He was an exceptional iron player, especially from bad lies. He had a knack for picking the ball very cleanly from muddy and cuppy lies. Instead of digging the ball out of bad lies, he made his ordinary swing, which happened to be very precise. He rarely hit the ball fat.

Wind meant nothing to him. There are many ways to deal with howling winds like those you see in the British Open, such as hitting knockdown shots, curving the ball into the wind, or letting the ball drift with it. Watson never bothered to do that. He would just hit his normal shot, and the ball flight was so pure that the wind had surprisingly little effect. His ball just plowed through it.

He also loved the crazy bounces you get in a British Open. Most golfers can't help but expect justice when they hit a good shot, and they become annoyed when the ball caroms off a knoll or hillock. But bad luck didn't faze Watson one bit. I asked him once how he was able to play so well in the British Open, what with the lousy weather, bad bounces and all, and he answered, "I love bad bounces," and walked away. He actually was empowered by the bad bounces, bumpy greens, outrageous bunkers, screaming wind, and bone-chilling cold that are endemic to the British Open. While everyone else was moaning and groaning and complaining, he just smiled ruefully and carried on. Everyone got flustered except him, and that was a big advantage. It was a powerful psychological tool that was so simple. I envied Watson for that. I won one British Open, but if I'd learned to take a masochistic pleasure in adverse conditions the way he did, I might have won more.

Watson is a proud, principled man with a strong belief system that won't be compromised. His stand to support Henry Block, the first Jewish member nominated for membership to Kansas City Country Club was typical of him. When there was resistance to admitting Block into the club, Watson resigned his membership, much to the disappointment of his father, with whom Watson had a close relationship. Watson was married at the time to the former Linda Rubin, also Jewish, and discrimination was something he wouldn't stand for. The club later caved and admitted Block, and you'd have to think it was because of Watson's stand.

He's a tough guy. When he played the tour, he wasn't chummy with a lot of players. Like me, he was a lone wolf, though I think Tom had a harder edge to his personality than me. During a tournament I called for NBC, Watson hit a big block to the right. I asked for a slow-motion replay, and explained how Tom's shoulder had come up suddenly on the downswing, causing him to undercut the ball through impact, which in turn left the clubface open and resulted in the block. Some time later we asked Tom for an interview, and he refused. He resented that we had criticized his swing on live television.

Politically, he's followed an interesting course. When he joined the PGA Tour in 1971, he was known as being the only Democrat on tour. Today, he's a Rush Limbaugh fan with a strong conservative bent. "If you're young and not a liberal you've got no heart," he says, paraphrasing a Churchill quote. "If you're old and you aren't conservative, you've got no brain." I think that conservatism came to bear in the matter involving Gary McCord and his expulsion from CBS's Masters telecast. McCord had made those jokes about the mounds concealing "body bags," and how the greens were so slick it seemed as though someone treated them with "bikini wax." Watson wrote a letter recommending that McCord be removed. When it came to a hallowed institution like the Masters, Watson had no sense of humor at all. He was a traditionalist all the way.

That traditionalist mind-set cost Watson dearly, because he was very reluctant to try an alternative putting style when his yips were at their worst. Using a long putter wasn't for him. Like Ben Hogan, he would do it the "right" way or not at all. Watson's case of the yips was as bad as any I'd ever seen. For years he was in denial about it, insisting his problem was only mechanical as opposed to being rattled nerves. I was almost surprised when he finally admitted publicly, in 2001, that he in fact had the yips. It was the last thing he wanted to admit to anyone, himself especially. It was like the yips were some kind of character flaw or something. Hey, the yips are the yips. I have no problem admitting that I fought them for thirty years, and that under pressure they are likely to come back with a vengeance. If they're good enough for Ben Hogan, Byron Nelson, and Sam Snead, they're good enough for me. Harry Vardon, who won a record six British Opens, said about the yips, "Once you've had 'em, you've got 'em," meaning they never really go away.

If you put his spotty putting aside, Watson is one fabulous player. His swing is a reflection of his personality in that it has a very fast tempo. He used to be criticized for swinging too fast, but I thought his tempo was just fine. He swung in a distinct one-to-two beat, his backswing and downswing seeming to take the same amount of time. There's nothing wrong with a fast swing—Lanny Wadkins, Hubert Green, Nick Price, and a bunch of other great players had very rapid tempos. The trick is to make your body parts work in the correct sequence, and Watson did that very well.

Watson has been a fabulous senior golfer and the experience has been rewarding for him. After I watched him lose a thrilling playoff to Don Pooley at the 2002 U.S. Senior Open—where he putted beautifully, I might add—I no longer questioned his desire to compete. The Champions Tour is a bit more relaxed, which takes the edge off his nerves and enables him to putt well. He's still extremely long and is a much more accurate driver than he was twenty or thirty years ago. And after the drama of seeing him take the first-round lead in the

2003 U.S. Open with his terminally ill friend, Bruce Edwards, carrying his bag, my mind was changed for good. Go for it, Tom.

Nick Faldo

Triumph of the Will

The Nick Faldo that was the best player in the game in the late 1980s and beyond was not particularly inspiring to watch. At his best, he rumbled along more like a huge semitruck than a sports car, plowing his way to six major titles without ever entering the passing lane. His game was grinding, inexorable, and utterly devoid of dash; he rarely shot in the low sixties and seldom had runaway victories. But here's the bottom line: Given one guy to play a head-to-head match on a tough course for all the marbles, I'd take Faldo. You can throw in Nicklaus and Woods, and still I'd be very comfortable.

Only a purist could appreciate Faldo. Even in his prime he didn't drive the ball very far and he hit a funky, knuckleball-like shot that sort of fluttered into the fairway. His iron play was precise but restrained. His short game was good but not magical, and his putting was only above average. What Faldo excelled at was consistency, course management, determination, a technically perfect golf swing, and an unmatched ability to handle pressure. Like his idol, Ben Hogan, the whole of his game was greater than the sum of its parts. Like a big python, he slowly squeezed you to death. As Greg Norman and many others found out, there was little point in trying to struggle. If you lost your composure just a bit and tried to fight him off, he just killed you faster.

Faldo was the most ruthless player of his era. When Norman was in the midst of blowing that six-stroke lead to Faldo in the 1996 Masters, one couldn't help but get the feeling that Faldo was enjoying it. He was very sporting after it was over, hugging Norman and whispering warm words to him that neither player has revealed to this day. But while it was happening, you could see that Faldo relished it.

Historically, Faldo made a number of contributions that haven't really been acknowledged. He was part of that generation of European players who revived the Ryder Cup competition and restored pride to the Continent. Seve Ballesteros gets most of the credit for this—and deservedly so because he was so inspirational and colorful. But Faldo was the more complete player. Nick played in eleven Ryder Cups, the most in history, and won twenty-five points. Seve won twenty-two-and-a-half points, but twelve of those came in team competition with Jose Maria Olazabal as his partner—Faldo didn't usually have partners like Jose Maria. Both players won three British Opens, but Faldo won three Masters to Seve's two. Ballesteros never finished better than third in the U.S. Open; Faldo at least got to a playoff in 1988, losing to Curtis Strange. Seve is regarded as the better player in many circles, but I don't buy it. Faldo played well everywhere he went, winning nine events on the PGA Tour and thirty other times outside the United States.

Faldo was the ultimate swing technician who committed himself totally to becoming the best player possible. I don't think Hogan was any more dedicated. In addition to retooling his swing under David Leadbetter, he practiced relentlessly. He always was in fabulous physical condition. His swing was easy and controlled; there was very little differentiation in effort between his 5-iron and driver. He *painted* his iron shots, meaning he rarely applied more than 60 percent of his power. The fact that he swung his driver with equal ease may ultimately have been a drawback. I've often wondered if he might have won even more had he risked getting thirty more yards with the driver.

But overall he was sensational. One shot in particular points up how solid that swing was and how much Faldo trusted it. In that same 1996 Masters, Faldo stood in the 13th fairway with the green easily within reach of his 5-wood. Faldo addressed the ball, then backed off and chose his 2-iron. Now, the 2-iron is exponentially more difficult to hit than a 5-wood, but Faldo saw that as the correct play. With everything at stake, he nailed the 2-iron onto the green, matched Norman's birdie, and averted the chance of a Norman comeback. It was an extremely gutsy, difficult shot that only a great champion would have the nerve to play.

From a public relations standpoint, Faldo was never very effective. In person he had a tremendous sense of humor and he showed a bit of mirth on the course once in a while. But he was rarely forthcoming with the media, and the public didn't sympathize much with his divorce in the 1990s and soap-opera episodes with the college student he dated some time later. He had few friends on the American and European tours, and often ate breakfast alone. Today, his game is in decline, though he contended briefly in the 2003 British Open. He shows signs of warming up; he is remarried now and has been more open with the press and public. In a way, Faldo is saying hello to us when it's time to say good-bye, but that doesn't diminish his standing in my mind as one of the greatest players of all time.

Seve Ballesteros

Golf's Greatest High-Wire Act

In the euphoric months following my 1976 British Open victory, one memory really stayed with me. It was of a long-limbed, dark-eyed, charismatic, nineteen-year-old Spanish kid who I played with in the final round. He arrived at the first tee with a two-stroke lead and brimming with confidence. He didn't play well that day. He drove the ball all over the golf course and fought like crazy to shoot 74. But he never gave up. On the last hole, after missing the green with his approach shot, he got my attention with one of the best shots I've ever seen. He played a delicate chip that ran between two bunkers and trickled close to the hole for a tap-in birdie. The crowd went wild. The boy's name name was Severiano Ballesteros. I had a hunch I would be seeing more of him.

I certainly would. My manager at the time, Ed Barner, signed Seve to a contract, and over the next few years we got to know each other well. My career was in full flower and Seve was very deferential. He was a precocious, nice young guy who was cocksure of himself but also had an air of innocence about him. His English wasn't very good, but I spoke some Spanish and we had no trouble communicating. I like to think I helped him mature socially and become savvier about business and life in general.

One thing I did not help him with was his golf game—not that it needed any help. In all my life, I never saw a golfer like him. He played purely by feel, trust, ego, and inspiration. Like no other golfer in history, Seve willed things to happen. He played every shot with a burning intensity and exuded a strong psychic power that seemed to put good luck in his corner. Difficult shots were easy for Seve and easy shots were difficult; he was at his best when he had to work the ball or manufacture a shot from around the green.

He was enormously flawed in some ways. He had very limited success in America, winning only six times in the United States. Tight fairways and tall, moist rough was not for him because he never was a good driver of the ball. He had long arms and legs, and his swing, though rhythmic, looked like someone dumping a bowl of spaghetti. He was just too wild. He had three top-five finishes in the U.S. Open, but never did threaten seriously. Seve was at his best in Europe, primarily at the British Open, where softer rough and the absence of trees played more into his hands.

Seve was and is a proud man who saw himself as larger than life. It annoyed him no end that PGA Tour commissioner Deane Beman never granted him a free ticket to play in America any time he wanted. Beman demanded that Seve either play fifteen tournaments in America or none at all—a pretty unreasonable stance on Beman's part and one that hurt the tour, I thought. Seve refused to cave, and played almost exclusively in Europe. That episode and a few like it gave Seve a peculiar mind-set. He always saw himself as the victim of some dark conspiracy and was sensitive to personal affronts, real and imagined. He had the power to foist his sense of pride and persecution on his teammates in the Ryder Cup, and they used it as motivation to give the spoiled, arrogant Americans their comeuppance.

There never was a better match player than Seve. He won the World Match Play a record-tying five times and had great success against the Americans in the Ryder Cup. Seve would do almost anything to win. He thought nothing of using gamesmanship, crossing his feet within eyesight of an opponent just as the guy started his takeaway. He developed a cough at the most opportune moments. It took a special personality to handle him. In the Dutch Open one year, I developed a temporary habit of beginning to walk toward my ball just as my playing partners were midway into their downswings. Seve, who knew all the tricks of gamesmanship, was sensitive to it being done by others. He mentioned it to me quietly, knowing I wasn't doing it on purpose. I stood still after that.

Of the American players, Paul Azinger was the best at giving Seve a taste of his own medicine. When you put Azinger and Ballesteros together, sparks were bound to fly. It was great theater, watching these two. They clashed over a ball-substitution incident at Kiawah Island in 1991, and there was more trouble at The Belfry in 1989, when Ballesteros thought Azinger fudged an advantageous drop on the 18th hole of their match. Calling the matches for NBC was great fun when those two went at it. It was a fascinating sideshow, and we tried to give as much of it as possible.

It didn't surprise me that Seve burned out early. After going hard at it for twenty years, his game fell apart. Not long ago Seve told me, "When I was young, I was very aggressive and it was good because no matter where the ball went, I always had a shot to the green, or at least a full swing. It was always a good bounce I got. Now when I hit it off line, I am always dead." He summarized the state of his game and his mind with a simple sentence, expressed with sadness. "There is no magic," he said.

It didn't help that he tried to investigate swing mechanics. Seve is an artist, and when an artist tries to become a technician, it just doesn't work. His full swing has been a mess for years now. I'd love to spend an hour with him on the practice range. Given the chance, I'd tell him one thing: All that matters is impact. If the clubface is square and the clubshaft is perpendicular to the ground when the club meets the ball, the laws of physics promise a good shot. I'd tell Seve to forget working on his stance, posture, ball position, and even his backswing. I'd tell him to focus purely on that nanosecond of impact. With his extraordinary feel and great ability to visualize, it would help him immensely.

Seve told the famed sports psychologist, Bob Rotella, "I used to cry after eighteen holes because there was no more golf to play. Now I cry after nine holes because I know I must play nine more." Still, Seve never lost his will to win. In 2000, at the Seve Ballesteros Trophy competition at Sunningdale in England, he beat Colin Montgomerie when Monty was at his very best. His match against Tom Lehman in the 1995 Ryder Cup was one of the most entertaining I've seen from the broadcast booth. Seve's game was shot full of holes by then and his drives soared forty yards off line. He hit it like an 18-handicapper. But he played his recovery shots, chips, and pitches like a plus-8, and kept the match close until being overwhelmed by Lehman at the end.

Playing against Seve was very helpful to me. You couldn't help but draw from his energy and acknowledge the existence of something supernatural about the way he played. My experience with Seve at the 1982 Million Dollar Challenge in South Africa was nothing short of remarkable. We wound up tied at the end of regulation play, and entered a playoff to see who would win the $500,000 prize for first place—a lot of money in those days, let me tell you.

Earlier in the week, I had met a woman named Rene Kurinsky, who was something of a precursor to sports psychologists. During the course of the conversation, she told me that the mind is very powerful and full of energy, and that the energy can be transferred from one person to another. She told me to never project positive or negative thoughts to an opponent, because subliminally they will feed off either one. I thought of this during the playoff with Seve when on several of the early holes he had very makeable putts to win the playoff. In those situations, it's human nature to think like the gallery did in the movie *Caddyshack*—"Miss it, Noonan!" But having talked to Kurinsky, and being especially attuned because I was playing with a guy whose game was black magic anyway, I kept my mind quiet. I didn't think a thing either way. And darned if Seve didn't miss. And miss. And miss again. Finally, on the ninth extra hole, I won the playoff.

Today, Seve's game from fifty yards and in is as good as ever. His full swing is a wreck, of course, and it's hard watching him suffer. But the memory of what he once was makes for some very pleasant reminiscing.

Hale Irwin

Persistent, Patient, Omnipresent

Irwin may be remembered as the greatest player in Champions Tour history. That's a great accomplishment, but in a way it's like being remembered as the world's tallest midget. His record as a senior is amazing—he's won a record thirty-seven times, including two U.S. Senior Opens and three Senior PGA Championships. The amount of money he's won is just mind-blowing. It's hard to believe, but Irwin has won more than $17 million on the Champions Tour in just nine years, compared with $6 million won in twenty-eight years on the PGA Tour.

To me, Hale's legacy on the PGA Tour surpasses what he's done as a senior. In that tough, golden era of the 1970s and 1980s, he won twenty times. Moreover, he won three U.S. Opens, just one short of Jones, Hogan, and Nicklaus. He did it, I think, without possessing an overload of natural golf talent. Hale was a very good athlete and was an All-American defensive back at Colorado, but his golf game wasn't super dynamic. He beat you with intellect, perseverance, stubbornness, physical stamina, great course management, and old-fashioned mental toughness. For a big guy—he's six feet tall, bigger than average for his era—he didn't hit the ball very far. He hit a slap upshoot fade that bordered on being an out-and-out slice. One time I asked Hale why he played such a big cut shot all the time and he said, "I try to hook it and it slices anyway, so I just go ahead and slice it." He was a decent ball striker, but not a great one. Irwin accepted this and never tried to overhaul his swing. He had the good sense to know that what he had was good enough, and the fact is, his swing today is almost identical to his swing forty years ago.

Irwin had plenty of assets to complement his game from tee to green. He was and is an extremely good putter, especially under pressure. His short game was solid. His greatest strengths were psychological. He won the 1974 U.S. Open at Winged Foot (the toughest Open ever, for my money) because he hung in there strong and simply outlasted everyone else. He won the 1979 U.S. Open at Inverness even though he was leaking oil at the end. His last U.S. Open victory, at Medinah in 1990, came because he made a forty-five-foot putt on the final hole to force an unexpected playoff against Mike Donald, which he won with more grinding persistence.

Irwin never looked like he was having much fun on the course. He carried the studious, slightly tortured expression that told you he had to concentrate furiously to play well enough to win. For a long time he wore glasses that made it difficult for him to have a lot of cosmetic appeal and make a lot of money through endorsements. Hale didn't really care. He knew that flamboyance was not his style, and he focused on letting his clubs do the talking.

When Irwin contended briefly at the 2001 U.S. Open at Southern Hills, I wasn't the least bit surprised. Nor was I stunned when I read recently that Hale still thinks he can win another U.S. Open. His belief in himself has always been ironclad, which may be his greatest asset of all.

Gary Player

Mind over Matter

I watched Ben Hogan play but never got to play with him, which I'll always regret. But in a sense I *did* play with Hogan, because I played so much with Gary Player. Those two men were mirror images of each other, if not in their technique then in their overall approach to playing. They both succeeded through constant practice and sheer determination, but Gary took Hogan's commitment to excellence and improved on it.

With his small size—he stood five foot seven and weighed 150 pounds—Player needed every edge he could get, not just to succeed as a golfer but to survive. He practiced relentlessly, exercised like a fiend, and watched his diet religiously. These three things weren't enough; a lot of players have dieted, exercised, and practiced themselves to death. For Player, these things were merely a platform, a jumping-off point that enabled him to exercise the traits that made him one of the top ten players in history and maybe one of the best five.

Player's dedication set the stage for him to employ his extraordinary mental and emotional powers. He had a frightening air of conviction about him. It didn't matter that his swing wasn't very good, that he didn't hit the ball very far, or even with stunning accuracy. He was the first player I saw who actually *willed* things to happen. Watching the man in black win by sheer force of will convinced me that the mind can move mountains.

Gary won nine major championships, including all four of them at least once. He won his first major in 1959 and his last in 1978, a remarkable testament to his longevity. Twenty years later, in 1998, he won again on the Champions Tour at age sixty-two. He was as good at match play as he was at stroke play; he won the World Match Play Championship a record five times.

He is the greatest raw competitor I ever saw. I played against Gary in one of those World Match Play events at Wentworth in England, and got a good taste of his competitiveness. On one hole Gary hit his shot into a bunker. I was on the green. Gary played his shot and his ball came to rest right in my line. I waited for Gary to come out of the bunker and mark his ball. And waited. When I looked over, there was Gary, raking the bunker, slowly. He took forever, and the delay upset my rhythm. Was it gamesmanship? I suppose it was, but it was within the bounds of competition and I didn't think less of him for it. I don't remember who won the hole. I just remember thinking that this was a guy who knew how to get an edge.

Gary was the best bunker player I ever saw, bar none. Give him any kind of lie—buried, half buried, downhill, wet sand, fluffy sand—it didn't matter. When he waded into the sand, you held your breath, hoping he didn't hole the darned thing. And his putter, a cheap old thing he bought out of a barrel in Japan, was nothing short of miraculous. The more pressure you put on him, the better Gary putted. His 1978 Masters victory in particular featured one of the best displays of putting ever seen. Gary shot 30 on the back nine to win, holing putts from all distances.

He was and is a great man. During the late 1960s and early 1970s, when controversy raged over apartheid in his native South Africa, Gary was treated miserably everywhere he went. Vandals burned slurs about Gary into the greens at tournaments. Spectators threw cups of ice in his face. He received death threats. Through it all, he handled himself with class. And although he denounced apartheid, he refused to denounce his country. He is one of the most courageous people I've ever met, in or out of golf.

I always thought Gary would have been at least as good a politician as he was a golfer. When it came to making a persuasive argument, or mollifying a crisis of some kind, or promoting things, he made Bill Clinton look like a hack. The phrase, "This is the best course of its kind I've ever played" was made famous by Gary, who was as good with words as he was with his golf clubs.

Lanny Wadkins

A Moment in Time

In my early days as a pro, guys tended to hang out in cliques. I used to joke that there were two groups on tour, those who fooled around on their wives and those who didn't, but in truth there were a number of informal clubs consisting of guys who got along well and played practice rounds together, traveled and ate together, and so on. Lanny was part of a clique that included Grier Jones, J. C. Snead, Jerry Heard, Jim Simons, and me. We were all about the same age except for J. C., who was a little older. We all had a lot in common.

I was very fortunate to be exposed to Wadkins on a regular basis. The great teacher Harvey Penick used to have a saying: "Go to dinner with good putters." What he meant was, if you hang out with good players, it will elevate your performance. The converse is also true; if you fraternize with people who complain all the time, have low goals or a lousy work ethic, that will rub off on you as well. Wadkins had a lot of traits that lifted me up, especially as a golfer.

For a moment in time, Lanny was as good as anybody I ever saw. He and Bobby Clampett were the best nineteen-year-old golfers in history. Lanny could do things with a golf club nobody else could do. He could play his ball from a divot using his driver—and hit the ball straight up in the air. His iron play was phenomenal; like me he had a knack for getting red hot and knocking down the flagsticks, hole after hole. And he couldn't tell you how he did it. Golf was instinctive for Lanny. He was a total feel player who flew by the seat of his pants.

Lanny was cocky. He walked with a swagger, had an edgy personality, and played a bold, daring game. He just loved to beat up on Hall of Famers. His favorite victim was Arnold Palmer. Lanny had Arnold's number. They both had gone to Wake Forest and had played a lot of money games against each other. Arnold could still play in the 1970s, but he couldn't beat Lanny.

When Lanny first came on tour, he had one of the worst putting strokes I'd seen. He aimed the putter left of the hole, took it back shut, screwed the face open through impact, then closed it quickly again on the follow-through. It was awful. The weeks he made anything at all, he won. After he turned thirty, his putting stroke got better and he wound up with twenty-one PGA Tour victories, including the 1977 PGA Championship at Pebble Beach. He also played on eight Ryder Cup teams and had a very good record. Had he putted better earlier in his career and then staved off the various injuries that bothered him for many years, I believe he would have been the best of his era.

Raymond Floyd

That Air of Royalty

Confidence is a huge asset in golf, and no player ever believed in himself more than Ray Floyd did. He loved to put his game on the line anytime, anywhere. When he was playing well, his eyes would get big and he would stride down the fairways with his back erect and shoulders back, his visor tucked low over eyes. When you saw him walk that way, you knew he meant business. Floyd was a gambler and confrontational guy who relished playing for his own money in practice rounds. He thought he was a better player than everybody else, which was apparent not in his words—he was always sportsmanlike—but in his demeanor. When he got "the look" and started taking those mincing little steps, you knew you were in trouble. He carried himself as though he were royalty and everyone else was a commoner.

Floyd was one tough customer. He didn't have an athlete's body, but he had superb touch and great nerves. The greater the pressure, the better he played, with only one exception. He lost the 1990 Masters to Nick Faldo by stumbling on the last two holes of regulation and then hitting the ball into the water at number eleven in the playoff. It was a surprising lapse, because he very rarely choked. He had a bit of trouble when it came down to match play; his Ryder Cup record was only mediocre. But the fact he was named to eight Ryder Cup teams and captained one of them says something about the kind of player he was.

Raymond won twenty-two times on tour and is one of only seven players to win the U.S. Open, the Masters, and PGA Championship. He won the PGA twice for a total of four career majors. A player has to have a deep belief in himself to pull through in a major, and he always had his game and emotions under control.

When it came to his golf swing, Floyd was unconventional, to say the least. He pulled the club back to the inside, set it high at the top, then lunged on the way down. He didn't release the club through impact so much as hold on to it. He liked to hit the ball high, and he had excellent power. But he also was versatile. Raymond played a lot of punch shots and could hook it or fade it at will. Around the greens, he was just terrific. He still stands as one of the best three chippers of the ball I've ever seen. If his ball were two feet off the green, he'd prefer to chip it rather than putt it, which I didn't have the nerve to do. His putting was also interesting to watch. His putter was unusually long—maybe it had something to do with his arms being so short—and he gripped it at the end of the handle. He had the touch of a safecracker, and was especially good from ten feet and in.

Floyd won his first tour event at age twenty, and for years led the life of a playboy. He loved wine, women, and song, and it probably cost him. His getting married in 1973, after he'd been on tour for ten years, was the smartest thing he ever did. His wife, Maria, motivated him and made him focus. Once he put himself on a shorter leash, he became one of the toughest competitors in history. And he's kept it going since joining the Champions Tour, winning fourteen tournaments and finishing in the top three an amazing fifty times.

Hubert Green

Odd Swing, Sound Results

Of all the guys I played against, Hubert was the least appreciated. On one hand I can see why. He didn't do many instruction articles for the golf magazines, wasn't a particularly lively interview, wasn't movie-star handsome, and was colorful only in that he regularly wore green clothes to match his name. Privately, he was a very smart guy with a lot of good ideas, but he didn't relate well to the public.

Hubert emoted through his golf game, which was as effective as it was fascinating to watch. His swing was a series of ungainly loops and twists. He took the club back to the outside, looped it down and in on the downswing, then went back outside on the follow-through. For a tall guy, he "played small," with plenty of knee flex and bend at the hips. His swing arc was small yet very circular; he was a short hitter but extremely accurate. He was very versatile and could work the ball either way. And he was one of the best chippers I ever saw.

Hubert had a habit that was similar to Sergio Garcia's interminable gripping and regripping the club. At address, he'd pump the club up and down and swivel his head back and forth again and again, until you thought his head might fly right off his body. Somehow, it looked cool rather than annoying.

His odd swing and idiosyncrasies notwithstanding, Hubert was one sweet player. He won nineteen tournaments on the PGA Tour. Hubert also won the 1977 U.S. Open and 1985 PGA Championship, and could have won another major had he not been victimized by some bad luck. At the 1978 Masters, Hubert needed to hole a three-foot putt to tie Gary Player, who had come in with a record-tying 64. Hubert was a good short putter and I was certain he'd make it, but a radio announcer stationed by the green started yakking away and distracted Hubert. He backed off the putt, which was the smart thing to do, but then he missed it.

Hubie had guts. At the 1977 U.S. Open at Southern Hills, he played the closing holes knowing someone—a bettor, perhaps—had phoned in a death threat. At the '85 PGA, he had to hold off Lee Trevino, which by itself would have made a lot of players choke.

When Hubert had the lead, you pretty much kissed off the idea of trying to catch him. He was one of the great frontrunners of all time. He also could get red hot at times. During one stretch in 1976, Hubert won three tournaments in a row.

Billy Casper

The Invisible Genius

When people think of golf in the 1960s, they think of the Big Three of Arnold Palmer, Jack Nicklaus, and Gary Player. To the public, it seemed then and seems now like no other pro golfers existed. It's been pointed out that, from 1965 through 1970, the Big Three combined for a total of thirty-eight victories on the PGA Tour.

But Billy Casper won twenty-three all by himself during the same period. And because he continued to play well through a good part of the 1970s, I'm inclined to include him on my list.

Casper in my mind is the most underrated golfer of all time, hands down. Billy won fifty-one times on the PGA Tour from 1956 to 1975. Only five players in the history of the game won more tournaments, and Billy's victories came against some of the best golfers of any era. He won the U.S. Open twice, in 1959 and 1966, and won the Masters in 1970. He played on eight Ryder Cup teams and captained another. He won the Vardon Trophy for low scoring average five times. He was sensational.

Casper wasn't the most flamboyant guy around, which is why he didn't get much attention from the press or much adulation from the public. After he joined the Mormon Church in the early 1960s, he cared even less about being famous and wasn't much inclined to promote himself. He wasn't particularly witty, entertaining, or demonstrative. All he cared about was golf, church, and family. And what a family it was—he and his wife, Shirley, raised eleven children. The trait that caught the public's imagination was Billy's diet. He had some nasty allergies to many foods, which he kept at bay by eating exotic things like buffalo and lion. Thank goodness for that little quirk; without it he would have received even less media attention than he did.

When we played on tour together, Billy and I were as close as two golfers could be. I played more practice rounds with him than I can count, which was both entertaining and inspiring, because his game was pure magic. He was a genius at golf, especially with the putter. He was probably the most confident putter who ever lived. And I saw him do things that were hard to believe. For example, if he missed a putt he thought he should have made, and was left with a three-footer coming back, he would walk up and slam that three-footer so hard it would hit the back of the hole, pop up in the air, then fall in. He did that all the time. If he ever missed one of those, the ball would have gone ten feet by the hole. But I never saw him miss. And he was even better on long putts. On thirty-, forty-, and even sixty-foot putts, he would roll the ball to within two feet, on average. When he won the 1959 U.S. Open at Winged Foot, he played the third hole, a difficult par 3, in a peculiar way. Instead of aiming for the green, which is flanked by deep Tillinghast bunkers, Billy deliberately laid up. He then chipped on to the green and putted for his par. He did this in all four rounds, and each time he one-putted for his par. That takes confidence.

He was a magician with the long clubs, too. Billy loved to work the ball. He would fade the ball with his driver and then curve his approach shot either way. The only thing that held Billy back from immortality was his lack of length. Had he been twenty yards longer throughout his career, his major championship victories could have run into the high teens. I'm very serious when I say that. Other than his lack of length, Billy had no other weaknesses whatsoever. The strange thing was, Billy never took a lesson in his life. He was entirely self-taught and swung by instinct and intuition.

In competition, Billy never choked. Every great champion has thrown away a tournament or two somewhere along the line, but Casper is the lone exception. If you found yourself playing head-to-head against him, you were in very deep trouble. He had almost no ego, and he didn't get nervous. He didn't care if you outdrove him or hit your second shot inside him. He would grind along in a very businesslike way, rarely making a mistake, and eventually he would beat you. Many remember when Arnold Palmer blew the 1966 U.S. Open at Olympic to Billy by blowing a seven-stroke lead on the back nine. But people forget that Billy shot 32 over the final nine holes—which is quite an accomplishment. In the playoff it was much the same thing. Arnold led by two after nine holes but Billy played that bulletproof game of his and eventually overtook Arnie and won. I always thought that if Arnold were playing against almost anyone else in those last two rounds, he would have won. But against Billy, Arnold knew he couldn't afford to make a mistake, which had to intensify the pressure he was already feeling. Billy had a way of doing that to people. He was a persistent, remorseless player who could stand up to anyone, anytime, anywhere.

Although he was a fairly droll individual, Billy also had an edge. On the 72nd hole of that U.S. Open at Olympic, Palmer left his birdie putt a few feet short of the hole. It was by no means a gimme, and Arnold now needed par to at least make the playoff. Palmer, a bit undone by the pressure, asked Casper if he could finish off the short putt, even though Casper was away.

"Go ahead, Arnold," said Billy. "Finish while you're hot."

Arnie shook in the short putt, which, after that unexpected barb by Billy, was quite a feat.

CHAPTER 11

A Real Junior High

Paving a Path for Kids

A COUPLE OF YEARS AGO I accompanied my youngest son, Todd, to a junior tournament in northern California. As usual, I roamed the course freely, observing not only Todd but the other players in the field. Watching kids play golf is my favorite form of spectating. It isn't the best golf I see by any means, but it's fascinating on many levels. The kids try so hard. You see them discovering new things every minute, from shotmaking to etiquette to trying to control their emotions. It's inspiring, like watching a baby walk for the first time. I was especially glad I was there that day, because I witnessed an incident that was apart from reality.

One of the kids, who looked to be about twelve years old,

faced a shot of sixty yards over a lateral water hazard. A series of yellow stakes, each a couple of inches in diameter, were spaced thirty yards apart along the margin of the hazard. The kid didn't look at all comfortable with this simple shot. Sure enough, he topped the ball badly and sent it skittering toward the hazard. I cringed and waited for the splash. But incredibly, the ball hit one of those skinny little stakes dead center, caromed backward toward the fairway, and settled into the prettiest lie you ever saw. Now, phenomenally lucky breaks happen from time to time, but the irony of this one made my jaw drop. One week earlier, at another junior tournament, I had seen the exact same thing happen to another player—a kid bounced a ball off a hazard stake and not only averted a penalty, but wound up with a perfect lie. In my thirty-four years as a pro, I never saw two lucky bounces like that happen so close together. It was like someone dropping a dollar into a slot machine for the first time and winning a million-dollar jackpot.

Neither of the kids thought much of it. They reacted as though they more or less expected it. And that's one thing that makes children special. Their perspective of the game is pure and unblemished. They aren't experienced enough to realize that bad bounces outnumber good bounces by two to one, and that deflecting your ball off a hazard stake is a one-in-a-thousand proposition. Golf to them is fun, pure and simple. They see it as mind over matter, a wishful, optimistic pursuit devoid of the scars of failure.

Somewhere along the way, we adults become cynical about the game. We tend to remember our bad shots more vividly than our good ones. Years of battling a slice, watching countless putts curl out of the hole, and seeing the wind grab the ball and knock it into the water leave dark stains on our psyche. The bottom line is, we know how hard golf is. Children, on the other hand, do not. For years I've recognized this and tried to make my attitude regress to those halcyon days, but I never could do it. No golfer I've seen, with the possible exception of Tom Watson, has successfully preserved that childlike outlook.

I had that outlook once, though. There was a time when I didn't realize that every putt shouldn't go in the hole. If there were a better putter in the world than me when I was twelve years old, I'd like to have seen him. I had nine putts for nine holes many times, and at Harding Park, the public course I played at in San Francisco, I once had just sixteen putts for eighteen holes. I remember one magical day when my dad took me to Golden Gate Park. It was exactly like Chevy Chase in *Caddyshack*. I literally could not miss. He started calling people over to watch. The distance of the putt was meaningless—from ten feet, or twenty or thirty, every putt went in. Everyone just stood there watching, not saying a word. I must have made twenty in a row from all distances. What can I say? I was a kid. But by the time I got to college, my best putting days were well behind me.

One of my life missions is to impart that magic to kids today. I've done it with my own children to a very satisfying degree. By exposing my kids to the game, I've given them a great gift, one that will give them pleasure for the rest of their lives. It's taught them character, confidence, patience, self-reliance, creativity, self-discipline, honesty, respect for their bodies, and respect for other people. It's given us something we can share together as a family. There is just no end to the joy we've experienced, all through a game. All four of my sons are accomplished players and one, Andy, just played a full season on the PGA Tour. But being a star has never been the end-all for any of them. Linda and I see their success in competition as only a by-product of the better things our kids and their parents have derived from the game.

For some years now, I've served as honorary chairman of the Utah Junior Golf Association. I volunteer my time with them every year, and try to contribute to kids in other ways in other places. I perform clinics, give speeches, and sprinkle a little money here and there. I try to walk the walk, and it isn't hard when you go to junior tournaments and see the efforts put forth by hundreds of grownups. I see it all as payback for what the game has given to me.

The Millers' Tale

I didn't start swinging a club at age one like Tiger Woods did, but I started early enough. When I was five, my dad put a golf club in my hands for the first time. By the time I was eight years old, I knew I was going to be a champion golfer. Many kids dream about it, but somehow I knew I was destined to be something special. The story of how I evolved into a top professional golfer contains several lessons on how to be a good golf parent. I can't imagine anyone being nurtured as well as I was. My upbringing in golf was so perfect it would have been an upset if I hadn't succeeded.

My father, Larry Miller, didn't take up golf until he was in his late twenties. He fell in love with the game and became a good enough player to win the Sportsman's Flight of the San Francisco City Amateur. It was just one notch below championship flight, and my dad only regretted he hadn't taken up the game earlier.

Dad decided that all his children were going to take up golf. He was a very smart, devoted parent and an independent thinker who had strong ideas about how a child should be raised. His number one rule was to always be positive. Dad had a saying: "Four parts praise, one part pruning." He knew that children who are complimented constantly bloom like flowers, whereas those who are criticized and chided develop all sorts of problems with self-esteem. From the time I can remember, he called me "Champ." He treated me as though I were something special. He didn't spoil us by any means. There was discipline around our house and all his children were given responsibilities very early on. But he imbued in me a very deep faith in myself and a belief that I could become anything I aspired to be.

When I was five Dad went down to an Army surplus store and bought a big green canvas tarp, which he nailed to the ceiling in our basement. He installed a large mirror and set three instruction books on a nearby table, a large one by Sam Snead, one by Byron Nelson called *Winning Golf*, and Ben Hogan's *Five Lessons*. He told me to copy the positions I saw in the books, to read as much of them as I could, and to ask questions. For the next three years, I never set foot on a golf course. I just hammered away at balls in that basement, memorizing the correct grip, stance, and posture, and matching my swing positions to the ones I saw in the books. I never got too immersed in where the ball was going, because it only traveled a few feet before slamming into that tarp. I developed a good sensory awareness of how solidly I was striking the ball and learned the importance of balance and tempo. I dreamed about the day I would finally get to go to a real course.

Finally, just before I turned eight, Dad decided to get me started formally in real golf. He orchestrated a plan. He took me to John Geertsen, the head pro at San Francisco Golf Club, the most prestigious club in the Bay Area. He told John, "I got a boy who's got a great swing. I wonder if you wouldn't mind taking a look at him." I made some swings, Mr. Geertsen liked what he saw, and he became my teacher from that moment until I turned pro. I can't say enough about how much he helped me.

My next lucky break happened when I was eleven, when Dad got me playing at the Olympic Club with the other junior members. That gave me two tremendous courses to cut my teeth on. My game really blossomed. In high school, I was undefeated in three years of matches. Along the way, as my reputation grew, I met many interesting people. Golf has a very rich tradition in the Bay Area. Ken Venturi, Tony Lema, Bob Rosburg, and hundreds of other very good golfers competed in the eras before, after, and during my formative years there.

The Man with the Goatee

An interesting thing happened when I was nine. The city of San Francisco used to have a big hole-in-one contest at Lincoln Park. They would paint a five-foot circle around the hole on a par 3 and install a big, thick flagstick in the cup. The pin was so wide there was barely enough room for a ball to fit in the hole. It was a very short hole, only 100 yards or so, and downhill. You signed up, and were given three balls.

When my turn came, I hit all three balls inside the circle. One of them bounced off the flagstick and would have gone in if the darned thing weren't so thick. As it was, I finished third and won a pair of FootJoy golf shoes.

When we finished, an odd-looking gentleman with a goatee approached my father. He told my dad he was an engineer at General Electric and worked as an inventor on the side. He said, "Your boy is a good player and there's no telling how good he could be if he used one of the putters I just invented." My dad replied, "All right, where's the putter?" The man said he didn't have one with him, it was at his home. He was insistent that we accompany him to his workshop and give it a try. So we piled in the man's little Citroen car and he drove us to his garage.

He had all types of weird-looking putters sitting around. He chose one, raked a ball in front of him, and said, "Let me demonstrate." At impact the putter emitted a loud chime like a doorbell. The man smiled and said, "What do you think?"

My dad looked like he'd just bitten into a lemon. He immediately said, "Forget it. My kid makes everything with his little Bulls Eye, and I think we'll just stick with that." The man was disappointed, but he accepted my father's reaction and very politely drove us home.

This happened in 1956. Many years later, some odd-looking putters started surfacing on the PGA Tour. One day I saw a man standing near the putting green, encouraging players to try them. It was the same guy we met in San Francisco—Karsten Solheim, whose Ping putters probably were the most famous and innovative of the twentieth century.

Karsten still had the goatee. I still had my Bulls Eye. It wasn't much longer before Karsten made millions off his irons and putters, which led me to chide my dad about his refusing to let me try that putter. That prototype, wherever it is, has to be worth a small fortune.

The 1964 U.S. Junior

In California, kids tend to think the sun rises in one part of the state and sets in another. There's so much great golf in the state, and the competition is so good, that not every kid aspires to break out and compete nationally. That certainly was the case with me when I turned seventeen. When the USGA announced that the 1964 U.S. Junior Amateur Championship was going to be played out west in Eugene, Oregon, I really had no intention or desire to enter. Then Bill Powers, an influential golf guy locally, urged me to sign up.

My game at that time was pretty good, though not overpowering. I didn't hit the ball very far, but I was a good iron player and, as I said, a very good putter. It was time to take my game on the road and see how it stood up against other kids in the country. After qualifying with a 71 at Olympic, which won the medal, I was given the opportunity to find out.

I flew to Oregon with Bill and four other boys who had also qualified. My dad, who then as now was my biggest fan, didn't make the trip. He was afraid to fly because of an experience he'd had on an airplane during World War II. So he stayed home but promised to phone every night to see how I did.

Once in Eugene, I again won the qualifying with rounds of 71-68, a record that stood until 1996. Being the medalist gave you a big advantage. You got to go off first when match play got under way. I was a very fast player then, and my matches averaged two hours, ten minutes—and I had no blowout victories. We all played more quickly then, something kids today could take a lesson from. I'd tee off at seven in the morning, be off the course a little after nine, then hang out until my afternoon match. I never came close to getting tired.

My biggest match came in the quarterfinal against Bobby Barbarossa from Florida. He was a very good player with a great reputation. Our match was all square at the 14th hole, a par 3 with the branches of a big tree overhanging the green. I pulled my tee shot into the tree, where it hung up in those branches for what seemed like an eternity. Then the ball suddenly plopped onto the green and stopped six inches from the hole. Poor Bobby was totally unnerved by that. I went on to win the match, one up. Years later, someone told me that Bobby was still talking about that shot.

The championship match against Enrique Sterling from Mexico City was thrilling, but it had a bittersweet ending. It was a close match, but I won, two and one. I was thrilled, but I'll always remember Enrique's father escorting his son off the green, telling him that by losing he had let his country down. I was very sad for Enrique. Whenever I encounter a pushy parent—which isn't often—I think about Enrique Sterling.

The competition was terrific. The camaraderie was even better. We stayed in a hotel in downtown Eugene and, as kids are wont to do, cut loose pretty good. You know that segment on the David Letterman show where they roll a bowling ball through a TV set, just to see what will happen? Our version of that was dropping a huge jug of root beer from a seventh-floor balcony, just to see what would happen when it hit the pavement below. Good, clean fun.

Not long after I came home, colleges came calling with scholarship offers. The University of Houston was a golf powerhouse in those days, and their coach told my mom and dad I'd get a full-ride scholarship and a new Mustang convertible if I signed with them. But I ended up choosing BYU.

I still have the MacGregor driver, my old Tommy Armour irons, and the Bulls Eye putter I used that week. For years my dad kept the shoes I wore as a memento. Not every trophy I've won has a lot of sentimental value, but everything from that week does.

Then and Now

The trip I made to Eugene when I was seventeen was a huge deal for me. It was like a little kid from New York going all the way to Disneyland. The world now is completely different. Golf has evolved to an amazing extent. When I began going with my kids to American Junior Golf Association tournaments, I could hardly believe what I was seeing. A lot of juniors are like miniature touring pros. Some make their own travel arrangements. They know how to budget their money. By the time they get to the PGA Tour, they are very familiar with life on tour, because they've already lived it.

When I came on tour, I knew so many guys with incredible talent who just couldn't handle the lifestyle. They hated the motels. They missed home-cooked meals. They missed their parents, wives, or girlfriends. It was culture shock. Even college golf didn't prepare them adequately, because there was a support system there. In college you do things as a team. If you play horribly there's someone there to pick you up. You have a security blanket wrapped around you.

The competition in junior golf today is exceptionally good. When my son Scott who played for BYU, was playing extremely well in the Tucker Invitational a few years ago, I felt he performed well enough to win. The kid who beat him, David Gossett, was just better. Gossett was a freshman, a small guy physically, but he had the game of a tour pro. His course management was superb, like he'd been playing for thirty years. *Golf World* magazine asked me to do a prediction column at the outset of the 1999 season, in which I picked who'd win the men's and women's majors as well as the U.S. Amateur. My pick for the U.S. Amateur was David Gossett, and when he won, people thought I was Kreskin. But I'd seen Gossett play. I knew how good he was.

Is there a downside to exposing kids to serious competition at an early age? I'm reluctant to take a hard position either way. I think that depends on the kid and the parents. It shouldn't be done at the expense of school. They should have plenty of activities at home to make them well-rounded people. The parents shouldn't put the kid in a position where there's the tremendous pressure of having all the eggs put in one basket. Like I said, golf is a means to an end. That end is happiness and fulfillment in life.

The Lessons I Learned

It's one thing to be on the receiving end of a great golf upbringing, quite another to impart those values to your own children. Every kid is different and so is every parent. It isn't earthshaking news to report that when I had my own children, I had to find my own way when it came to passing along the values that were imparted to me. Of course, I had a big advantage coming from a stable home environment, and the memories of how my father taught me came flooding back when I began introducing my eldest son, John Jr., to golf. As the other five kids came along, my skills at being a golf parent improved.

Here's what I learned:

Use the foolproof starter's kit. Dad had me down in that basement pounding balls for two and a half years before he took me to the golf course. The anticipation of wanting to play almost made me crazy. Parents who want their kids to love the game as much as they do, but are reluctant to force it on them, can learn something by that. I know I did. The memory of that experience led me to formulate my own plan for introducing kids to the game that is guaranteed to hook them forever. It is absolutely foolproof. It is especially effective for kids between the ages of three and eight, when they are most impressionable.

Here's how it works: Take the kid to the course along with a bag of old balls and a child club or two. One more thing: The course has to have a pond or stream.

When you get to the course, rent a golf cart. Put the kid between your legs on the driver's side and let them steer out onto the course. That alone will give them a huge rush. Don't let them drive the cart unassisted, of course. Just let them steer a little bit. Drive out to the pond, where you aren't in anybody's way, and stop at a spot at the water's edge.

Dump a few balls on the ground and have them make a few practice swings, brushing the grass with the clubhead. Then let the kid hit the balls into the water. I don't know why, but there's something about watching the ball splash that makes a little kid ecstatic. They won't get discouraged at all; all they can think about is making the ball splash in that water!

Remember, there are two kinds of shots. If they hit the ball well, you say, "Great shot!" If they whiff the ball or dribble it only a few feet, you say, "Great swing!" That's it. Remember my father's saying: Four parts praise, one part pruning. You sneak in a suggestion here and there, such as, "That was great. Let's see if you do that standing a little taller."

After five or ten balls, stop the game. Go to the water's edge and look for a couple of bugs. Let them catch a frog. Tell them a story about something in nature. Explain how fish breathe, or the fact that insects have six legs and spiders have eight legs. It doesn't matter.

Now go back to hitting balls. Spread six balls on the ground and let them have at it. After they've hit four balls, announce, "OK, time to go," and pocket the remaining two balls. The child will object. He will plead to hit those last two balls. But the answer is no. Tell them, "We'll do this again, but it really is time to go home." Let them steer the cart again on the way back to the clubhouse.

The idea is to leave before it's really time to leave. You want to give them a taste of something delicious, but just enough to whet their appetite. You want to do a lot in a short period of time, with golf as the focal point. The next time you plan to go, give forty-eight hours' notice. The anticipation will be almost more than they can handle. When you go out, repeat your first experience, adding a feature or two—for example, you might want to bring your fishing pole and fish for twenty minutes.

What can you expect from all of this? A desperate desire to go to the golf course that will last, approximately, for the rest of their lives.

Quality time beats quantity time. I was a touring golf professional for more than twenty years. Next to having a parent in the military, I can't imagine a profession that places greater time constraints on the parent–child relationship. We live in an age where quality time is viewed as an acceptable substitute for *total* time, and I accept that grudgingly, if at all. I know everything would have been easier had I been working nine to five like normal people. Because I didn't, I was forced to make the most of the time I had with my kids.

My dad was a busy fellow, and I look back on the sacrifices he made with awe. Setting up the basement with the green tarp and getting the instruction books . . . taking me to meet John Geertsen . . . accompanying me to the par-3 contest . . . going to Karsten Solheim's garage. These were time commitments he made, and they didn't all involve being physically at my side. He reflected a lot, pondered what would be the best way to reach out. When he couldn't be with me, such as the trip to the U.S. Junior, he arranged for me to be taken care of and put me in the good hands of respected people.

Had my dad spent all his waking hours with me but had

been impatient or too demanding, the extra time wouldn't have done any good. He made the most of the time we had together.

Golf is a means to a greater end. Dad didn't choose golf as our primary game merely because he loved it. He saw in it an opportunity to connect with his children on other levels. It wasn't all golf, all the time. We talked about a million things on the car rides to and from the course, and of many things when we played together. It made us closer. Moreover, he encouraged me to have other hobbies and interests. Needless to say, I was obsessed with the game and it took up the lion's share of my thoughts. But dad only allowed it to the extent that it was healthy.

Seek a qualified instructor. If you're an average golfer yourself, you probably are qualified to teach a child how to position their feet at address. But don't go much further than that. My dad, though he had become very knowledgeable, took me to John Geertsen because he had the humility to know his limitations as an instructor.

This is an important step. Not only do you want them to learn the swing correctly, you want the stuff taught to them by a party who has a little separation from the child emotionally. Parents tend to tell a kid too many things. They sometimes get impatient. I feel I did a good job teaching my kids, but I always kept myself in check and exercised a lot of restraint. If I were teaching my kids a game I wasn't so adept at, such as tennis, I wouldn't have tried teaching them anything beyond the rules. I would have sought out an instructor.

Preserve the magic. I've mentioned what a phenomenal putter I was at a young age. I had faith, optimism, and hope.

Putting was all so simple. As an adult, I got to a point where my attitude was just the opposite. Here's how it progressed: I learned that on a perfect surface, a putting machine can only make the same fifteen-foot putt six times out of ten. Then I learned about spike marks and how they can deflect the ball off-line. Psychologically, the chances of making that fifteen-footer dropped to only four out of ten. Then I learned about grain. That dropped the percentage chances to two out of ten. Then I realized I wasn't a putting machine who stroked the ball exactly the same way every time. Psychologically, the odds of making the fifteen-footer dropped to one in ten. And with the poor attitude in general, I was lucky to make even that many.

Kids, of course, live in another world. They don't see the spike marks or the grain. They rely on faith, optimism, and hope, and darned if it doesn't work. My father saw this in me, and he handled it very delicately. He only complimented me and never let on that what I had going was truly magic. He didn't spoil it by teaching me all sorts of putting mechanics or fooling with my stroke.

Do things nobody else does. My dad saw in me a high level of creativity. All kids have it to one degree or another, but he knew I leaned toward expansive thinking rather than linear thinking. So, although he left the mechanical teaching to John Geertsen, Dad taught me how to teach myself. He used to take me out and put me in all kinds of trouble. He'd stick my ball under the lip of a bunker, or in an ice plant, or behind a tree. This taught me true cause and effect in golf—how a sand wedge behaves when it enters the sand, how deep rough turns the clubface closed, what causes a slice or hook and how to produce one on purpose.

I learned a lot about golf by these drills. But there was another by-product that was even more valuable. I realized that I was doing things no other kids were doing. I knew deep down that I was paying a price they weren't paying. When I began competing, I felt I *deserved* to win.

No more sledgehammers. My dad, bless him, didn't have access to the wonderful children's clubs available today. We used adult clubs that were sawed down to make them shorter. They were too darned heavy. The grips were too big. They were all we had, so I took it in stride, but I'd never do that today. I'm convinced that one reason kids don't always fall in love with golf is because swinging the club is too much work.

Save some money and invest in a set of junior clubs. They don't cost nearly as much as an adult set and small children don't need a full set anyway. Four clubs—a little 3-wood, a 7-iron, pitching wedge, and putter—is all they'll need until they get to be about nine. They won't need a full fourteen-club set until they reach puberty.

Do we have a volunteer? Too often, parents hand their kids over to a junior program and let it go at that. I can tell you, the experience for you and your child will be ten times more rewarding if you get involved. It doesn't matter on what level, whether you help with scoring at a tournament, arrange a golf club donation program, or take a group of kids out for milkshakes after they play nine holes.

There just is no substitute for helping out. Along the way, you'll see your child exposed to everything positive about the game and be able to point it out and emphasize it as being good. You'll also see a few things that aren't so positive. Lost tempers, pushy parents, and the occasional example of poor sportsmanship are all part of the show. But you'll be there to discuss everything with your child and encourage them to learn from what they see and experience—even the bad stuff.

Most of all, you'll see your child grow up in the best possible environment, amid the best values set forth by the best people.

CHAPTER 12

Rules for Fools

Time to Clean up the Rules of Golf

DURING MY PRIME YEARS ON the PGA Tour, there was a rules official named Joe Black who was respected for his knowledge of the Rules of Golf and skill at administering them. Joe knew the rules inside out and rarely was tripped up by a peculiar rules situation. He also had an authoritative way of speaking that removed doubt in the player's mind as to whether he was interpreting a rule correctly. He truly was one of the best. But my encounter with Joe at the 1976 World Series of Golf led me to give him the nickname "Mr. Beauty." The nickname was extreme perhaps, but so was Joe. And so were the rules of golf he was charged with enforcing.

I was playing head-to-head against Tom Watson. Waiting

to play on the 17th hole, my mind drifted a bit to what a good year it had been. After all, I'd won the British Open and two other tournaments. And although it was clear I wasn't going to win the World Series, I stood to make a fat check. At that point, my caddie, Andy Martinez, sidled over to me with a look on his face I didn't like.

"I think we've got a problem," he said.

Andy pulled from my bag a little cut-down Bulls Eye putter that belonged to my six-year-old son, John Jr. The putter was eighteen inches long, almost too short for him. I had no clue how it got in my bag, but I had a feeling it meant trouble.

I showed the club to the PGA Tour brass before I signed my scorecard, just in case. I wanted to make sure I hadn't violated the rule limiting the number of clubs you can carry to fourteen. Most of the officials laughed. That can't be a club, they said. But then Joe Black walked over and took a closer look.

"Let me see," Mr. Beauty said. "It's got a grip . . . it's got a shaft . . . it's a got a clubhead . . . by golly, it's a golf club! That's four shots, Johnny."

He meant a four-stroke penalty—two for every hole I had the extra club in my bag, to a maximum of four strokes. I couldn't believe it. The other officials had exercised the spirit of the game, but Joe Black was going by the letter of the law, as usual.

In truth, my problem wasn't really with Mr. Beauty. My problem was with the Rules of Golf themselves. The fact I was penalized severely for carrying a club I had no intention of using and in fact couldn't use if I tried, was beyond the pale. But the Rules of Golf, unlike the rules that prevail in a criminal courtroom, don't contemplate intent. There are no mitigating circumstances. They are based purely on what transpires physically, on the course and sometimes off it. There can be no leeway, no equivalent of Michael Jordan taking four steps without a dribble while driving the lane or a first baseman pulling his foot off the bag an instant before the runner reaches first base. The Rules of Golf are remorseless, the strictest in all of sports—more so because when possible you try to call the infraction on yourself.

I've had other penalties, almost all of them deserved, and many close calls. At the 1982 Colonial National Invitation, play was suspended one day just after I'd completed the 10th hole. I wasn't happy with my clubs that day because I felt the shafts were too soft. So, with some time on my hands, I went to the equipment trailer and had a fellow install stiffer shafts in several of my irons. Just before play resumed, it was pointed out that I couldn't make alterations to my equipment during the round, which technically was still in progress. I quickly took the offending irons out of the bag, and finished the round with only my 5-, 6- and 7-irons, sand wedge, woods, and putter. I played those last eight holes in 1 over par—not bad for having half a set of clubs. It certainly beat getting disqualified.

On the whole, I'm a fan of the Rules of Golf. But they can be unbearably complicated. There are thirty-four rules in all, most having clauses and subclauses. There also are sections devoted to Definitions, Local Rules, Clubs and Balls, the Rules of Amateur Status, and more. On top of *that*, there is the voluminous *Decisions on the Rules of Golf*, a six-hundred-page book that contains hundreds of special rulings for thorny episodes the rules themselves don't cover. (For example: What if you are on the green and you drop your towel, and the wind blows the towel into your ball, causing it to move—is there a penalty? Answer: Yes, because the towel is deemed to be part of your equipment.) To become a true expert on the rules, a person needs to apply the effort equivalent of two years of college.

It's only a matter of time before a rules catastrophe decides the outcome of an important pro tournament. When that happens, the whole game will suffer. Golf will be depicted as silly, unfair, and not worth playing. Sportswriters who cover golf only occasionally and don't know it very well have ridiculed the game before, and the public tends to believe what it reads. At San Diego in 1987, Craig Stadler kneeled on a towel to play a shot from under a tree. He was deemed to have been "building a stance"—a two-stroke penalty—and was disqualified for signing an incorrect scorecard. The media had a field day.

A rules episode in 2003 nearly resulted in a public relations nightmare for the U.S. Golf Association and the game in general. It occurred at the U.S. Women's Open at Pumpkin Ridge's Witch Hollow Course, which I covered for NBC. On the par-5 18th hole in the final round, Annika Sorenstam was tied for the lead when she hit her second shot to a wooded area short and to the right of the green. Her ball was near a boundary fence surrounding portable toilets, which was considered a temporary immovable obstruction and afforded the player relief with no penalty. To the left of the toilets was a scoreboard, which also is a temporary immovable obstruction. Sorenstam was entitled to two separate drops, one for the toilets and another for the scoreboard. But figuring out *where* Annika was supposed to drop her ball took a full fifteen minutes, which seemed like forever. The ruling should have taken five minutes, max.

The slowdown was significant because back in the fairway, cooling their heels, were Hilary Lunke, a qualifier who had never finished higher than 15th in an LPGA tournament, and Angela Stanford, a fine young player who had been riding a crest of momentum coming into the tournament. At that moment, Lunke was tied for the lead with Sorenstam and Kelly Robbins, with Stanford one behind. The pressure was magnified because Lunke and Stanford had to wait for a resolution to Sorenstam's drop. It was similar to a basketball team calling a time-out to freeze a player standing at the foul line. Lunke's rhythm must have been affected, because when play resumed she hit a terrible second shot well to the right and into a fairway bunker. Fortunately she saved par to get in a playoff, and Stanford also made the playoff with a long birdie putt. But the delay very nearly cost Lunke the achievement of a lifetime.

The complexity of the situation was partly to blame for the delay. Kendra Graham, the USGA rules official at the scene, was also culpable. Graham first and foremost wanted to avoid making a mistake, which would have been more tragic than a delay. But her slow reaction time, exacerbated by constant pleas and queries by Sorenstam and her caddie (who should have kept his nose out of it) kept Graham from thinking quickly and clearly. In the end, the slowdown could have spelled disaster for Lunke and Stanford, which I didn't hesitate to point out over the air when play concluded for the day.

I'm not sure how the event could have been avoided, but it certainly was symptomatic of the rules' complexity. It's an especially big issue on the pro tours because there are so many local rules in effect. We deal with things the everyday player does not, like the temporary immovable obstruction Sorenstam dealt with. There also are temporary *movable* obstructions, such as cranes, trucks, and the like. Ernie Els was allowed to move his ball away from a crane that impeded his line of sight in the 1994 U.S. Open, took advantage of the ruling, and made a par. But in fact, his ball should have stayed where it was and the crane should have been moved. It was a mishap that may have saved him a stroke and got him into the playoff, which he won.

In many cases, the content and language of the rules leads to outright rules violations that cost the players dearly. There *is* a solution to that. If the U.S. Golf Association and Royal and Ancient Golf Club of St. Andrews, Scotland (the joint rule-making authorities) were on the ball, they'd simplify a few of the rules right away. I'm not suggesting a major overhaul; most of the rules are easy to understand and exist for a purpose. But I have a few suggestions of where they could start.

1. Let players keep their own scorecards.

At the 2003 British Open at Royal St. George's, Mark Roe and Jesper Parnevik forgot to exchange scorecards at the beginning of the third round. It is customary for an official to hand each player their scorecard at the beginning of the round, after which the players then exchange cards so they keep score for each other. Roe and Parnevik forgot to trade cards that morning, and wound up getting disqualified. It was especially tragic for Roe, who would have been only three shots off the lead had he remembered to switch cards with Parnevik. The error cost him his best shot at winning the British Open.

This aspect of Rule 6 is suspect and the punishment brutal—it's like getting the death penalty for forgetting to sign your income tax return. Why can't players mark their own scorecard during the round and then check it with the fellows they're paired with before signing and turning it in? It would simplify things enormously, and the only downside is the prospect of a player lying about his score. But that has only happened once in the history of the PGA Tour, when in the early 1970s, Rogelio Gonzales was booted off the tour for altering his hole score. Golf is the most honest sport extant, and I can't imagine a tour player risking his career by deliberately writing down a different score than he actually made. Even if he or she tried in an era of omnipresent TV cameras and computerized scoring, it would be next to impossible to escape without getting caught.

These scorecard fiascos occur every year. The most famous incident occurred in the final round of the 1968 Masters, when Roberto De Vicenzo paid a heavy price for signing an incorrect scorecard. Tommy Aaron was keeping Roberto's score that day, and he wrote down a par on a hole where Roberto had actually made a birdie. When you sign for an individual hole score that is higher than what you actually made, the higher score stands. Roberto would have tied Bob Goalby for the lead and forced a playoff, but his mishap relegated him to second place. If Roberto were keeping his own scorecard, what are the chances he would have written down a par instead of a birdie? About zero. A similar thing happened in the final round of the 1957 U.S. Women's Open, when Jackie Pung signed an incorrect scorecard—this time for a hole score lower than what she actually made. That is much more serious—Pung was disqualified and her one-stroke "victory" over Betsy Rawls turned to ashes. The penalty was outrageous. A two-stroke penalty would have sufficed. It would have cost her the victory, but at least her week wouldn't have been a total waste.

2. *Soften disqualification penalties.*

This falls in line with the scorecard disasters I just discussed. Although most rule violations cost the player a one- or two-stroke penalty, certain infringements carry a penalty of disqualification. Missing your starting time is one. Seve Ballesteros was disqualified from the 1980 U.S. Open at Baltusrol because his alarm clock was off by an hour and then he got stuck in traffic, causing him to miss his starting time. I have no problem with that particular disqualification, because Seve knew his starting time and was responsible for being at the first tee when his name is called. And what could have been done—let Seve join the next group off?

But there are other violations for which the disqualification penalty is too severe. Practicing on the course prior to your starting time or during a rain delay packs a disqualification, which is way too harsh. A two-stroke penalty would be sufficient. After all, what player would knowingly hit shots to a hole and pay a price of two strokes? In 2003, Fuzzy Zoeller was disqualified for hitting a few shots for a cameraman during a delay. Ouch. Why give him the death penalty for a misdemeanor?

3. *Get rid of Rule 29.*

The Rules of Golf are constantly criticized for being too long and too numerous. Rule 29, which covers "Threesomes and foursomes," should just be dropped. Heck, do many people even know what that type of golf is? If you follow the Ryder Cup, you may know a "foursome" is alternate-shot format. I understand a few people play alternate shot for recreation in Great Britain, but in my entire life in America, I have never encountered teams of two people taking turns hitting the ball. It's an antiquated rule that takes up space. It should go in a handbook of *Rules for Special Formats*, along with scrambles, Pinehursts, and other hit-and-giggle formats.

4. *Modernize the verbiage.*

Rule 14 declares that the ball "must be fairly struck at and must not be pushed, scraped or spooned." If you trimmed "scraped and spooned," everyone would still get the point. Spooning is what I do with my breakfast cereal; I have no idea what it means in golf. The language is antiquated and not very specific—the same as Rule 4-1d on clubheads, which states they must be "generally plain in shape." What do you call plain? Was the PowerPod driver "plain in shape"? Surely they can be more specific than that.

Another rule ready for a rewrite is Rule 5-3. It says, "If a ball breaks into pieces as a result of a stroke . . ." You can stop right there, reading the rest isn't necessary. Modern golf balls do not break into pieces. I have not seen it happen in many years. Range balls are an exception, but people who take range balls on the course are unlikely to know the rules anyway.

I wish there were more flexibility in the terms used to describe certain things in the game. I alluded to the term *foursome*, which to me describes four people playing golf together more than it does an alternate-shot format. But what about *four-ball*, the term used to describe what 99 percent of people think of as "better ball?" There's a certain snootiness with the terms used in the rule book. The USGA refers to a match as being "all square" and that's fine, but I don't see why you can't refer to it simply as "even." The list goes on. You can't say "pin," you must say "flagstick." You can't say "trap"; the correct term is "bunker." Come on. Let's move into the twenty-first century!

5. Every drop should be two club-lengths, period.

Dropping procedures scare the heck out of most players, even tour pros. A lot of them won't make even the most rudimentary drop until a rules official comes over to supervise. That's because a wrong move can cost them a small fortune. So why risk it?

The rule of thumb on drops is that if you're dropping in a nonpenalty situation you must drop within one club-length from the nearest point of relief. If you're dropping in a situation where you're penalized—say, away from a water hazard—you drop within *two* club-lengths. If you happen to get your club-length limits mixed up, drop the wrong way, and give the ball a whack, you get whacked in return to the tune of a two-stroke penalty.

That's pretty cruel, and it would hardly ever happen if *every* drop were two club-lengths. What's the problem? The extra club-length you're granted in relief situations would rarely result in a meaningful advantage in terms of being closer to the hole. And it would save a lot of time and confusion.

The two-club-length rule for penalty situations came in handy for me once, and demonstrated how the rules can be turned to work in your favor. At the Bing Crosby tournament at Pebble Beach in the early 1970s, my drive on the par-4 10th hole skittered over the precipitous cliff to the right. A red line denoting a lateral water hazard was painted just inside the margin of the cliff. It was impossible to play my ball from the rocks below, so I elected to take the drop with a one-stroke penalty. In most situations, you want to drop as far away from the trouble as you can. But this time the grass at the farthest point of the two-club-length limit was bare, the ground irregular. If I dropped my ball there, it could have bounced into a very difficult lie. On the other hand, if I dropped just inside the red line, where the ground sloped toward the hazard, my ball likely would bounce into the hazard itself, which would permit me a redrop without penalty. With Joe Dey, the commissioner of the PGA Tour and the most knowledgeable man on the Rules of Golf I ever met looking on, that's what I did. I dropped twice, and the ball bounced into the hazard each time. After that I was permitted to place the ball by hand rather than drop it, and I set the ball down into a nice, fluffy lie. Joe Dey, Mr. Golf himself, gave me an approving nod and walked away. I then lashed a 4-wood onto the green and holed the putt.

5. *Range finders should be permitted.*

Long ago—and I mean decades—players ascertained the distance to the green purely by eye. Only in the early 1960s, when Gene Andrews and Jack Nicklaus popularized measuring actual distances, and tying it in with how far they hit each club, did playing by yardage become widespread. Today there are yardage markers alongside every fairway, numbers stamped on sprinkler heads, and (in tournaments, anyway) printed sheets showing the exact location of the flagstick on every hole.

I say it's time to make range-finding devices legal. It's a no-brainer, really. It would speed up play, for one thing, because you'd know in an instant how far from the hole you are and wouldn't have to waste time looking for a sprinkler head. It would be much more convenient and in the end wouldn't give you any information that isn't available already. The skill of determining how hard to hit a shot would still be preserved, especially from the tough distances inside sixty yards or so.

6. *Eliminate drops within a hazard.*

You hit your ball into a bunker, which is partially filled with casual water because of heavy rain. Your ball goes into the part covered with water. You're entitled to relief under Rule 25-1b, but you have to *drop* the ball within the bunker. But what happens when you drop your ball from shoulder height into the sand? *Splat*. A buried lie. And now you've got no shot at all.

If the bunker is completely filled with water and there's no place to drop it within the bunker, the rules permit you to drop outside the bunker—with a one-stroke penalty. You might as well have hit your ball into a lake. My solution is to allow you to *place* the ball in the bunker when it's partially filled with water, or if your ball is unplayable for any reason. You can at least hit the ball that way, and it's fair because the next shot is still no piece of cake.

7. *Enough of caddies lining up their players.*

It only happens on the LPGA Tour for some reason, but several players have their caddies stand on their line of play while they address the ball, to check their alignment. Obviously, the players feel they are so inept they need their caddies to help them. Rule 8-2 allows it, so long as the caddie moves off the line before they play the shot. But it's like legalized cheating. It runs totally contrary to one of the fundamental challenges of the game.

I've always felt I was responsible for the part of the rule that requires the caddie to move off the line of play before the player begins his swing. In the 1970s, I used to have my caddie crouch on my line of play when I putted. It wasn't because I needed help lining up my putter, however. I merely wanted Andy Martinez to tell me, after the fact, if my ball had started on the line I'd chosen. It drove the TV people nuts, because they often position a handheld camera down the line of play in order to provide viewers with a great shot of the player and his target. But when they tried to get that down-the-line shot of me putting, all they got was a wonderful view of Andy's back. I think the TV people complained about this to the USGA, because soon the rule was tweaked to require the caddie to move off the player's line before they actually pulled the trigger. Think about it: What difference does it make if the caddie is there when the player hits the ball? The caddie has already helped line up the player. As a broadcaster I realize that TV coverage is pivotal to the game's growth and exposure, and I'll always believe the interests of commercial television, along with Andy and me, had something to do with that rule.

In any case, I was fine with the USGA changing the rule and requiring the caddie to move off the line. In fact, I believe they should go further. Whether it's on the putting green or on a full-swing shot through the green, the caddie should be prohibited from lining up the player *at any time*. What's more fundamental than aiming at the target?

These suggestions do not represent a wholesale overhaul of the rules. There are radicals who believe the stroke-and-distance penalty for hitting a ball out of bounds is too severe. They argue that the worst shot in golf—a whiff where you miss the ball completely—only costs you one stroke, so why should a 280-yard drive that misses the fairway by only ten yards cost you two strokes? I disagree with them; if you know out-of-bounds is present, it isn't asking too much to aim the ball away from it, put the O.B. stakes out of your mind and put the ball into play. There are those who believe you should be permitted to tamp down spike marks on the putting green; I disagree with that, too. But a sensible review of the rules, performed with an abiding spirit of what is fair, would result in changes that improve the game for everyone.

CHAPTER 13

Moving Forward

Some 2020 Visions

YOU KNOW YOU'VE MADE YOUR mark in sports when you alter the way others approach the game. To some extent I've been able to do that. My legacy isn't the equivalent of Wilt Chamberlain's forcing the NBA to widen the free-throw lane, but I did have an impact. In the prime of my career, I shot an awful lot of very low scores. I mean 61s, 62s, and 63s. I was the first guy to do that, and it raised the expectations of other players. Low scores had been shot before, but not with regularity. Once I broke that barrier, the fear of going low was erased. It was similar to when Roger Bannister broke the four-minute mile—a ton of people soon followed.

When I shot 63 in the final round of the 1973 U.S. Open,

it was regarded by some people as a fluke. It didn't matter that we were shooting at Sunday pin placements, that Oakmont was perhaps the toughest course in the nation, or that only three other pros broke 70 that day. Many writers (and some players) were incredulous and sought ways to diminish it. The most notable complaint was that the course was softened by rains earlier in the week. As I saw it, a soft Oakmont was a lot tougher than your basic PGA Tour course under the hardest conditions. But the following year, I started shooting very low numbers regularly. I shot 61 three times, and shot 64 or lower fifteen times. I won the 1975 Phoenix Open by fourteen shots. When that happened, they knew my going low was not an anomaly. More important, they concluded that if I could do it, they could, too. And the tour started to see a lot of scores in the low 60s. That will always be my legacy, and I'm very proud of it.

The next barrier was 60, which Al Geiberger broke with a 59 at the 1977 Danny Thomas Memphis Classic. That score has been matched several times since then on the PGA, LPGA, and Nationwide tours. Today, players aren't afraid to shoot as low as they possibly can. The only thing holds them back is ability and a couple of putts that refuse to fall.

The reason for bringing this up is to speculate on what we might see over the next two decades. In my opinion, we are going to witness a lot of sea changes in golf. We'll see them in equipment, performance levels, and the way the game is played. The essential character of the game will never change because it will always consist of whacking a ball with a stick toward a hole in the ground. But every aspect of the game, be it the ability of the best players, the character of golf courses, to hi-tech devices that will expedite play and help us perform better, is filled with possibility.

Equipment has the most potential for innovation. When I

won the British Open at Royal Birkdale in 1976, every club in my bag except my putter had an Alidila graphite shaft. Two other pros—Gene Littler and Gay Brewer—had tried graphite shafts in their drivers, but I was the first to have them installed in the irons, and I remain the first and only guy to win a major using graphite exclusively. At the time, graphite was at the far end of the technology frontier, and I couldn't imagine an innovation surpassing it.

Boy, was I naïve. It never occurred to me that within twenty-five years, we'd have even better graphite shafts that could be matched perfectly to a player's swing. I couldn't imagine multipiece golf balls that didn't cut or titanium clubheads with springy faces that launched the ball amazing distances. I couldn't even envision metal woods. I never conceived there would be portable launch monitors that would detect exactly how fast the ball was coming off the clubface, and how fast it was spinning.

Thirty years ago I couldn't have told you that metal spikes would become almost extinct, that there would be rain suits that were actually waterproof, umbrellas that worked in the wind, rubber grips that hardly ever wore out, and laser devices that told you exactly how far you had to the pin. I couldn't imagine pesticides that weren't toxic, or that greenskeepers would be able to aerate a green without taking huge plugs out of the turf. Because personal computers were still ten years away, it was impossible to conceive that teachers would use computerized swing models to help players improve. And even the Internet, which allows you to follow a PGA Tour event in real time, was a pipe dream.

So much has happened, so fast, that most of us have become inured to the novelty of the next new thing—which seems to hit the marketplace every month. The speed at which these technological advances are being made means the game we play today will be quite a bit different twenty years from now. And I see no end to the renaissance we're experiencing with continuing evolution on the technology and performance fronts.

Here's what my crystal ball reveals:

Artificial turf. If it can happen in baseball and football, it can happen in golf. I'm loathe to imagine a golf course without grass, but I think it's inevitable. I don't think many existing courses will make the transition, but new ones will pop up with a unique type of artificial turf. The surface will be quite different from Astroturf; it will have to be more pliable, durable, and lifelike, like the Nexturf now used on pro athletic fields and city parks around the country. Except it will behave like real grass when a golf ball lands on it. Already there are practice ranges that feature a type of artificial grass that is realistic and very resilient.

The turf will cost a fortune at the outset, but it will be a one-time expenditure. It will cost very little to maintain and ultimately will be cheaper than having to groom courses the way we do today. A machine similar to a street sweeper will give it a once-over grooming every morning, and twice a year they'll spray it with a chemical to prevent mold and mildew. The surface will enable people to play in winter—you can just plow away the snow—and will still be able to accommodate trees, creeks, and ponds.

Three-dimensional TV. It's not much of a stretch to imagine, but with high-definition television still out of reach for most people, it's still a long way away. But one day the technology will be such that the viewer will be able to discern breaks in the greens, get a feel for elevation changes, and be able to appreciate how long a shot is. When this happens, golf will be the best sport of all to watch on television. Basketball, football, and baseball, with their confined, linear playing arenas, won't be nearly as enjoyable.

I expect that TV screens will be much larger as well, and may very well be semicircular. Cameras will reveal a scene that is 180 degrees in scope, giving you the feel that you're on the course with the player. Sound, too, will be more sophisticated. If a fan hollers something from the stands on the right, you'll hear the sound emitted from the same location.

The novelty item, the equivalent of players being miked today, will be tiny cameras mounted on a player's hat. They'll provide a first-person view of the action—when Tiger Woods stalks a putt and looks at it from four different angles, you'll stalk it right along with him and see what he sees. The cameras will be almost weightless and won't distract the player at all. You've probably seen the helmet cams in football, and umpire and catcher cams in baseball. The "cap cams" will be similar.

No more bug bites or sunburns. There will be tiny electronic devices that will be even more effective at warding off mosquitoes, no-see-ums, and other pests. Sprays and lotions will become obsolete; every spring you'll buy a battery for the device that will last the entire season.

Exposure to the sun will be devoid of risk. As the ozone layer continues to diminish, science will be forced to address the increasing incidence of skin cancer. A lotion will be developed that is similar to a car wax that lasts a long time. You'll apply it once a week, and be able to play without a hat, without a worry. Eyedrops will come along that function in a similar way—you apply them in the morning, let them soak in for a few minutes, and not have to worry about the sun damaging your eyes.

Virtual golf. The rudimentary simulated computer golf games we see today will be surpassed by highly realistic virtual golf games. A person will be able to walk into a studio in the dead of winter, don headgear, and "play" Pebble Beach. They will have a 360-degree view of the surroundings, will be able to hear the ocean roar and seals bark, and eventually even smell the beach. The golf will be realistic, too. The player will grasp an electronic wand—the "club"—and its movements will play out perfectly in what you see through the headset. You'll take divots, hit shots fat and thin, hook and slice, even top the ball. The feel of the particular shot will be transmitted through the handle.

Hi-tech apparel. Clothing styles of late have gone full circle from when I played the tour. The thigh-hugging slacks worn by Jesper Parnevik, Charles Howell, and others are back in vogue, at least on tour. Tiger Woods wears a collarless shirt that predates my era by thirty years—collarless shirts were quite popular for a time in the 1940s.

Twenty years from now, ordinary fabrics will be water-repellent. Shoes will be made entirely of synthetic materials and be as comfortable as house slippers. Shirts and trousers will not wrinkle. Golf gloves will be made of a material that is impervious to wear; a single glove will last a whole season. If it gets dirty you'll just throw it in the washing machine. Jackets will contain an interior lining that is similar to a space blanket; heat from your body will be reflected back on you only more intensely. The result is that you'll never get cold on the course.

Instant energy. Golf is underrated for its demands on a player's strength, stamina, and energy. Tour players walk enormous distances over the course of a week, probably a total of forty miles. A lot of tournaments have been lost because a player ran out of gas. This has become an accepted fact among top players, more than half of whom work out religiously and watch their diets. A few guys hang out at the bar, smoke cigarettes, and so forth, but darned few nowadays.

The emphasis on conditioning will lead to advances in nutrition. Energy bars are a nice innovation, but we've only scratched the surface. In the future, each person will be able to obtain a profile of their unique metabolism and body chemistry. Their diet will be specialized. And I think that golfers will be able to obtain a custom-made snack that will kick in five minutes after eating and fuel them for a four-hour round. These fuels will be digested almost immediately. And they'll taste good, which can't be said for a lot of energy bars on the market today.

The idea behind all the dieting and exercising is to improve performance. What the future holds there is especially intriguing. Over the next ten years, all kinds of records are going to fall. The arrival of Tiger Woods has put us on the cusp of some extraordinary breakthroughs. When I look even further down the road, I believe we'll eventually look back on current players the way we look at Old Tom Morris.

Here's what we'll see.

Someone will shoot 59—in a major. Ben Hogan told of having a dream in which he made seventeen consecutive holes-in-one, then lipped out his drive on the 18th hole and shot a 19. He also once said, "There's no reason a man can't birdie every hole." That's pretty grandiose by any standard. The fact is, the scoring barrier is still 59. Except that it comes with one important corollary: Someone has yet to shoot it in a major championship. The 63 I shot at the 1973 U.S. Open has held up for more than thirty years. Tom Weiskopf and Jack

Nicklaus tied it at the 1980 U.S. Open, as Vijay Singh did in 2003 at Olympia Fields.

It's a formidable barrier. It's one thing to shoot 59 at the Bob Hope Chrysler Classic, like David Duval did in 1999 or at Las Vegas, where Chip Beck shot a 59 in 1991. It's quite another to do it in a major, on a tough course under tremendous pressure. But it's going to happen. There won't be fleets of them because courses are getting harder. And it may not happen for a number of years. But it's going to happen in my lifetime.

The greatest putter of all time. I've always believed that using the extralong putter is the best way to putt. It's the only stroke that is a true pendulum motion. Although the extralong putter has saved the career of many a player, we've yet to see someone putt lights out with one. The main reason is that people are reluctant to use them. It's like a public admission that you've got the yips, and players are still self-conscious about it. Another reason is that people don't give it a real chance to work. For the long putter to work, you've got to pay your dues. You have to hit a thousand putts with one before you get comfortable. People tend to give up after five hundred putts or so.

But it is a superior method, and a player will come along who has used the long putter from day one and will be a talented putter anyway. On the pool table surfaces players will be putting on in twenty years, this player will absolutely run the tables. He will make every putt he looks at. He will consistently one-putt half the greens every round. He will make putting look as easy as stroking a cue ball into the corner pocket. Then there will be renewed caterwauling that the long putter is unfair, and a movement to ban the long putter for good.

A player better than Tiger Woods. As great as Jack Nicklaus was, Tiger Woods at his best is better than Jack was. Some people thought that would never happen, but it has. And it's inevitable that at some point over the next two decades, someone will come along who is even better than Tiger. It's a scary thought.

Millions more kids will have taken up the game by 2020. A select few will be enormously talented. They'll be bigger than Tiger, stronger, and have an even better head start. As well-nurtured as Tiger was—he had a sports psychologist when he was a teenager, had a great instructor in Butch Harmon before he was a college freshman, and early on played in the best tournaments using the best equipment—this kid will have even more advantages.

But this player, though clearly the best, will not dominate the game the way Tiger has. The competition will be too good.

The Presidents Cup will be folded into the Ryder Cup. This is more a plea than a prediction. I always thought it was a shame that international stars such Gary Player, Nick Price, and Greg Norman couldn't play in the Ryder Cup. The advent of the Presidents Cup in 1994 figured to add a greater international dimension to great team competition, and to an extent it has. The 1996 Presidents Cup, in which the American team defeated the International team by one point, was particularly thrilling. Realistically, however, there's no way the Presidents Cup will ever surpass the Ryder Cup in terms of prestige or public interest. The format is too similar. It doesn't have the history and tradition. It's a success, but I wouldn't call it a runaway success.

Even the players lack enthusiasm. The season is so long and is packed with so many tournaments anyway, that's it's difficult for the Americans to get excited about venturing halfway around the world to compete. They're too saturated with golf.

This was apparent at the 2003 Presidents Cup in South Africa, a terrific battle I felt privileged to announce for NBC. The competition wound up tied, and unlike the Ryder Cup, a tie-breaker had been put in place. Tiger Woods and Ernie Els locked horns in a sudden-death playoff, and the world waited on pins and needles for a resolution. Then it got dark. And everyone agreed to call it a tie and just go home. If the Presidents Cup is so important, how could the players refuse to stay an extra half day and see who wins? Certainly, there is no such thing as a tie in the U.S. Open. But, personal schedules being what they are, and players itching to get home, the respective team captains, Jack Nicklaus and Gary Player, threw up their hands. South Africa is a long way to go for a tie.

Eventually, I'd like to see the International team join the current Ryder Cup and make it a three-way competition. That would be a like an Olympic Games for golf. Traditionalists may scream about destroying one of the great institutions in golf, but a similar transformation has been made before. In 1973, Ireland was allowed to participate for the Great Britain team for the first time, and in 1979 all of continental Europe joined the side. So the evolutionary precedent is there.

I think the three-way format would be compelling. I would make it all four-ball match play and singles match play, and do away with the alternate-shot format, which I never liked. The excitement would be immense and victory would be more meaningful. If I were king, I'd make the change tomorrow.

The Grand Slam will remain untouched. It says something about Tiger Woods's greatness that he held all four major titles at one time. But he didn't win the classic Grand Slam of all four majors in one season, and I seriously doubt anyone ever will. The odds of that happening are roughly a million to one.

Nor do I think anyone will win three of the four majors—the Triple Crown—in a calendar year again. It's a remote possibility, but if someone's going to do it, they better do it quickly. Within ten years, the talent pool will be so deep that winning two majors in a year will be a huge accomplishment, certainly bigger than it is now.

I want to make one more prediction. In 2020, golf will remain the greatest game in the world. No other sport fosters honesty, integrity, character, and sportsmanship the way golf does. It is the most fun, relaxing, exhilarating, and healthy pastime ever devised. There is no end to the things it gives you. I can't count the number of friends and business associates I've met through the game. It's enabled me to make a good living for my family and has brought me closer to my children. It has enabled me to travel, to experience other cultures, and gain a unique perspective on the world.

That's what golf has given me as a player. As a spectator—and as a TV analyst I am mainly observing—I've been witness to more thrills than the law should allow. The entire experience has made me feel deeply indebted to the game and the people in it.

I do know that long after my TV career is finished, I'll still play and teach the game, read about it, watch it on television, and talk about it constantly. As long as I'm calling the shots, golf will remain part of who I am.

Afterword

IN CLOSING, I'D LIKE TO SAY that champion athletes possess traits everyday people do not. Sure, the great golfers I've observed and competed against clearly were blessed with sound bodies, good instructors, and the physical means necessary to pursue a path to success. But I believe they're endowed with something more. They have a special aura about them. They possess a set of intangibles that makes them highly motivated, competitive, single-minded, unafraid, determined, and confident. They see themselves as people of destiny.

The source of the mind-set varies. Usually it can be traced to an influential person, a significant life event, or the environment they grew up in. Often it's a combination of all three. In my case, I've mentioned the advantages of growing up in the competitive arena of San Francisco, of having access to decent equipment, and being assigned a good teacher at an early age. I had a great deal going for me—deep roots, as it were.

But the biggest influence was my father. Dad just passed away in January 2004, but three years before he left us, at the age of 86, he wrote a letter to my son, Todd, outlining the values and perspectives a person needed to become successful. Dad wasn't a writer by trade, but through this letter was able to articulate the approach to life one needed to achieve their dreams.

I'm printing that letter here, unedited, for everyone to see. Read the lines (and between them), and you'll glean what makes individuals such as Tiger Woods and Jack Nicklaus—and Johnny Miller, for whatever I accomplished—the people they are.

THE DO'S AND DO-NOT'S

Why some make it, while others do-not.

The ones that do are the POSITIVE THINKERS, WHILE the DO-NOT'S ARE WRAPPED UP WITH NEGATIVISM. DON'T PLAY "CHICKEN." If you do, you will REMAIN IN THE BARNYARD!

THE PLAYER THAT RIPS IT IS THE ONE THAT GETS IT! GRANDPA SAYS RIP IT! THEN GO AFTER IT! SHOW ARNIE PALMER YOU ARE JUST LIKE HIM. FANS LIKE RIPPERS.

CRAP is for toilets, not for golf.

Yes, make it WORK, WORK, and more work. The easy way is the way to the DUMPS, I say. You got to have a Reason/Purpose for being OUT THERE each and every day. "WILLY-NILLY" is defeating I say. You gotta be careful and NOT NOT NOT NOT let yourself be caught HORSING AROUND carelessly, for it becomes a HABIT—Down the Tube Charlie Boy . . . YES, YES, thank GOD that a person never gets something for NOTHING in this life of worth just by horsing-around. INTENT AND PURPOSE is the ONLY way to get it BIG, BIG, BIG . . . Reminder: If a Guy can take His Knocks/Lumps like a man, then he belongs out there. . . . If he can't Fight Back, then DOWN THE TUBE CHARLIE BOY. Just a warning to anyone who wants to make it BIG out there.

I say, set your sights for the STARS and don't settle for the MOON. Winners are set apart from the crowd, and someday they will stop and watch you perform and that will be your Testimony of Greatness well done. (footnote: On your way to the stars, take your knocks like a man and fight back. That will get you there, sooner.)

You must be diligent all of the time, never letting in NEGATIVE thoughts or thinking enter your PSYCHE, for it is here where you will either MAKE IT or fail, and that goes for everyone else. The PSYCHE must always be receiving the VERY BEST thoughts and courage. You just CANNOT mix JUNK with good thinking and expect to become a champion, it just cannot be done. Go down the straight road and you can't fail.

A parable and/or axiom is: In order to get to Heaven one must travel the straight and narrow road of life. So it is with anything one must do in every-day living. And that is as it should be. There is NO NO compromise or FREEBIES to it, and that too is as it should be. . . . Verily: Good will always be GOOD, Bad will always be Bad. VERILY! ENOUGH BE SAID.

"AYE" verily, not only golf but everything you do in LIFE. "Work-Ethics" is what gets the Job done. NO substitutes will ever do it better.

GRANDPA'S Wisdom: The strongest man is a man who loses but fights back. . . . He is HARDENED like steel. . . . SMILE inside. Fight outside, Champ.

Verily I say: You are that glorious AGE where ALL things are Beautiful for Self, so make the VERY BEST of each day. Never fall into a life of Gloom and Doom. Meet each day POSITIVELY.—Yes, even where your Game of Golf is concerned, treat every THOUGHT, every good and every NOT so good with RESPECT, and go on Forward to the NEXT one. Remember that a Smile is something very SPECIAL in a persons LIFE, so do NOT treat any one lightly. Be of GOOD CHEER every time you get up in the morning and/until night, be an inspiration to SELF and unto others. You will be blessed by God for that even More than all of the Trophies you might Glean from this game. And, remember that you are NOT NOT NOT the only one who misses shots or has bad days, they are all part of growing up and showing your WORTH unto Life. Be a Great Man, in ever part of life you enter and HELP others along the way. You will be so blessed that you cannot fail. So it is with US all in life. Each of us are Challenged and Each of us are Blessed according to our efforts. Proud of Champ and All of you in this wonderful Family of God.

—GPA

Afterword for the Paperback Edition

I'M NOT AVERSE to making predictions now and then, but when it came to guessing what might transpire in golf in 2004, I'm glad I kept my thoughts mainly to myself. If someone had told me that Tiger Woods was going to experience his most disappointing season as a pro, or that the U.S. Ryder Cup team, playing on home soil, would receive its worst trouncing ever, I'd have assumed that that person was smoking something illegal. That Vijay Singh would turn in one of the most dominating performances of the last fifty years at the relatively advanced age of forty-one? That Phil Mickelson would win his first major—the Masters—by becoming a precision player, and one of the better drivers in the game? I may call the shots, but long shots like those are too crazy to contemplate.

Actually a more astute observer than I might have seen these things coming. When I completed the hardcover edition of this book, Mickelson was already hard at work tightening his swing with instructor Rick Smith and had gotten off to a fast start with a win at the Bob Hope. Vijay was doing what he usually does, pounding balls from dawn to dusk, but even in 2003 there were signs he was finding the kind of form that would produce nine PGA Tour victories. As for the Ryder Cup team, there was a long way to go before the team would be decided—after the PGA Championship—but none of the team members were playing inspired golf. As for Annika Sorenstam, who won her seventh major championship in June at the McDonald's LPGA Championship, there was no telling what kind of year she was going to have, because the LPGA schedule doesn't get going until mid-March.

Those were the big stories in golf—Tiger's slump (if you could call it that), Vijay's dominance, the American Ryder Cup team's dismal performance, Annika's ongoing quest for immortality, and Mickelson winning the major that was long overdue. There's a compelling explanation behind each one.

Mickelson at the Masters: Same Man, New Plan

Nothing is more rare than the world-class player who totally reinvents himself, one who retools his swing and overhauls his strategic approach to playing the game. Many top players tweak their swings a bit, sometimes for the better, often for the worse (see chapter 6 on "The Grand Canyon Syndrome"). But the guy who rebuilds his swing almost from the ground up is seldom seen, and for good reason. If you've made millions of dollars and won more than twenty PGA Tour events, the tendency is to say, "Why change?"

Phil Mickelson did change, however, and the result was his first major championship. He transformed not only his full swing and short game, but revamped his basic strategy. Over the course of five months, the gambling, go-for-broke Mickelson, who swore he would never back off from his proclivity for taking crazy risks, became one of the shrewdest, smartest players on tour. And it resulted not only in his winning the Masters, but finishing second in the U.S. Open, third at the British Open, and tying for sixth in the PGA Championship.

The first thing Mickelson did was shorten and tighten his

swing, especially with the driver. Never an accurate driver of the ball, he sacrificed distance (which he had in abundance) in favor of hitting a high fade that found more fairways. He still drove the ball farther than most guys, and by accepting a few more middle-iron shots from the fairway instead of short-irons from the rough, he putted for birdie more often. He hit more greens and because of that, made fewer bogeys and double bogeys while making about the same number of birdies he always had.

The second change was his strategy from ninety yards and in. From this zone Mickelson has always been deadly, and he continued to be aggressive at the area of the game he was best at. He practiced hard to perfect a three-quarters swing that improved his distance control and ability to control trajectory. It really paid off.

Phil also changed his shot selection around the greens. For years he'd been in love with the flop shot, the high-flying, soft-landing beauty that few guys could play as well as he could. It saved him a lot of shots but it cost him some, too. Working with short-game teacher Dave Pelz, Mickelson decided to play the flop only when it was absolutely necessary. The turf at Augusta National is extremely fast and firm, and the flop shot, which requires a long swing, allows very little room for error. The two decided on a low-risk strategy on these shots, and although there now would be lesser chance of the big-hero reward—a hole-out from off the green—it surely would mean fewer scorecard-wrecking double bogeys. The change was evidenced on the 18th hole on Saturday, when Mickelson missed the green by fifteen feet to the right. The hole position was also to the right, so he didn't have much green to work with. Phil being Phil, the assumption was he'd either chip or try a flop shot. Instead he used his putter, the old "Texas wedge," and got the ball close enough to save par. It was a gutsy, defining moment for him. Rarely has a shot in the third round of a major championship meant so much to a champion.

The final change, though it was more a modification than anything, was in his putting routine. Erratic short putting may have cost Phil the 2002 Masters, and he began adopting a practice drill he learned from eighty-one-year-old Jackie Burke, the Houston pro who won the Masters in 1956. He placed several balls in a circle around the hole, each about two feet away, and judiciously putted each one, getting the feel for the small differences in break with his eyes and feet. He became almost automatic on short putts and was more confident and effective from all distances. On the last hole on Sunday, needing a downhill fifteen-footer to sew up the tournament, he nailed the putt dead center.

Mickelson's changes took courage and a huge commitment psychologically. Phil seemed to lose his enthusiasm toward the end of the year, and had a poor Ryder Cup, among other lackluster performances. But he won his first major, the hardest one of all. And it leads me to say publicly that he'll win a few more majors—including another big one this year.

Champions Tour: The Walrus Rules, Hale Fascinates

On one hand I'm not surprised that Craig Stadler won five tournaments on the Champions Tour and was the leading money winner. After all when he turned fifty in 2003, he not only won three times in his rookie season on the Champions Tour, he pulled off a rare feat by winning the B.C. Open on the PGA Tour. But when you look beyond the results and examine his swing, you can't help but be surprised and also inspired, because he is not the type of player you would think would age very well. His broad, chunky body wasn't an impediment when he was younger, but as he moved into his 40s, you had to wonder if he might lose some strength and flexibility, which can wreak havoc with the golf swing. But it never did bother him, partly because his swing is unique to begin with. It isn't pretty, but it repeats time after time.

The reason Stadler won more than two million dollars is because he has always been blissfully disinterested in the mechanics of the golf swing. If he'd ever tried to unravel the mysteries of that swing and became mechanics-oriented, he might not have been able to play at all. He possesses great hand-eye coordination, pretty good flexibility for a fellow with his body type, and a what-the-heck attitude about results. He can get pretty steamed when he hits a bad shot, and I've seen him bury a club or two into the ground when he hits one off the planet. But his temper has always been short lived. He recovers and moves on. The bottom line is, he has a temperament that reveals a fiery desire to win.

It helps that Craig's standard shot is a fade, which is easier to control and sets him up with a lot of juicy approaches into the greens on the shorter courses the seniors play. His putting has also held up very well. He always has run hot and cold with the putter, but he doesn't seem to have accumulated too much scar tissue from his failures. Finally I think he's been inspired by the progress of his son, Kevin, who has the stuff to be a star on the PGA Tour. It takes a special confluence of factors for a guy like Stadler to dominate, and in 2004 he had them all.

Stadler is an interesting case study, but next to Hale Irwin, the Walrus pales. I've talked about Irwin at length, but his performance in 2004 was terrific and led me to compose a new theory about what makes him tick. Irwin won two tournaments, including the Senior PGA Championship, which pushed his career total to forty senior victories, a number that may never be beaten. He was second only to Stadler on the money list, and has won more than twenty-six million dollars on the Champions Tour alone. As I've said, he is the greatest senior golfer of all time and has rewritten the record book. He may still be the best player on the tour, and he turns sixty years old in June 2005.

Irwin is the most intense, driven, motivated player out there, and I'm fascinated as to why. Some players, like Dana Quigley, play for the sake of playing, because they love the lifestyle, the competition, and the fundamental act of hitting a golf ball. But Hale seems to be pursuing a greater mission than that, and I'm not sure what the mission is. I have a lot of respect and admiration for Hale but, as a former player myself, I wonder what makes him compete so furiously. When you're a young player, there are certain things you want to accomplish, such as winning majors, making the Ryder Cup team, becoming financially secure, and so on. Hale already has all those, and no matter how many U.S. Senior Opens he wins, they can't possibly match up with the three U.S. Open titles he won years ago. The bottom line is, the things a player accomplishes as a senior are really a footnote to your earlier achievements.

My feeling is that Hale enjoys showing up at a senior tournament knowing he's the best, and being acknowledged as the best. He's not an egotistical person per se, but I believe he gets a bigger rush than most people by knowing he's the king; even though Hale is one of the greatest golfers of all time, he never was the best in the world at any point in his career. Throughout the 1970s, either Jack Nicklaus, Tom Watson, Lee Trevino, or myself was better. Someone always stood a bit taller than him in the 1980s, whether it was Curtis Strange, Nick Faldo, or Seve Ballesteros. It's odd for a man who won three U.S. Open titles to never have been the number one player in the world, but that mantle has strangely always eluded him. So, I think Hale in a way is really relishing the fact that he is the best senior golfer who ever lived—including being the best today. Whatever the reason, we're all benefactors of his desire, because watching him play is a thrill.

Tiger Woods: A Man on the Precipice

Watching Tiger Woods closely throughout 2004, I had the sense I'd seen a player like this before. A player who could shoot 66 while hitting only three fairways. A player with tremendous imagination, a brilliant short game, and a knack for willing the ball into the hole. A fantastic competitor who never gives up. A wild driver who seemed to succeed in spite of himself.

I saw—and still see at this writing—Seve Ballesteros. Tiger has officially become a poor driver of the ball, much like Seve was for most of his career. Tiger's ability to post low numbers despite finishing the year ranked 187th in driving accuracy is a testament to his phenomenal ability in other departments of the game. His year wasn't an abject failure; he finished fourth on the money list and did win the World Golf Championship Match Play. But it was disappointing by his outrageously high standard, and it all was the result of his inability to keep his tee shots on the short grass. Countless times in 2004, Tiger would drive the ball fifty yards off line, only to hit a brilliant recovery shot and save par. In the final round of the Byron Nelson, Tiger couldn't hit a fairway to save his life, yet he almost won the tournament. Had any other player driven the ball as crooked as Tiger, he would have missed the cut—another tribute to how superlative the rest of his game is. For the year, had Tiger driven the ball as accurately as Vijay Singh, he possibly could have had a better year than Vijay did.

For those of you who missed seeing Seve in his prime, this is how he played golf. He had an outstanding career and few players were as exciting to watch. But until Tiger sorts out the swing problems that have plagued him for the past couple of years, my prediction that he won't break Jack Nicklaus's record of eighteen professional major wins will come true without even being threatened. At the majors especially, the driver is the most important club in the bag. Right now Tiger doesn't have it. It's cost him tactically, of course, but it's also robbed him of another weapon: his ability to intimidate. The fear he instilled in other players is gone because they know his wild driver makes him vulnerable.

It's amazing, really, that Tiger can drive the ball so crookedly. He has played golf virtually his entire life and has tremendous knowledge of the swing. He is extremely athletic and possesses extraordinary hand-eye coordination. He has access to the best equipment available and practices more than most players. You'd think his driving would improve as his career progressed, as was the case with Ben Hogan and many others. Instead he's gotten worse, and has arrived at a critical juncture in his career. Seve drove the ball worse as he got older, and eventually got to a point where his driving was so erratic, and his confusion over the source of it so great, that he lost his confidence forever. For Seve it was a psychological issue as much as a mechanical one, and he never really recovered. Tiger has arrived at a similar make-or-break threshold where the swing changes he's been working on for the last couple of years will either kick in or let him down completely.

Most observers feel Tiger made a mistake by leaving Butch Harmon. I agree with them, although Tiger has so much innate talent he would be successful even if Stevie Wonder coached him. The thing about Harmon is that he's not merely a brilliant instructor, he understood Tiger's swing better than Tiger himself. Tiger used to play all sorts of shots with his driver: cuts and draws, high shots and low. He pretty much hits just one shot now because he doesn't have the confidence to work the ball with his old versatility. Tiger's best shot is a high fade but, for whatever reason, he plays a lot of right-to-left draws. I don't understand it.

Whatever personal issues exist between Tiger and Butch, Tiger definitely would be well served if he went back to Butch and said, "I'm sorry for thinking I could do it alone. I need your help." He needs to find a way to set their differences aside and get back to work. At stake in this decision is a bunch of major championships and a larger place in history. A show of humility is a small price to pay for at least a reasonable shot at Jack's record.

Vijay Singh: One of a Kind

In winning nine tournaments, including the PGA Championship, Vijay Singh very quietly shattered what remained of two long-standing assumptions about professional golf. First, he proved once and for all that tall, sturdy guys are not only here to stay, they are here to dominate. Only forty years ago, it was widely held that tall golfers were at an inherent disadvantage. Golf is a precision game, and longer limbs mean a wider arc and longer range of motion. That supposedly should make controlling the club unwieldy, like writing your name with your fingers locked at the eraser end of a long pencil. Virtually every great golfer, including Jones, Hogan, Nicklaus, Player, and Palmer, stood less than six feet in height. There always is an exception to the rule but, Byron Nelson notwithstanding, golf had very few good tall players.

There has been a noticeable trend toward the better players standing taller than six feet. Tiger, Mickelson, Els, Goosen, Love, and others all are tall, but there hasn't been conclusive proof that this is more than an anomaly. But in turning in one of the best year-long campaigns in recent history, Vijay, who stands six foot three, has solidified the notion that bigger is better.

Not only does he hit the ball a mile, something the tall guys do with greater ease than shorter players, he is also extremely precise. None of the taller players today are especially straight drivers, but Vijay is one of the most accurate long hitters in the game today. In fact, he would hold up very well in any era. When I joined the tour in 1969, a straight hitter like Lee Trevino seldom missed fairways when he was on his game. Trevino, in fact, hit every fairway the year he won the PGA Championship at Tanglewood in 1974. As guys have gotten bigger, they've lost a lot of that precision. In their defense, when you're carrying the ball three hundred yards or more, there is a lot more time for the ball to drift off line. Still, none of today's tall players have great control of their driver—except Vijay. And he's also a wonderful iron player who controls distances very well, especially with his wedges.

The other myth he's exploded is that a guy over forty years old can't dominate the game. Ben Hogan is given credit for dominating in 1953, when he won three majors and one other tournament, but he played a fairly short schedule. At age forty-one, Vijay not only played in twenty-nine events, he practiced like a demon when he wasn't competing. He's durable by any standard, and the combination of experience and physical stamina was devastatingly effective.

In some ways, Vijay is a throwback to the great Hogan. No man practices more. He usually is the last guy to leave the range at a tour event, and when he takes a week off (which isn't often), he spends his leisure time at his Jacksonville home—doing what else?—hitting balls. I admire his commitment, because he doesn't immerse himself in golf at the expense of his wife and teenage son. When Vijay isn't playing golf, he's with his family. You have to love that work ethic.

In other ways he shows a great flair for innovation. Vijay won a bunch of tournaments early in the year putting with a belly putter. When he arrived at the PGA Championship, he brought with him a conventional putter and won his second major by putting conventionally. Imagine, changing your putting style in the middle of a hot streak like the one he had! When Vijay felt like the belly putter might be getting the slightest bit shaky, he stayed a step ahead of the curve and went with the conventional model. Very often, when you switch to a new putter, the freshness of the look and feel makes you think you can hole everything, and for a while that's what happens. I did that myself in the second half of my career, switching putters and styles at the drop of a hat. It worked, too. Vijay utilized that quick burst of confidence wonderfully. In the future, I think we'll see more players routinely learning two or more strokes with several putters, and more willingness to change from week to week.

How could Vijay improve? It's hard to pick on his golf game, that's for sure. I do think he might try being a little more engaging with fans and the media. He's never seemed entirely trustful of reporters, a wariness that may be traced to the treatment he received following accusations that he knowingly broke the rules in a tournament long ago. But he seems to be loosening up a bit. During an interview at the Tour Championship last fall, he was a joy to listen to. His buddies say he has a great sense of humor and is a loyal, generous friend. It would be nice for the world to see that side of him.

The Ryder Cup: Anatomy of a Blowout

In the weeks leading up to the 2004 Ryder Cup at Oakland Hills in Michigan, I didn't see how the American team could lose. On paper, we had a team that was better from top to bottom. Add to that the extra motivation the Americans felt after losing in 2002, and the fact that we were playing at home, and I actually saw the possibility of a blowout victory. And it *was* a blowout—an 18½ to 9½ drubbing by a European team that was more enthusiastic, tougher, more team-oriented, and even more motivated than the United States.

My feeling that the Americans had better players and could win easily was a big mistake. The truth is, the top players in Europe definitely have caught up with the Americans. They are every bit as good and in team competition they play like it. The reason they were underdogs is that they don't play as well individually in top competition within America. A European player hasn't won the U.S. Open since 1970, Colin Montgomerie has yet to win in America, and the rest of the players on the continent still don't feel comfortable playing against top fields in the United States. It doesn't make sense, really, because the scores they shoot on the European Tour are every bit as good as the scores you see on the PGA Tour. But there's a mental block there that the European players still haven't overcome as individuals.

Put the Europeans together as a team, however, and they're dynamite. Europe now has won four out of the last five Ryder Cups, and right now they are superior in this form of competition. The main reason is that they are closer to each other. They travel together, eat and drink together, and truly like each other. You don't see much of that among the Americans. Usually they travel alone on their private jets. They fraternize some, but for the most part keep to themselves and their inner circles of agents and families. There was a telling moment in the Ryder Cup when the camera presented an interesting scene around the 18th green. There were the European players and their caddies and wives encircling the green, all of them linked physically, either holding hands or draping their arms around each other's backs. The Americans, meanwhile, stood alone or in small groups. It was if they were wearing signs that said, "Don't touch me." The Americans are individuals. They don't like to be touched; they don't like anyone intruding in their space. Tiger Woods is not a touchy-feely guy. Not many of them are. The Americans avoided the crowds at Oakland Hills, while the Europeans freely signed autographs. While Phil Mickelson practiced alone with his new equipment on Oakland Hills's other eighteen-hole course, the Europeans clung together.

You would have to go back many years to find a Ryder Cup that was decided earlier than this one. The outcome was pretty much determined after Europe built a 6½ to 1½ lead on the first day. The Americans, who for the most part showed up looking and sounding disinterested in the whole thing, appeared to be in shock. The Europeans, meanwhile, were behaving like kids in candy store, filled with joy, energy, and powerful feelings of camaraderie. The attitude of the players is very important in team competition, and Europe's couldn't have been brighter. The Americans seemed fragmented and depressed. A collection of first-team college All-Americans would have gotten more than 1½ points on the first day. I'm serious. The Europeans were not unbeatable that first day; the Americans were just pathetic.

The pairing of Tiger Woods and Phil Mickelson was a huge gamble on the part of American captain Hal Sutton, and it blew up in his face when Tiger and Phil lost both of their matches. Sutton has been second-guessed to no end in the aftermath of that whipping, but to me the pairing was barely worth trying to begin with—even if the two had won. Here's why: If Tiger were paired with any other player the first two matches, in all likelihood he and his partner would have won at least 1½ points. The same goes for Phil; the worst he and another teammate would have done was win 1½ points. By pairing Phil and Tiger (who don't exactly love each other) together and watching them come up empty, Sutton possibly lost more than the three points that appeared on the scoreboard. In a sense he also lost the points the two could have produced had they been paired with other players. The setback was exponential.

The United States rallied slightly in the Saturday morning four-balls, winning 2½ out of 4 points. At that point the overall score was 8–4 for the Europeans, and the Americans appeared to have a fighting chance. But then came a crucial decision by the United States. The team of Chris Riley and Tiger Woods had won their match that morning, and now Riley was saying he was too tired and emotionally spent to play again that afternoon. I was incredulous. Here's a guy in his twenties who is playing well and, almost more importantly, making the taciturn Woods smile and loosen up a bit. And he decided he couldn't handle another match. Instead, Jay Haas, at age fifty, played for the fourth time. It immediately brought to mind the criticism I leveled at Jeff Maggert for choosing to sit out during the 1999 Ryder Cup at Brookline. I was tempted to speak out against his decision not to play, but then I thought better of it. The matches, like I said, were as good as over at that point. It wasn't worth sticking my neck out and getting in trouble over. So I bit my tongue the rest of the way, not only on the Riley episode but on the Americans' performance as a whole. The United States lost three of four matches in the afternoon to face an insurmountable 11–5 lead heading into the final day's twelve single matches.

The Americans didn't make a charge that last day and lost by a whopping nine points. Who was to blame for the loss? Certainly you can't blame Hal Sutton. His players should have overcome the ill-advised Woods–Mickelson pairing. And what can you do when one of your players—I'm speaking of Riley—doesn't feel inspired enough to play? In the end, the captain doesn't swing the clubs, and can't be blamed for the loss. Dave Stockton had a big impact when he was captain in 1991, and Tony Jacklin was a great captain for Europe a couple of times, but they are exceptions.

Nor do I blame Mickelson, who took a lot of heat for signing a new equipment contract and switching clubs just before the Ryder Cup. It's a long year for players these days, one virtually without end when you factor in the non-official events at the end of the year, and he had to make the switch sometime. What the heck. He wasn't playing well enough to have won more with the clubs he was used to using.

I can't give credence to the claim by the American players that they can't get up for an international event every single year. It's true that they have to play the Presidents Cup and Ryder Cup in alternate years, whereas the Europeans have two years to prepare for only the Ryder Cup. But getting psyched up for the Ryder Cup shouldn't be that hard. If they simply showed up and made the event fun and exciting the way the Europeans do, maybe it wouldn't take so much out of them.

No, the reason the United States got beat is the me-first, money-oriented culture it embraces. Remember when the Americans made a big issue a few years back about getting some of the revenues from the Ryder Cup? And how they won the day, and now receive money that goes to their favorite respective charities? Here's an idea that Tom Lehman, the captain for the U.S. team in 2006, might adopt: He should gather the team on Thursday night and say, "You guys aren't very good playing for each other, but you're very good when it comes to playing for cash. Money is the one thing you understand and are motivated by, so I'm going to take all your Ryder Cup charity money and put it in a pot. Those of you who win matches will get a percentage of the pot that you can contribute to your charity. Those who lose get nothing."

I don't think Tom will take that advice. But since pride, patriotism, and fighting for each other haven't worked, what else is left?

Annika: Move Over, Jack

Annika Sorenstam had another monster year in 2004, winning eight tournaments including her seventh major. That brings her career total to fifty-six wins, and she's still only thirty-four years old. It goes without saying she is the best player of her era, but the nature of accomplishments are such that she is moving into Jack Nicklaus territory. Meaning, she's closer than ever to being considered the greatest female golfer of all time.

Annika is a long way from matching Kathy Whitworth's total of eighty-eight career victories. She also has a way to go before she matches some of Mickey Wright's remarkable contributions to the record books. But in 2004 Annika won those tournaments against the best fields in the history of women's golf. The quality of play on the LPGA is far higher than it's ever been. The players are simply better than their predecessors and there are more of them. When Whitworth and Wright were winning tournaments in the 1960s, a typical field only included six or seven players capable of beating them. Fields improved over time and in the 1990s were darned tough. But the collection of players out there now—Grace Park, Cristie

Kerr, Lorena Ochoa, Karrie Webb, Se Ri Pak, and perhaps ten others—are capable of winning in any given week and can beat Annika if she isn't at the top of her game. I have all the respect in the world for Whitworth, Wright, Patty Berg, Nancy Lopez, JoAnne Carner, Pat Bradley, and all the rest. Like Bobby Jones, whose Grand Slam has always been slightly suspect because of the quality of the fields in the U.S. Amateur and British Amateur, it isn't their fault. All you can do is beat the best of your era, and they did that. But Annika, by way of her physical conditioning, attention to nutrition, and constant practice, has shown a greater commitment to her craft than players of previous generations.

She still has a ways to go, however. Seven majors is impressive, but I'd have to say she's underachieved in that area. Even though she won the U.S. Women's Open in 1995 and 1996, it's been eight years—her very best years, by the way—since she won her last one. The total doesn't reflect her surpassing skill or dominance.

Her ability notwithstanding, Annika is a big reason women's golf is pretty healthy. I hear from time to time about crowds at LPGA events not being as big as on the men's tour, but then again, how can they be? A big percentage of their fan base is female, and since there are fewer female golfers in the nation than male golfers, it isn't possible to lure as many fans through the turnstiles. Comparisons between women's tennis and women's golf aren't fair because the women's tennis events are held concurrently with men's events at the same site. I wish there were a premier men's and women's golf championship played the same week at the same site. The LPGA deserves a pat on the back for doing as well as they have. And I'm sure the fan base will continue to grow, thanks largely to Annika.

The irony is, Annika may not be there to experience the

glory days that potentially lie ahead for her and the LPGA. There's still a good chance she'll go into semi-retirement sometime in the next few years in order to start a family. Even if that happens, she's established a standard the rest of the players will be chasing for a long, long time.

JOHNNY MILLER

Salt Lake City, Utah
November 2004

Acknowledgments

IT'S CUSTOMARY AT THE END of a long telecast to "roll the credits"—mention those who you don't see or hear, but who play pivotal roles in bringing the production to fruition. For my career in general, and this book in particular, I'm happy to acknowledge the encouragement, guidance, and support extended by my friends, family, and associates.

First and foremost, I'm grateful to my wife, Linda, for standing by my side for the last thirty-five years and for giving me six great kids. Thanks also to the Miller children—John Jr., Kelly, Casi, Scott, Andy, and Todd—for keeping me young at heart.

Special thanks to Fran La Voie, my assistant and loyal friend, for keeping the train on the tracks and running on time. I don't know how she does it.

I'd formally like to thank John Geertsen, my golf instructor from age eight, and the members at San Francisco Golf Club and the Olympic Club. They planted the seeds that enabled me to flower.

Two golf legends have had a marked influence on my life. I'm grateful to Billy Casper for being such a fine friend and great mentor. I also am indebted to Jack Nicklaus for setting a great example for a young pro to follow, and for always being there for me.

My admiration and thanks to Tommy Roy, executive producer for NBC Sports. His commitment to excellence inspires me to always do my best. Thanks also to my colleagues in the booth, past and present, for shepherding their teammate along.

My business associate, Bob Stanworth, has made so many of my off-course ventures interesting, challenging, and always worthwhile. Brent Turley, my friend and associate for many years, also helped me a great deal during my "second career."

This book was a challenge. Guy Yocom, my co-author and colleague at *Golf Digest* for over ten years, has a gift for putting words to music. Our literary agent, Scott Waxman, did a fine job putting the project together. Thanks, guys.

Finally, I extend my sincere thanks to my readers and viewers. Without you, there would be no shots to call.

The lead golf analyst for NBC Sports for the past fifteen years, Johnny Miller has won twenty-four PGA titles and is a member of the World Golf Hall of Fame. He has also designed many award-winning golf courses and writes a monthly column for *Golf Digest*. Johnny divides his time between Napa, California, and Salt Lake City, Utah.

Guy Yocom is senior writer for *Golf Digest* and lives in Connecticut.